American Contract Bridge League

Introduction to Bridge
Introduction to Duplicate Bridge
"Spade Series"

by Audrey Grant

88973

ISBN 0-943855-09-8

The American Contract Bridge League

presents

 # *The ACBL Spade Series*

"Introduction to Duplicate Bridge"

This is the fourth book in the four–book series that forms the basis of the ACBL teaching program. The other books:

♣ *The ACBL Club Series* — "Bidding: An Introduction"
   (Published in the summer of 1987)

♦ *The ACBL Diamond Series* — "The Play of the Hand"
   (Published in the summer of 1988)

♥ *The ACBL Heart Series* — "Defense"
   (Published in the summer of 1990)

American Contract Bridge League
2990 Airways Boulevard
Memphis, TN   38116–3847

(901) 332-5586

The American Contract Bridge League

The American Contract Bridge League (ACBL) is dedicated to the playing, teaching and advancement of contract bridge.

The current membership of 187,000 includes a wide range — from the thousands who are just learning the joys of bridge to the most proficient players in North America.

ACBL offers a wide variety of services. These include:

• Tournament play. Thousands of tournaments — North American Bridge Championships (three a year) as well as tournaments at the regional, sectional, local and club levels — are sponsored annually.

• A monthly magazine. *The Bulletin* offers articles on tournaments, card play, the Laws, personalities, special ACBL activities, etc.

• A ranking plan. Each time a member does well in any ACBL event, whether it be at the club level or at a North American Bridge Championship, that member receives a masterpoint award. Players achieve rankings and prestige as a result of their cumulative masterpoint holdings.

• A teaching program. This book is one of a series of volumes being used in this program.

• A charity program. Each year the ACBL designates a charity as its Charity of the Year, and all clubs cooperate to raise money for this charity.

• A college program. The ACBL cooperates with the nation's colleges in making bridge instruction and play available to college students.

• A supply department. The ACBL offers a wide variety of bridge supplies, books and other bridge-related items for sale to members.

• Membership in the World Bridge Federation. Each year the ACBL sends premier players to compete in the world championships.

ACBL has long been the center of North American bridge activity — in 1987 the League celebrated its 50th anniversary. We invite you to enjoy our second half-century with us.

TABLE OF CONTENTS

Introduction

The American Contract Bridge League's *Spade Series* Student Text is the last in a four-part series of bridge books for beginning players. It focuses on introducing the player to duplicate bridge.

This series of books is unusual in the field of bridge writing for several reasons. First, they were written by a professional educator, Audrey Grant, who also happens to be a bridge player. Accordingly these books encompass all of the sound principles that facilitate learning any subject and are built on the firm foundation of a basic understanding of the game of bridge.

Next, the technical approach to these books was determined by surveying a cross section of North American bridge teachers. This means that whether a student learns bridge from this book in Vancouver, British Columbia; St. Louis, Missouri; or Orlando, Florida, he'll be able to play bridge with virtually any other bridge player.

Third, the effectiveness of the teaching principles was field-tested in five cities prior to the publication of the first book in this series (*The Club Series Text, 1987*), with more than 800 actual bridge students and at least 25 bridge teachers involved.

Finally, it is the first time in the 50-year history of ACBL that the sanctioning body for bridge in North America has produced its own basic bridge texts. The end result of the joint effort of Audrey Grant and ACBL is a four-book series that enables the reader to learn bridge (or update his game) in a logical and progressive fashion. More importantly, the reader will have fun while learning the fundamental concepts of good bridge bidding and play which will be beneficial for a lifetime.

LESSON 1
Getting Started

Duplicate Bridge Is Fun
Starting Out
Scoring
Matchpointing
Summary
The Finer Points

Workshop Material
Group Activities
Sample Boards

♠ *DUPLICATE BRIDGE IS FUN* ♠

Duplicate Bridge! This can be an emotionally charged topic. For some, it represents an unpleasant experience; for many others, one of life's fondest memories. Why the disparity? Many bridge players are introduced to the game under unfavorable circumstances. They are unprepared for the new format and, having had one bad experience, never return. Those who go into the game prepared for the experience usually find that it opens up an exciting new world.

There are many questions people ask. What is the difference between duplicate bridge and rubber bridge? Is duplicate the same as contract bridge? Do the players bid different-ly? How do you keep score? In this lesson series, we will introduce you to the world of duplicate bridge and set you on a journey you will be glad you did not miss.

What Is Duplicate Bridge?

Duplicate bridge, commonly referred to as *duplicate*, is a form of the game in which each deal is bid and played by two pairs and then the same deal is bid and played by a number of other pairs. Each time the deal is replayed, the original conditions are "duplicated." Because the deal has been played more than once, the various results can be compared to see which partnerships performed best. Duplicate is slightly different from *rubber bridge*, the type of bridge usually played in the home. In rubber bridge, each deal is played only once. The players accumulate points as they bid and make their contracts and defeat the opponents' contracts, but there is no way by which they can compare their performance.

Why Play Duplicate?

There are more than six billion possible deal combinations. When you play a deal of rubber bridge, the deal is gone forever, even in the memories of most of the players. You may be pleased about that! On the other hand, you may be curious and wonder how some-one else would have bid and played with your hand. You may wonder what an "expert" holding your cards would have led.

Trying to remember your cards and those of your partner is challenging enough, but when you attempt to reconstruct the entire bidding and play of a deal, your memory can play tricks. Did your opponent lead a spade or a heart after winning the third trick? Duplicate offers an advantage in this situation. A deal is no longer bid and played never to be seen again. The same deal is played more than once, sometimes a dozen or more times. This helps to improve your game. For example, suppose you are confident you did everything possible to make your 4♥ contract but ended up being defeated. It seems that the con-tract could not be made. Playing rubber bridge, that would be the end of the story — it's on to the next deal and nobody is any the wiser. In a duplicate game, however, you can see how other players have done with the same deal. If you find that most other declarers were successful in taking 10 tricks, you may want to take another look at the deal. It will still be there at the end of the game and you will be able to discuss it with the other players.

Rubber bridge can be frustrating when you are losing to players who always seem to get all the good cards. They keep piling up the points, bidding games and slams, while you never hold enough to open the bidding. Even recalling the phrase "lucky at cards, unlucky at love" doesn't help. In duplicate bridge you are trying to do better than the other players who hold the same cards as you. It may be discouraging to pick up a deal with no high cards, but your competitors will be faced with the same problem. You are not at any disadvantage. The winner will not be the lucky player who gets the good deals but the player who makes the most of what he is dealt.

There is also the never-ending search for the fourth player to make up enough for a game. Have you had that experience? Organizing a bridge party is not for the fainthearted. You decide on two tables, make sure you have eight people coming, and at seven o'clock, with the party set for eight, the phone rings. For some reason, one player or a couple can't make it. Time to panic. It is just as difficult for the people on the other end of the phone. They have committed to play bridge but something comes up and they have to cancel, knowing the party can't be the same without them.

Duplicate bridge is the answer. Your days of trying to get together the right number of people to have a successful game are over. In fact, you do not even have to find a partner. In every city and almost every town across North America, and in many parts of the world, there are *duplicate bridge clubs* which are in the business of finding a fourth for bridge. Some run games once a week, others are open every afternoon and evening every day of the week. The *American Contract Bridge League*, referred to as *ACBL*, with its headquarters in Memphis, will not only provide you with a booklet listing almost 5000 clubs but will even organize your bridge holiday. Every year there are hundreds of local and regional duplicate tournaments and three North American Bridge Championships. There are events for the experienced players and for the world champions which you can watch (*kibitz*), but most tournaments specialize in games catering to those who are new to duplicate bridge. The tournaments are held in some of the finest hotels in the world. Are you convinced that duplicate bridge is for you? Let's look at how you get started.

♠ STARTING OUT ♠

In future lessons, we will look at how you go about finding a local duplicate game and what to do when you first arrive. For this lesson, however, we will assume you are already sitting at the table, with your favorite partner, ready to start playing. We will start by looking at two of the items that will be sitting on the table in front of you and then present the mechanics of bidding and playing a hand.

The Guide Card

In a duplicate game, each partnership is given a *pair number* and a *direction*, either North-South or East-West. For example, a pair may be assigned to *"7 N-S,"* representing pair number 7 in the North-South direction. This corresponds to their starting position for the game. Pair 7 N-S would be seated at Table Number 7 with one member of the partnership sitting in the North position and the other in the South position. On each table there will be a *guide card* that looks something like this:

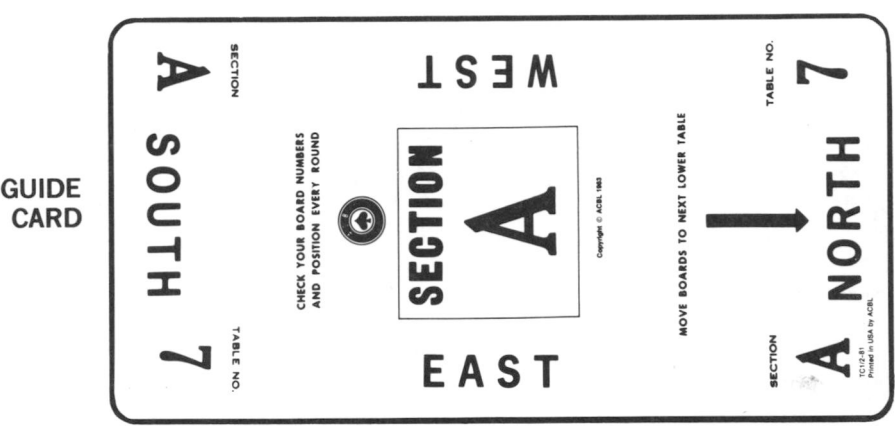

The first thing to notice on the guide card is the *table number*. There will be several tables in play at a duplicate game and each table is assigned a different number. The tables will normally be laid out so that Table 2 is right next to Table 1 and so on. Also displayed on the guide card are the directions: North, South, East and West. North may not point toward the geographic North Pole. All tables, however, will have North pointing in the same direction. A very large game or tournament may be divided into a number of *sections*. Each section will be identified by a letter and each table within the section will have a number. For example, you may be assigned to "A 8 E-W," representing Section A, Table 8, East-West. Each section will have its own set of guide cards with the section displayed on them. The guide cards for one section are usually a different color from those of another section to help you easily identify the section in which you are playing.

The Duplicate Board

In addition to the guide card, there will be one or more *duplicate boards* placed on the table in front of you. A board is used to hold the cards for each deal. Since the same deal is going to be played at more than one table, the board is designed to keep the original hands intact and make it easy to pass it on to another table. It will look something like this:

**DUPLICATE
BOARD**

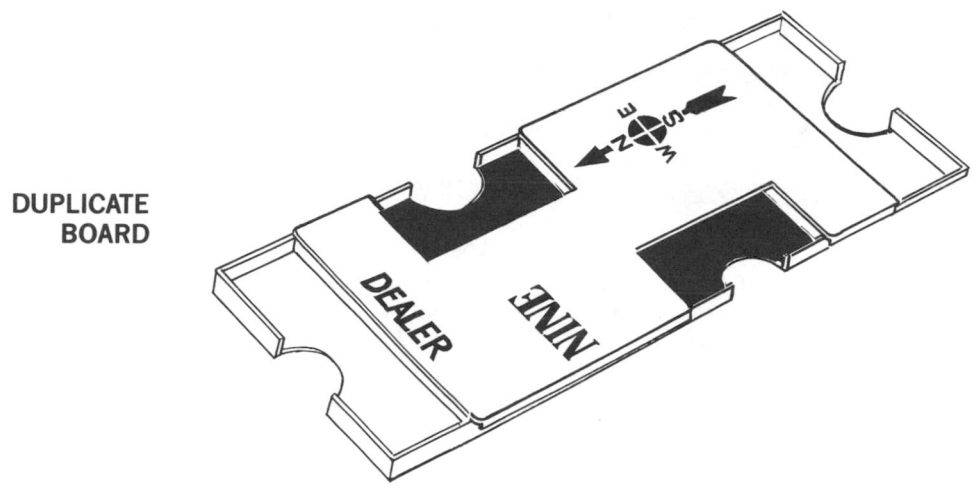

The board has four pockets, each capable of holding a hand of thirteen cards. On each board there is a *board number* so that you keep track of each deal that you play. The board numbers usually range from 1 to 36, although you play only some of the boards during a game and fewer boards may be in play (1–20).

On the board are marked the directions, normally with an arrow pointing toward the North (N) hand. The board is placed on the table with North aligned in the same direction as marked on the guide card. North (N), South (S), East (E) and West (W) each then have their own hand in the pocket in front of them. It is the responsibility of the player sitting North to see that the board is correctly placed on the table.

DEALER or DLR is also marked on the board. Since the hands are going to be played more than once, they are dealt only once, at the start of the game, and kept intact thereafter. The dealer marked on the board, therefore, does not refer to the player who actually deals the cards. Instead, it represents the player who will start the bidding (as though he dealt the cards). On Board 1, North is always shown as the dealer. On Board 2, East is the dealer, followed by South on Board 3 and West on Board 4. The dealer continues to rotate clockwise around the table on the subsequent boards, as would be the case in a rubber bridge game, giving each player in turn the opportunity to start the bidding.

In a rubber bridge game, both partnerships start out as *not vulnerable*. If a partnership bids and makes a game, it becomes *vulnerable*. When a side is vulnerable, the penalties for being defeated in a contract are increased, but if the vulnerable side bids and makes another game, it wins the *rubber*, receiving a bonus in the scoring. Then a new rubber starts, with both sides not vulnerable again. Whether a side is not vulnerable or vulnerable, therefore, depends on the state of the game.

In duplicate bridge, each deal stands by itself and is scored independently of the other deals that are played. Therefore, whether or not a partnership is vulnerable on a particular board has to be predetermined. Vulnerability is assigned so that each partnership is vulnerable half the time and not vulnerable the other half of the time. It has nothing to do with the results achieved on an earlier hand. If your side is vulnerable, the word "VUL" (VULNERABLE) is marked beside your pocket on the board, or the pocket or lettering is colored red. If there is nothing marked beside the pocket and/or the pocket is not colored red, then you are not vulnerable. On Board 1, both sides are not vulnerable. On Board 2, North-South are vulnerable while East-West are not vulnerable. On Board 3, it is East-West's turn to be vulnerable while North-South are not vulnerable. On Board 4, both North-South and East-West are vulnerable. A similar pattern continues for the remaining sets of four boards with some variances. The complete pattern is repeated every 16 boards.

Shuffle and Deal

When the boards are first placed on your table, one or more of the cards may be face-up in the pocket. This indicates that the cards have not yet been shuffled and dealt. Alternatively, the person running the game may instruct the players to "shuffle and deal." Shuffling and dealing the cards is not necessarily the responsibility of the player sitting in the position marked as DEALER on the board. Anyone at the table can shuffle and deal the cards for a particular hand. When there are several boards to be *made* (shuffled and dealt), each partnership shares the responsibility. For your partnership, for example, you may deal out the cards for one or more boards while your partner fills in the entry form.

The cards are taken out of each of the pockets and shuffled together. Before dealing them out, it is customary to have one of your opponents *cut* the cards, although you can do this yourself if no one at the table objects. The cards are then dealt face-down clockwise into four piles in front of you and then each hand of thirteen cards is put into its proper pocket of the board.

Bidding

When everyone is ready to bid and play the board, you each take your cards out of the pocket in front of you. Before looking at your hand, count your cards to make sure you have 13. Because the deals are played more than once, it is not uncommon for a card to have been dropped on the floor or inadvertently placed in the wrong pocket. Discovering the problem later, during the bidding or play, will not only prove embarrassing but could result in your side being penalized in the scoring of the deal. The player marked as DEALER on the board starts the bidding. The bidding then proceeds in the normal fashion, clockwise around the table.

If nobody opens the bidding, the deal is said to be *passed out*. You do not reshuffle and redeal the cards. Instead, you replace the cards in their pockets and get ready to bid and play the next board. The same deal is going to be played at other tables and one of the players there may choose to open the bidding. If a deal is passed out, it is a good idea to mix up the cards in your hand before replacing them in the pocket. Otherwise, when someone at another table takes the cards out of the pocket and sees them nicely sorted into suits, he may be able to guess that the deal was passed out at your table.

Play of the Cards

If you are going to pass the same deal to another table after it has been played, you cannot gather the cards together after each trick as you would in rubber bridge. You need to leave each hand intact so that it can be replaced in the appropriate pocket of the board.

Let's start with the opening lead. Instead of placing the card in the middle of the table, you place it in front of you. In duplicate bridge, the opening lead is normally made face down, rather than face up. That way, if you made a mistake and it was not actually your lead, no one has seen the card. When someone points out the mistake, you can pick up your card and the correct player can lead with no one knowing what card you attempted to lead. Leading face down also gives your partner the opportunity to ask for a review of the bidding, or any other questions about the auction, before seeing the card you chose to lead.

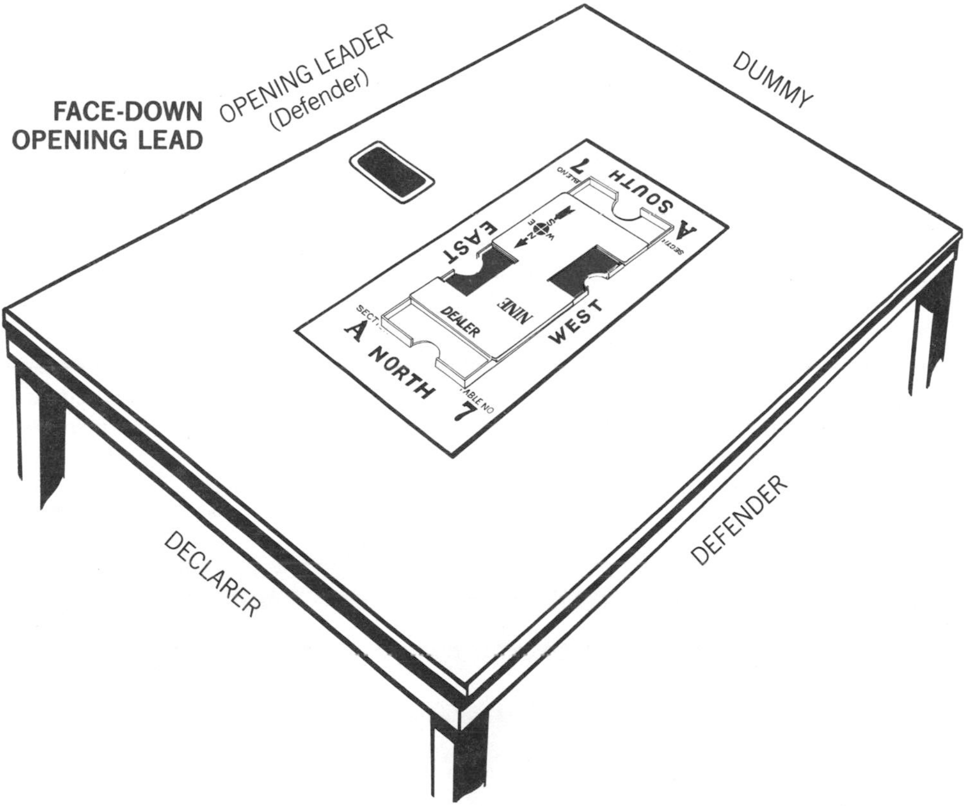

FACE-DOWN OPENING LEAD

OPENING LEADER (Defender)

DUMMY

DECLARER

DEFENDER

When everyone is satisfied that it is really your opening lead, the card is turned face up. Dummy then puts down his cards, face up in columns, similar to rubber bridge.

DUMMY COMES DOWN

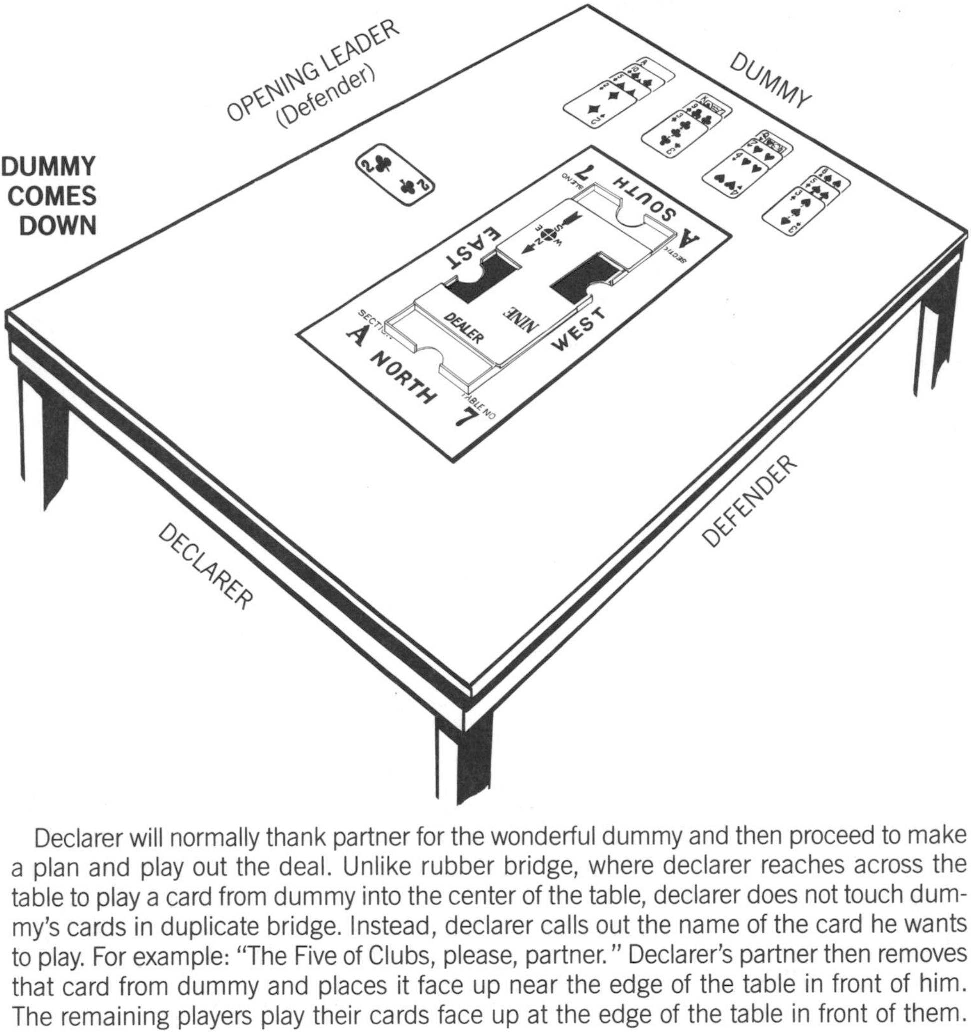

Declarer will normally thank partner for the wonderful dummy and then proceed to make a plan and play out the deal. Unlike rubber bridge, where declarer reaches across the table to play a card from dummy into the center of the table, declarer does not touch dummy's cards in duplicate bridge. Instead, declarer calls out the name of the card he wants to play. For example: "The Five of Clubs, please, partner." Declarer's partner then removes that card from dummy and places it face up near the edge of the table in front of him. The remaining players play their cards face up at the edge of the table in front of them.

**THE
FIRST
TRICK**

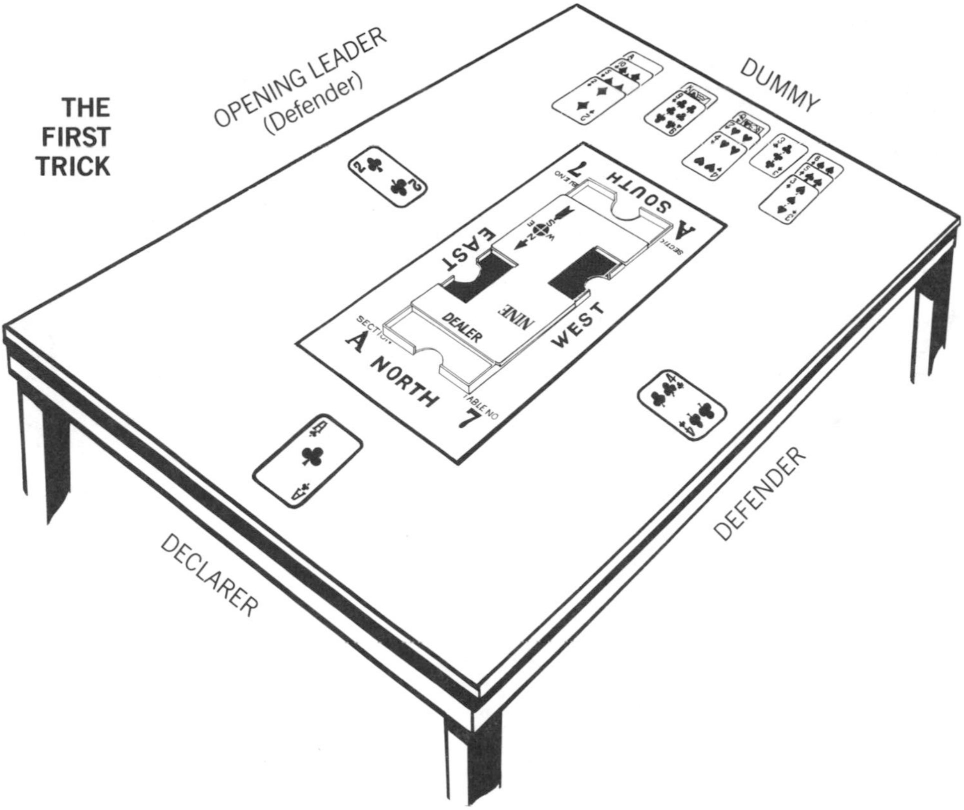

After all four cards have been played and it is clear who has won the trick, everyone turns his card face down in front of him. You should not turn your card face down, however, until you have had sufficient time to see all the cards played to the trick. Once you turn your card face down, **you may not require the players to let you see the cards played to the trick again**. As long as your card remains face up, you may require the other players to let you see their cards, even if they have turned them face down. Once all four players have turned their cards face down, no one may require that the cards be faced again until the end of the deal. This is a little different from rubber bridge where you may ask to see the cards played to the last trick even after they have been gathered up.

The pair who won the trick turn their cards face down in front of them pointing vertically toward each other. The pair losing the trick put their cards face down horizontally, pointing toward their opponents. The card played to the first trick is placed on the player's left, close to the edge of the table, and each subsequent card is displaced slightly to the right so that, at the end of the hand, each player has a neat row of cards in front of him.

AT THE END OF PLAY

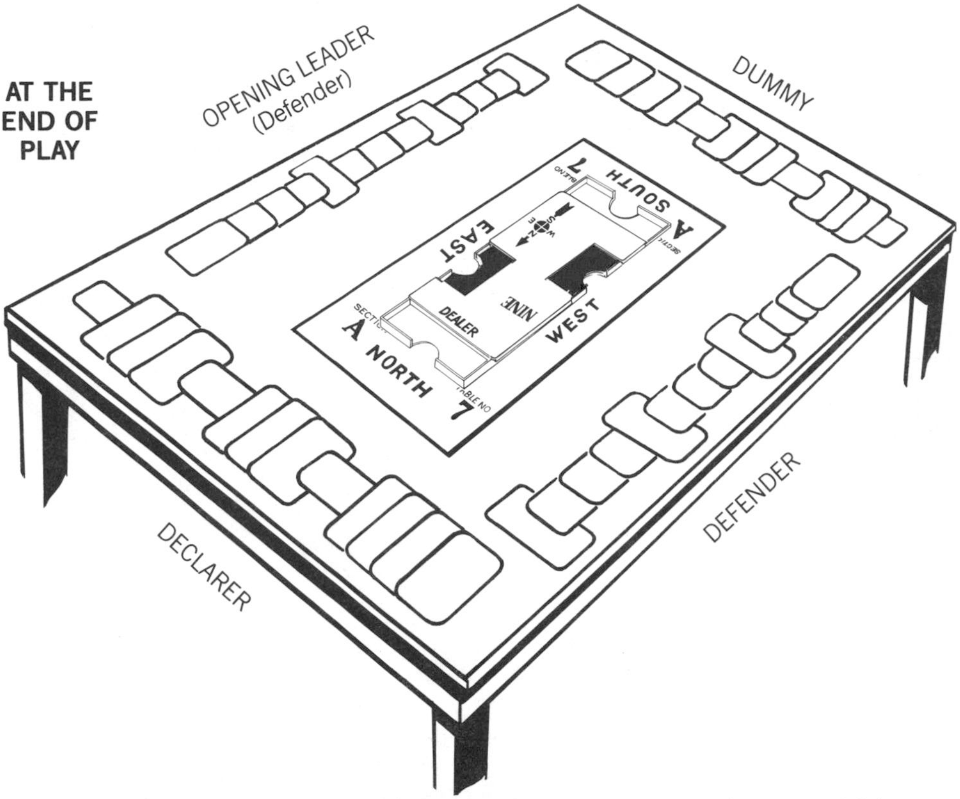

OPENING LEADER (Defender)

DUMMY

DEFENDER

DECLARER

By examining the cards in front of them, the players can agree on how many tricks were won for each side. For example, suppose North-South were in a contract of 4♠ in the deal illustrated in the above diagram. Did they make it? You can count the winners, the cards which are placed vertically in front of North and South. Both North and South have 10 cards pointing in their direction, indicating they won 10 tricks and made the contract. Three of their cards point toward East-West, representing the three tricks they lost. Notice how the East-West cards confirm this result. Both East and West have three cards pointing vertically in front of them, indicating that they took three tricks. Ten cards are pointing toward their opponents.

Playing the cards out this way makes it easy to resolve any discrepancies. If a player has one of his cards turned in a different direction than the other players, everyone can take out the card played to the trick and reconfirm which side won the trick. Similarly, it is possible to reconstruct the entire play of the hand if necessary. For example, there may be a question at the end of the hand as to whether or not one of the players failed to follow suit when he could have. This can be easily resolved.

Once the players agree on the number of tricks taken, each player can gather up the cards in front of him and put them back into the correct pocket in the duplicate board. After the deal has been scored, everyone is ready to bid and play the next board.

♠ *SCORING* ♠

When the deal has been bid and played, we need to record the result. It is time to look at how to determine the score on each hand. As with rubber bridge, the points are scored in three ways:

- Trick Score
- Bonuses
- Penalties

Because each deal is scored on its own, however, there are some minor differences between rubber bridge scoring and duplicate scoring. We will look first at how the score is arrived at and then at how to record it during a game.

Trick Score

The trick score is the same for duplicate and rubber bridge. The score awarded depends on the denomination of the contract as follows:

TRICK SCORE

- Clubs or Diamonds   20 points per trick
- Hearts or Spades   30 points per trick
- Notrump   40 points for the first trick
         30 points for each subsequent trick

The trick score is awarded only if you make the contract and only for those tricks beyond *book* (the first six tricks). For example, compare the trick scores for contracts of 2♣, 2♠ and 2NT. In each case, you have to take eight tricks to fulfill the contract.

- 2 ♣   20 + 20 = 40 points
- 2 ♠   30 + 30 = 60 points
- 2 N T   40 + 30 = 70 points

The small differences in trick score for the different denominations can have a large impact on the strategy in duplicate bridge. Your objective is to achieve a higher score than the other partnerships that hold the same cards. If your side can take exactly eight tricks, it is obviously better to play in a major suit contract (hearts or spades) than a minor suit contract (clubs or diamonds). It is even better to play in a notrump contract if you can take the same number of tricks. We will take a closer look at how this affects your strategy in future lessons.

Bonuses

There are bonuses awarded for bidding and making a partscore or game contract, for bidding and making a slam, for making overtricks and for making a doubled or redoubled contract. The size of the bonus often depends on whether or not your side is vulnerable.

As mentioned earlier, the vulnerability of both sides is predetermined before you start to play the deal and is indicated on the duplicate board. Unlike rubber bridge, there is no bonus for holding *honors* — four or all five of the top five cards in the trump suit or all four aces in a notrump contract.

Partscores and Games

When you make your contract, you receive a bonus. If the trick scores of the tricks contracted for total 100 points or more, you get a *game bonus*. If not, you get a *partscore bonus*.

GAME AND PARTSCORE BONUSES

	Not Vulnerable	Vulnerable
Game	300 points	500 points
Partscore	50 points	50 points

To get a sufficient trick score for a game bonus, you will have to bid to at least the five level in a minor suit (20 + 20 + 20 + 20 + 20 = 100), the four level in a major suit (30 + 30 + 30 + 30 = 120), or the three level in notrump (40 + 30 + 30 = 100). Otherwise, you receive only a partscore bonus.

Here are some examples, assuming your side is not vulnerable:

Contract: 3 NT	Trick Score	100	(40 +30 +30)
Result: 9 tricks	Bonus	300	(Non-vulnerable game)
	Total Score	400	

Contract: 4♥	Trick Score	120	(30 +30 +30 +30)
Result: 10 tricks	Bonus	300	(Non-vulnerable game)
	Total Score	420	

Contract: 5♣	Trick Score	100	(20 +20 +20 +20 +20)
Result: 11 tricks	Bonus	300	(Non-vulnerable game)
	Total Score	400	

Contract: 2 NT	Trick Score	70	(40 +30)
Result: 8 tricks	Bonus	50	(Partscore)
	Total Score	120	

Here are some examples, assuming your side is vulnerable:

Contract: 3NT	Trick Score	100	(40 +30 +30)
Result: 9 tricks	Bonus	500	(Vulnerable game)
	Total Score	600	

Contract: 4♠	Trick Score	120	(30 +30 +30 +30)
Result: 10 tricks	Bonus	500	(Vulnerable game)
	Total Score	620	

Contract: 5♦	Trick Score	100	(20 +20 +20 +20 +20)
Result: 11 tricks	Bonus	500	(Vulnerable game)
	Total Score	600	

Contract: 3♥	Trick Score	90	(30 +30 +30)
Result: 9 tricks	Bonus	50	(Partscore)
	Total Score	140	

The immediate awarding of a game or partscore bonus is the major difference between duplicate scoring and rubber bridge scoring. In rubber bridge, no bonus is awarded until one side has won two games (winning the rubber).

Slams

Additional bonuses are awarded for slams. A *small slam bonus* is given for bidding and making a contract in any denomination at the six level (6♣, 6♦, 6♥, 6♠ or 6NT). A *grand slam bonus* is awarded for bidding and making a contract in any denomination at the seven level (7♣, 7♦, 7♥, 7♠ or 7NT). The size of the bonus depends on the vulnerability as follows:

SLAM BONUSES

	Not Vulnerable	Vulnerable
Small Slam	500 points	750 points
Grand Slam	1000 points	1500 points

The slam bonus is awarded in addition to the game bonus. If you do not make your slam contract, however, you lose the game bonus as well as the slam bonus, suffering a penalty instead. Here are some non-vulnerable examples:

Contract: 6♣	Trick Score	120	(20 +20 +20 +20 +20 +20)
Result: 12 tricks	Game Bonus	300	(Non-vulnerable game)
	Slam Bonus	500	(Non-vulnerable small slam)
	Total Score	920	

Contract: 6 ♥	Trick Score	180	(30 +30 +30 +30 +30 +30)
Result: 12 tricks	Game Bonus	300	(Non-vulnerable game)
	Slam Bonus	500	(Non-vulnerable small slam)
	Total Score	980	

Contract: 7 NT	Trick Score	220	(40 +30 +30 +30 +30 +30 +30)
Result: 13 tricks	Game Bonus	300	(Non-vulnerable game)
	Slam Bonus	1000	(Non-vulnerable grand slam)
	Total Score	1520	

Here are some vulnerable examples:

Contract: 6 ♦	Trick Score	120	(20 +20 +20 +20 +20 +20)
Result: 12 tricks	Game Bonus	500	(Vulnerable game)
	Slam Bonus	750	(Vulnerable small slam)
	Total Score	1370	

Contract: 6 NT	Trick Score	190	(40 +30 +30 +30 +30 +30)
Result: 12 tricks	Game Bonus	500	(Vulnerable game)
	Slam Bonus	750	(Vulnerable small slam)
	Total Score	1440	

Contract: 7 ♠	Trick Score	210	(30 +30 +30 +30 +30 +30 +30)
Result: 13 tricks	Game Bonus	500	(Vulnerable game)
	Slam Bonus	1500	(Vulnerable grand slam)
	Total Score	2210	

Overtricks

When you make one or more *overtricks* in your contract, the trick score for each extra trick is added to your score.

Here are some vulnerable examples:

Contract: 4 ♠	Trick Score	120	(30 + 30 + 30 + 30)
Result: 11 tricks	Game Bonus	500	(Vulnerable game)
	Overtrick	30	(30)
	Total Score	650	

Contract: 2 ♠	Trick Score	60	(30 + 30)
Result: 10 tricks	Partscore		
	Bonus	50	
	Overtricks	60	(30 + 30)
	Total Score	170	

Contract: 3 NT	Trick Score	100	(40 + 30 + 30)
Result: 13 tricks	Game Bonus	500	(Vulnerable Game)
	Overtricks	120	(30 + 30 + 30 + 30)
	Total Score	720	

Notice that you do not get a game bonus if you are in a partscore contract and make enough tricks for game. Similarly, you do not get a slam bonus if you are only in a game contract and take 12 or 13 tricks. You must bid to a game or slam contract to be awarded the bonus.

Doubled Contracts

If you make a doubled contract, your trick score is doubled and you receive a special bonus of 50 points for the "insult" of being doubled. If you are in a partscore and your doubled trick score amounts to 100 or more points, you get the appropriate game bonus. Non-vulnerable overtricks are worth 100 points each and vulnerable overtricks are worth 200 points each. Here are some non-vulnerable examples:

Contract: 4♠ Doubled	Trick Score	240	(30 +30 +30 +30) X 2
Result: 10 tricks	Game Bonus	300	(Non-vulnerable game)
	Insult Bonus	50	
	Total Score	590	

Contract: 2♥ Doubled	Trick Score	120	(30 +30) × 2
Result: 9 tricks	Game Bonus	300	(Non-vulnerable game)
	Insult Bonus	50	
	Overtrick	100	
	Total Score	570	

The second example illustrates why it is dangerous to double a partscore contract unless you are quite sure that you can defeat it. If the 2♥ contract had not been doubled, the total score would have been only 140 (60 for the trick score, 50 for the partscore bonus and 30 for the overtrick).

A contract can also be *redoubled*. The effect on the scoring is to double again the trick score, insult bonus and overtrick score received for a doubled contract. For example, if the last contract above was redoubled, the total score would be calculated as follows:

Contract: 2♥ Redoubled	Trick Score	240	(30 +30) × 4
Result: 9 tricks	Game Bonus	300	(Non-vulnerable game)
	Insult Bonus	100	(50 × 2)
	Overtrick	200	(100 × 2)
	Total Score	840	

With doubled and redoubled contracts, the points can mount up quickly!

Penalties

Not all contracts are made, of course, and you can get points for defeating your opponents' contract. The size of the penalty depends on the number of tricks by which the contract is defeated (*undertricks*), the vulnerability and whether or not the contract is doubled or redoubled.

PENALTIES

	Not Vulnerable	Vulnerable
Undoubled	50 points per trick	100 points per trick
Doubled	100 points for the first trick 200 points for the 2nd and 3rd tricks 300 points for each subsequent trick	200 points for the first trick 300 points for each subsequent trick
Redoubled	200 points for the first trick 400 points for the 2nd and 3rd tricks 600 points for each subsequent trick	400 points for the first trick 600 points for each subsequent trick

Here are some non-vulnerable examples:

Contract: 2♥
Result: 7 tricks (down one) Penalty 50

Contract: 3NT
Result: 6 tricks (down three) Penalty 150 (50 +50 +50)

Contract: 6♣ Doubled
Result: 11 tricks (down one) Penalty 100

Contract: 4♠ Doubled
Result: 6 tricks (down four) Penalty 800 (100 +200 +200 +300)

Here are the same results when vulnerable:

Contract: 2♥
Result: 7 tricks (down one) Penalty 100

Contract: 3NT
Result: 6 tricks (down three) Penalty 300 (100 +100 +100)

Contract: 6♣ Doubled
Result: 11 tricks (down one) Penalty 200

Contract: 4♠ Doubled
Result: 6 tricks (down four) Penalty 1100 (200 +300 +300 +300)

Scoring Summary

Although you will quickly become familiar with the scores awarded for some of the common contracts, you do not have to memorize all the bonuses and penalties and be able to compute the total score in your head. Included with the material for this series is a Duplicate Scoring Summary. Similar summaries are available in most bridge clubs and at bridge tournaments. The Duplicate Scoring Summary shows the total score for all possible results. You find the row corresponding to the contract and the number of tricks made. You then look under the appropriate column depending on the vulnerability and whether or not the contract is doubled or redoubled.

♠ ♡ ◊ ♣ ♠ ♡ ◊ ♣ ♠ ♡ ◊ ♣ ♠ ♡ ◊ ♣ ♠ ♡ ◊ ♣

Bid	Made	Not Vulnerable			Vulnerable		
		Undbl	Dbl	Rdbl	Undbl	Dbl	Rdbl
1♠ – 1◊	1	70	140	230	70	140	230
	2	90	240	430	90	340	630
	3	110	340	630	110	540	1030
	4	130	440	830	130	740	1430
	5	150	540	1030	150	940	1830
	6	170	640	1230	170	1140	2230
	7	190	740	1430	190	1340	2630
1♡ – 1♠	1	80	160	520	80	160	720
	2	110	260	720	110	360	1120
	3	140	360	920	140	560	1520
	4	170	460	1120	170	760	1920
	5	200	560	1320	200	960	2320
	6	230	660	1520	230	1160	2720
	7	260	760	1720	260	1360	3120
1 NT	1	90	180	560	90	180	760
	2	120	280	760	120	380	1160
	3	150	380	960	150	580	1560
	4	180	480	1160	180	780	1960
	5	210	580	1360	210	980	2360
	6	240	680	1560	240	1180	2760
	7	270	780	1760	270	1380	3160
2♠ – 2◊	2	90	180	560	90	180	760
	3	110	280	760	110	380	1160
	4	130	380	960	130	580	1560
	5	150	480	1160	150	780	1960
	6	170	580	1360	170	980	2360
	7	190	680	1560	190	1180	2760
2♡ – 2♠	2	110	470	640	110	670	840
	3	140	570	840	140	870	1240
	4	170	670	1040	170	1070	1640
	5	200	770	1240	200	1270	2040
	6	230	870	1440	230	1470	2440
	7	260	970	1640	260	1670	2840

Bid	Made	Not Vulnerable			Vulnerable		
		Undbl	Dbl	Rdbl	Undbl	Dbl	Rdbl
2 NT	2	120	490	680	120	690	880
	3	150	590	880	150	890	1280
	4	180	690	1080	180	1090	1680
	5	210	790	1280	210	1290	2080
	6	240	890	1480	240	1490	2480
	7	270	990	1680	270	1690	2880
3♠ – 3◊	3	110	470	640	110	670	840
	4	130	570	840	130	870	1240
	5	150	670	1040	150	1070	1640
	6	170	770	1240	170	1270	2040
	7	190	870	1440	190	1470	2440
3♡ – 3♠	3	140	530	760	140	730	960
	4	170	630	960	170	930	1360
	5	200	730	1160	200	1130	1760
	6	230	830	1360	230	1330	2160
	7	260	930	1560	260	1530	2560
3 NT	3	400	550	800	600	750	1000
	4	430	650	1000	630	950	1400
	5	460	750	1200	660	1150	1800
	6	490	850	1400	690	1350	2200
	7	520	950	1600	720	1550	2600
4♠ – 4◊	4	130	510	720	130	710	920
	5	150	610	920	150	910	1320
	6	170	710	1120	170	1110	1720
	7	190	810	1320	190	1310	2120
4♡ – 4♠	4	420	590	880	620	790	1080
	5	450	690	1080	650	990	1480
	6	480	790	1280	680	1190	1880
	7	510	890	1480	710	1390	2280
4 NT	4	430	610	920	630	810	1120
	5	460	710	1120	660	1010	1520
	6	490	810	1320	690	1210	1920
	7	520	910	1520	720	1410	2320
5♠ – 5◊	5	400	550	800	600	750	1000
	6	420	650	1000	620	950	1400
	7	440	750	1200	640	1150	1800

♠ ♡ ◊ ♣ ♠ ♡ ◊ ♣ ♠ ♡ ◊ ♣ ♠ ♡ ◊ ♣ ♠ ♡ ◊ ♣

For example, the total score for 4♠ vulnerable making 12 tricks is 680. Similarly, the score for 6♦ doubled not vulnerable making all 13 tricks is 1190. See Appendix for the complete Scoring Summary (Instant Scorer).

The Scoreslip

Once you have calculated the score on a board, it is entered on a *scoreslip*. There are two basic forms of scoreslip: the *pick-up scoreslip* and the *traveling scoreslip*. A pick-up slip is used to record the results of the boards played by one North-South pair against one East-West pair. After the scores have been entered on the scoreslip, the slips are "picked up" and given to the person responsible for compiling all the scores for the entire game. The traveling scoreslip, or *traveler*, is so named because it "travels around" with each board and is used to record the result each time the board is played. After you have finished playing a board, you can look at the traveler to see how other pairs have scored on the same deal. Pick-up slips are normally used at tournaments and they are described in the "Finer Points" section at the end of this lesson. The traveler is commonly used in club games. It is interesting to see how you are doing compared to the other partnerships sitting in your direction. Before looking at the traveler itself, let's consider the information that will need to be recorded for every board that is played.

- The board to which the score applies.
- Which pair number was North-South and which was East-West.
- The contract and which player was declarer.
- The result. Did declarer make the contract? How many overtricks or undertricks? What was the total score awarded?

This seems like a great deal of information. Let's take a look at a sample traveling scoreslip and see how it is designed to record all the necessary information as economically as possible.

ACBL SHORT TRAVELING SCORE (Mitchell or Howell)									
Board No.									
N-S Pair No.	Contract	By	M a d e	D o w n	SCORE		N-S Match-points	E-W Pair No.	E-W Match-points
					N-S	E-W			
1									
2									
3									
4									
5									
6									
7									
8									

In the top right-hand corner is a space for the board number. This need be entered only once, when the board is first made up, since the slip will be traveling with the same board throughout the game. Each time the board is played, there will be a North-South pair playing against an East-West pair. Instead of using the names of the players, each pair is referred to by the pair number that was assigned at the beginning of the game. Down the left-hand side is a column containing the North-South pair numbers. Whenever a score is entered, it is entered on the line corresponding to the North-South pair that played the board. For example, if Pair 4 N-S was playing the board, the score would be entered on line number 4. Farther to the right is a column headed "E-W Pair No." In this column, the East-West pair number is entered. For example, if Pair 3 E-W was playing the board against 4 N-S, then "3" would be entered in this column on line number 4.

There is a column for the contract. The contract is entered in abbreviated form, with an "X" used to represent a double and an "XX" to represent a redouble. For example, "4S" would represent a 4♠ contract; "1N" would be a 1 NT contract; "2H X" would represent a 2♥ contract that had been doubled. The column headed "By" is for the declarer and is entered as "N," "S," "E" or "W," corresponding to the direction marked on the guide card and on the board for the player who declared the contract. There is a column headed "Made" to enter the number of tricks taken by declarer if he made the contract. The column headed "Down" is for the number of undertricks if declarer was defeated. If declarer was in a 4♥ contract and took 10 tricks, exactly making the contract, this can be indicated by placing a check mark or a dash (—) in the "Made" column, rather than marking "10" in the column. In this lesson series "4" would be entered to indicate that four tricks over the book of six tricks were taken. If declarer took 11 tricks, making one overtrick, this is indicated by marking "+1" or "5" in the "Made" column. If declarer took only eight tricks, being defeated by two tricks, this is indicated by marking "2" in the "Down" column.

The total score for the contract is marked in the "SCORE" column. If North-South were awarded points for making a contract or for defeating a contract, the points go on their side of the SCORE column, headed "N-S." Similarly, if East-West were awarded points for making a contract or for defeating a contract, then the points go on their side of the SCORE column headed "E-W."

The columns headed "N-S Matchpoints" and "E-W Matchpoints" are not filled out until the end of the game and we will look at what gets entered there in the next section. Let's take a look at a completed line on a scoreslip and see what it tells us:

	ACBL SHORT TRAVELING SCORE								
	(Mitchell or Howell)								

Board No. | 8

N-S Pair No.	Contract	By	Made	Down	SCORE		N-S Match-points	E-W Pair No.	E-W Match-points
					N-S	E-W			
1									
2	3 H	N	4		170			5	
3									
4									
5									
6									
7									
8									

This is the scoreslip for board number 8, as indicated in the top right. It has been played by North-South pair number 2 against East-West pair number 5. The contract was 3♥ (3H), played by North (N) and declarer made an overtrick (4 or +1). The North-South pair received 170 points — 90 for the trick score, plus 50 for the partscore bonus, plus 30 for the overtrick.

It is officially the responsibility of the player sitting in the North position to fill out the scoreslip once the play is over, but in an informal game, whoever is best at figuring out the score can enter it. Both partnerships, however, should examine the score and agree that it is entered correctly. The scoreslip is then folded and put back in one of the pockets of the board (usually by North), so that it can be passed with the board to another table. At the next table, the North player will leave the scoreslip folded so that no one at the table can see the previous results until the board has been played. After the play, North unfolds the scoreslip and enters the result. The other players at the table will usually be eager to look at the scores from other tables to see how they have fared.

At the start of the game, there will be no results on the scoreslip, but as the game progresses, the scoreslip will contain more and more results, making the comparisons much more interesting. For example, a scoreslip might look like this after a board has been played six times:

	ACBL SHORT TRAVELING SCORE (Mitchell or Howell)								

Board No. 2

N-S Pair No.	Contract	By	Made	Down	SCORE		N-S Match-points	E-W Pair No.	E-W Match-points
					N-S	E-W			
1	4 H	N	4		620			1	
2	3 H	N	4		170			3	
3	4 H	N		1		100		5	
4	4 S X	E		3	500			2	
5	3NT	S	3		600			4	
6	3 H	N	3		140			6	
7									
8									

Notice how varied the results might be. Not all pairs will bid to the same contract. Even when they do, it is quite possible that the declarers will not all make the same number of tricks. This is part of what makes the game of duplicate so much fun. When you pull out the scoreslip and see the results you may well wonder if everyone really was bidding and playing the same hand!

♠ *MATCHPOINTING* ♠

At the end of the game, each board will have been played a number of times and all the results will have been entered on the scoreslip. Now it is time to compare the results and see how each pair performed under the "duplicated" conditions.

Matchpoints

Suppose you and your partner were Pair 7 N-S, and on board number 1 you were in a contract of 3 NT, not vulnerable, making exactly nine tricks for a total score of 400 points — 100 in trick score plus 300 for the non-vulnerable game bonus. If the board was played nine times during the game, the scoreslip might end up looking like this:

| ACBL SHORT TRAVELING SCORE (Mitchell or Howell) | | | | | | | | | Board No. | 1 |

N-S Pair No.	Contract	By	M a d e	D o w n	SCORE		N-S Match-points	E-W Pair No.	E-W Match-points
					N-S	E-W			
1	3 NT	N		1		50		1	
2	4 H	N	4		420			3	
3	3 NT	S	5		460			5	
4	3 C	E		3	150			7	
5	4 H	N	5		450			9	
6	3 NT	S		2		100		2	
7	3 NT	S	3		400			4	
8	4 H	N		1		50		6	
9	3 NT	N	4		430			8	

How did you do? Since you were playing North-South, your score must be compared with those of the other North-South pairs who held the same cards. Your score of 400 points was better than that of four of the North-South pairs. Pair 1 N-S was defeated in their 3 NT contract, losing 50 points. Pair 4 N-S collected 150 points for defeating East's 3♣ contract by three tricks. 150 points was not as good a score as the score that could be made by bidding and making a game. Perhaps Pair 4 N-S should have doubled and collected 500 points! Pair 6 N-S lost 100 points for going down two tricks in 3 NT and Pair 8 N-S lost 50 points when they went down one trick in 4♥.

Because duplicate bridge is a comparative form of scoring, you are awarded one *matchpoint* for every pair you beat and half a matchpoint for every pair you tie. Since you beat four other North-South pairs, you would get 4 matchpoints on this board. *Matchpointing* each board is an easy way of determining how each pair fared. By adding together the matchpoints received on each of the boards you played, you will be able to see how well you did in comparison with all the other North-South pairs.

Let's see how the other North-South pairs fared on Board #1. Pair 3 N-S had the best result. They scored 460 points for making two overtricks in their 3 NT contract. They would receive 8 matchpoints for beating all eight of the other North-South pairs. Since this is the best result on the board, they are said to have scored a *top* on the board. The number of matchpoints you get for a top board will depend on the number of times the board was played during a game. In this game, Board #1 was played nine times, so a top was worth 8 matchpoints. If a board is played 13 times, top would be worth 12 matchpoints; if a board was played only three times, top would be 2 matchpoints.

Pair 5 N-S had the next best result, scoring 450 points, so they receive 7 matchpoints. Pair 9 N-S gets 6 matchpoints for scoring 430 points and pair 2 N-S gets 5 matchpoints for scoring 420 points. Then comes your result, worth 4 matchpoints. This is an *average* result on the board — four pairs did better, four pairs did worse. Pair 4 N-S gets 3 matchpoints for scoring 150 points, slightly below average. Pair 1 N-S and Pair 8 N-S both lost 50 points. They each get 1 matchpoint for beating pair 6 N-S plus half a matchpoint for tying each other. Pair 6 N-S did not beat any of the other pairs and get no matchpoints. This is referred to as a *bottom* on the board.

Here is how the scoreslip looks with the North-South matchpoints filled in:

ACBL SHORT TRAVELING SCORE
(Mitchell or Howell)

Board No. | 1

N-S Pair No.	Contract	By	M a d e	D o w n	SCORE N-S	SCORE E-W	N-S Match-points	E-W Pair No.	E-W Match-points
1	3 NT	N		1		50	1–	1	
2	4 H	N	4		420		5	3	
3	3NT	S	5		460		8	5	
4	3 C	E		3	150		3	7	
5	4 H	N	5		450		7	9	
6	3NT	S		2		100	0	2	
7	3NT	S	3		400		4	4	
8	4 H	N		1		50	1–	6	
9	3NT	N	4		430		6	8	

Half matchpoints are usually marked as a dash (—) rather than as ½. Pair 1 N-S and Pair 8 N-S each have 1½ matchpoints on the board. Of course, this is only half the story. Each of the East-West pairs also wants to know how well they did on the board. Looking at things from the East-West perspective, the best result was achieved by Pair 2 E-W. They scored 100 points and so receive 8 matchpoints for beating all the other pairs in their direction. Pair 1 E-W and Pair 6 E-W both get 6½ matchpoints for beating six other pairs and tying each other. Then comes Pair 7 E-W who lost only 150 points, receiving 5 matchpoints. Pair 4 E-W, your opponents on Board #1, get 4 matchpoints, the same average result that you received. Then comes Pair 3 E-W with 3 matchpoints for losing 420 points to North-South, Pair 8 E-W with 2 matchpoints for losing 430 points and Pair 9 E-W with 1 matchpoint for losing 450 points. Finally, Pair 5 E-W gets a bottom on the board — no matchpoints.

Here is the scoreslip with both the North-South and East-West matchpoints filled in:

ACBL SHORT TRAVELING SCORE
(Mitchell or Howell)

Board No. | 1

N-S Pair No.	Contract	By	M a d e	D o w n	SCORE N-S	SCORE E-W	N-S Match-points	E-W Pair No.	E-W Match-points
1	3 NT	N		1		50	1–	1	6–
2	4 H	N	4		420		5	3	3
3	3NT	S	5		460		8	5	0
4	3 C	E		3	150		3	7	5
5	4 H	N	5		450		7	9	1
6	3NT	S		2		100	0	2	8
7	3NT	S	3		400		4	4	4
8	4 H	N		1		50	1–	6	6–
9	3NT	N	4		430		6	8	2

Notice how the North-South and East-West matchpoints complement each other. When Pair 3 N-S got a top, their opponents, Pair 5 E-W, got a bottom. Similarly, when Pair 6 N-S got the bottom, their opponents, Pair 2 E-W, got a top. When you get an average result, your opponents also get an average result.

The players do not have to do the actual matchpoint calculation. That will be done at the end of the game by the person running it. However, you will soon get a feeling for whether you got a top or a bottom, or an average result.

Your True Opponents

From the discussion about matchpointing, it becomes apparent that your "real" opponents on a board are not the pair you are playing against. Instead, you are trying to beat all the other pairs playing in the same direction as you.

If your opponents bid and make a vulnerable 6♦ contract, scoring 1370 points, it may seem as though you have not done very well on the board. How well you do on the board, however, will depend on what happens at all the other tables at which the board is played. If all the pairs holding your opponents' hands also bid and make 6♦, you will end up with an average number of matchpoints. You might even get a top result on the board if the other pairs playing the hand make an overtrick, scoring 1390 points, or play in 6 NT, scoring 1440 points. Of course, if no one else bid the slam, you may end up with a bottom.

Recognizing who your true opponents are is very important when it comes to the tactics required to do well in a game of duplicate bridge. Always remember that you are trying to do better than the other players holding your cards. Losing points to the table opponents won't matter, provided you lose less than other pairs in your direction. Scoring points for bidding and making contracts won't be good enough if other pairs score more points holding the same hands. It becomes a test of your skill. In each lesson, we will take a look at some of the tactics you can use to improve your results.

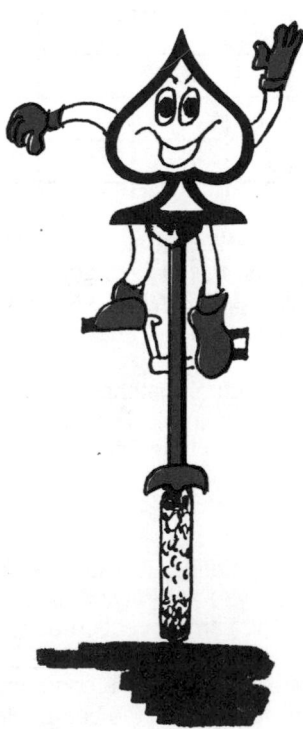

♠ *SUMMARY* ♠

In duplicate bridge, the same deal (board) is played at a number of tables. Each time the board is played, the result is recorded.

TRICK SCORE

• Clubs or Diamonds	20 points per trick
• Hearts or Spades	30 points per trick
• Notrump	40 points for the first trick
	30 points for each subsequent trick

GAME AND PARTSCORE BONUSES

	Not Vulnerable	Vulnerable
Game	300 points	500 points
Partscore	50 points	50 points

SLAM BONUSES

	Not Vulnerable	Vulnerable
Small Slam	500 points	750 points
Grand Slam	1000 points	1500 points

PENALTIES

	Not Vulnerable	Vulnerable
Undoubled	50 points per trick	100 points per trick
Doubled	100 points for the first trick 200 points for the 2nd and 3rd tricks 300 points for each subsequent trick	200 points for the first trick 300 points for each subsequent trick
Redoubled	200 points for the first trick 400 points for the 2nd and 3rd tricks 600 points for each subsequent trick	400 points for the first trick 600 points for each subsequent trick

When the game is over, the results on each board are matchpointed. You receive one matchpoint for each pair playing the board in the same direction that had a worse result than yours and half a matchpoint for every pair that tied your result.

♠ *THE FINER POINTS* ♠

Pick-Up Scoreslips

At tournaments, and in some club games, pick-up scoreslips are used to record the results, rather than traveling scoreslips. They are often used to allow the scores to be entered into a computer which can quickly calculate the matchpoints and overall results at the end of the game. A typical pick-up scoreslip looks like this:

AMERICAN CONTRACT BRIDGE LEAGUE

N – S PAIR	ALL DEALS PLAYED THIS ROUND WILL BE SCORED ON THIS CARD. CIRCLE DIRECTION OF DECLARER. E–W OK						E – W PAIR
N – S SCORE	MADE	DOWN	N – S CONTRACT	BOARD NUMBER	E – W CONTRACT	MADE	DOWN	E – W SCORE
			N S		E W			
			N S		E W			
			N S		E W			

Printed in USA by ACBL   FORM 102A REV. COPYRIGHTED 1971

The North-South pair number is entered in the top left-hand corner and the East-West pair number in the top right-hand corner. Each board that the pairs play against each other is scored on a separate line. The middle column is used to record the board number. If North-South declared the contract, it is entered in the column headed "N-S CONTRACT" and the declarer is circled (N or S). The result is then entered in the "MADE" or "DOWN" column on the North-South side. Similarly, if East-West declared the contract, it is entered in the column under "E-W CONTRACT" and the result is recorded in the "MADE" or "DOWN" column on their side of the pick-up slip. The total score is then entered under "N-S SCORE" or "E-W SCORE" depending on which partnership scored the points.

Here is a sample pick-up scoreslip where Pair #4 N-S played boards #5 and #6 against Pair #7 E-W:

AMERICAN CONTRACT BRIDGE LEAGUE

N – S PAIR	\multicolumn{6}{l}{ALL DEALS PLAYED THIS ROUND WILL BE SCORED ON THIS CARD. CIRCLE DIRECTION OF DECLARER. E–W OK *Bc*}	E – W PAIR
4							*7*
N – S SCORE	MADE	DOWN	N – S CONTRACT	BOARD NUMBER	E – W CONTRACT	MADE	DOWN	E – W SCORE

N – S SCORE	MADE	DOWN	N – S CONTRACT	BOARD NUMBER	E – W CONTRACT	MADE	DOWN	E – W SCORE
650	*5*		Ⓝ S *4S*	*5*	E W			
100			N S	*6*	Ⓔ W *3NT*			*1*
			N S		E W			

Printed in USA by ACBL   FORM 102A REV. COPYRIGHTED 1971

♠ *GROUP ACTIVITIES* ♠

Exercise One: The Guide Card

Take a look at the guide card on the table in front of you and answer the following questions:

1. At which table number are you sitting?
2. Which direction are you? (North, South, West or East?)
3. Where will North be positioned at the other tables in the room?
4. If the game has multiple sections, can you tell which section you are in?

Exercise Two: The Duplicate Board

Take a look at the duplicate board on the table in front of you.

    1. What is the board number?
    2. Is the board positioned correctly with regard to directions?
    3. Which player has the first opportunity to bid?
    4. Is either side vulnerable?

Exercise Three: Playing Out the Cards (Optional Exercise)

Take out the cards from the duplicate board in front of you. Assume South is in a contract of 1 NT (no matter how ridiculous that may be). Have West make an opening lead and North put down his cards as dummy. Play out a few tricks until everyone is comfortable with how to place their cards on the table. Then pick up your cards and replace them in the duplicate board.

Exercise Four: Calculating the Score

Fill in the chart below to determine the total score for each of the contracts:

Contract	Vulner-ability	Result	Trick Score	Game/Partscore Bonus	Over-tricks	Penalty Bonus	Slam bonus	Total Score
2♥	Not vul	8 tricks			−	−	−	
3NT	Not vul	11 tricks				−	−	
6♣	Not vul	12 tricks			−	−		
4♥	Not vul	9 tricks	−	−	−		−	
1 NT	Vul	8 tricks				−	−	
4♠	Vul	10 tricks			−	−	−	
3♦	Vul	7 tricks	−	−	−		−	

Exercise Five: The Duplicate Scoring Summary

Use the Duplicate Scoring Summary sheet (Instant Scorer) to look up the scores for each of the following results:

Contract	Vulnerability	Result	Total Score
4♥ Doubled	Not vul	10 tricks	
7♠	Not vul	13 tricks	
2♠ Doubled	Not vul	9 tricks	
5♦ Redoubled	Vul	10 tricks	
1 NT	Vul	11 tricks	

Exercise Six: The Scoreslip

Complete the scoreslip for Board #8, filling in the results below. The first two results have already been entered to guide you.

1. North-South Pair #1 played against East-West Pair #6. North played in a contract of 4♥ and took 10 tricks for a score of 420 points.
2. North-South Pair #2 played against East-West Pair #8. North played in a contract of 2♥ and took 10 tricks for a score of 170 points.

	ACBL SHORT TRAVELING SCORE (Mitchell or Howell)							Board No. 8	

N-S Pair No.	Contract	By	Made	Down	SCORE N-S	SCORE E-W	N-S Match-points	E-W Pair No.	E-W Match-points
1	4 H	N	4		420			6	
2	2 H	N	4		170			8	
3									
4									
5									
6									
7									
8									

3. North-South Pair #3 played against East-West Pair #2. East played in a contract of 3♠ doubled and was defeated two tricks, losing 300 points.
4. North-South Pair #4 played against East-West Pair #4. North played in a contract of 4♥ and made an overtrick for a score of 450 points.
5. North-South Pair #5 played against East-West Pair #7. North played in a contract of 4♥ and was defeated one trick, losing 50 points.
6. North-South Pair #6 played against East-West Pair #1. South played in a contract of 3NT and was defeated two tricks, losing 100 points.
7. North-South Pair #7 played against East-West Pair #3. North played in a contract of 3♣ and made an overtrick for a score of 130 points.
8. North-South Pair #8 played against East-West Pair #5. South played in a contract of 3NT and was defeated one trick, losing 50 points.

Exercise Seven: Matchpointing

Take a look at the scoreslip from the previous exercise and answer the following questions:

1. Which North-South pair got the best result? How many North South pairs did they defeat? How many matchpoints do they get?
2. Which North-South pair got the worst result? How many matchpoints do they get?
3. How many matchpoints do Pair #2 N-S get?
4. Pair #5 N-S and Pair #8 N-S had the same result. They beat Pair #6 N-S and tied each other. How many matchpoints do they each get?
5. Which East-West pair got the best (top) result? How many matchpoints do they get? How does this correspond to the matchpoints awarded to the North-South pair they played against?
6. Which East-West pair got the bottom result? How does this compare with the result of the North-South pair they played the board against?

♠ *SAMPLE BOARDS* ♠

The following pages contain the practice hands for the lesson. Each board is accompanied by a scoreslip showing sample results that might have occurred in an actual duplicate game. This gives you something to compare your result with. There is also a suggested auction to reach a reasonable contract and a suggested approach to the play of the hand. In practice, the actual auction and play might progress quite differently, depending on the judgment exercised by each of the players at the table.

BOARD #1

Dealer: North
Vulnerable: None

NORTH
♠ K 10 4
♥ A K J 4
♦ K 10 8 4
♣ Q 8

WEST
♠ Q 9 6 3
♥ Q 9 5 3
♦ A 6 2
♣ 6 4

EAST
♠ A J 8 7 5
♥ 8 6
♦ Q J 5
♣ 10 9 3

SOUTH
♠ 2
♥ 10 7 2
♦ 9 7 3
♣ A K J 7 5 2

ACBL SHORT TRAVELING SCORE
(Mitchell or Howell)

Board No. **1**

N-S Pair No.	Contract	By	Made	Down	SCORE N-S	SCORE E-W	N-S Match-points	E-W Pair No.	E-W Match-points
1	3NT	N	5		460			1	
2	3NT	N	3		400			3	
3	3NT	N	4		430			5	
4	5 C	S		1		50		2	
5	3 C	S	4		130			4	
6	3NT	N	3		400			6	
7									
8									

Suggested Bidding

WEST	NORTH	EAST	SOUTH
	1 NT	Pass	3 NT
Pass	Pass	Pass	

Even though South has a singleton spade, a notrump contract is still the best chance for a good score. Opener needs a balanced hand to start the bidding 1 NT. Responder, however, decides the final contract. South has 8 HCPs plus 2 points for the six-card club suit. Knowing there are at least 26 combined points, South wants to be in a game. Of the two choices, 3 NT and 5♣, notrump requires fewer tricks and is more likely to succeed.

Suggested Play

With no help from the bidding, East is likely to lead the ♠7, fourth highest from his longest and strongest suit. Dummy would play low, West would contribute the ♠Q, third hand high, and North would win the trick with the ♠K. North needs nine tricks. Including the spade trick, he has six club tricks and two heart tricks, enough for the contract. Of course, North must be careful to play the clubs starting with the ♣Q, high card from the short side.

Notes

Bidding and making exactly 3 NT would be worth 400 points (100 trick score plus 300 for the non-vulnerable game bonus). Looking at the sample scoreslip you can see that 400 points would be an average matchpoint score. Two pairs did better, two did worse and one pair did exactly the same. Pair #1 N-S has the best result so far for making two overtricks. Perhaps declarer led the ♥10 from dummy and took a finesse. If West did not cover with the ♥Q, declarer could repeat the finesse and end up with four heart tricks instead of two. Of course, if the finesse had lost, it would have been a different story. Pair #4 N-S decided to play in 5♣ instead of risking 3 NT. Not a lucky decision! They lost a spade trick and two diamond tricks for down one, giving Pair #2 E-W a good result on the board. Pair #5 N-S stopped in 3♣. Another poor decision, since they missed the game bonus they could have earned for being in 3 NT.

BOARD #2

Dealer: East
Vulnerable: North-South

NORTH
♠ A
♥ J 9 7 4
♦ K 6 3
♣ 10 7 5 4 2

WEST
♠ J 9 6 4
♥ A K 5
♦ 8 4 2
♣ Q 8 3

EAST
♠ Q 10 8 7 3 2
♥ Q 3
♦ A 7 5
♣ A K

SOUTH
♠ K 5
♥ 10 8 6 2
♦ Q J 10 9
♣ J 9 6

ACBL SHORT TRAVELING SCORE
(Mitchell or Howell)

Board No. 2

N-S Pair No.	Contract	By	Made	Down	SCORE N-S	SCORE E-W	N-S Match-points	E-W Pair No.	E-W Match-points
1	4 S	E	4			420		1	
2	4 S	E		1	50			3	
3	4 S	E	5			450		5	
4	4 S	E	5			450		2	
5	4 S	E		1	50			4	
6	4 S	E	6			480		6	
7									
8									

Suggested Bidding

WEST	NORTH	EAST	SOUTH
		1♠	Pass
2♠	Pass	3♠	Pass
4♠	Pass	Pass	Pass

The bidding is straightforward. Opener rebids 3♠ after partner's single raise because, counting 2 points for the six-card suit, he has a medium strength hand worth 17 points. West happily accepts the invitation to bid game since he has the top of his range for raising to 2♠.

Suggested Play

South will likely lead the ♦Q, top of a sequence. East counts his losers. There are two diamonds losers and two spade losers, one too many. Since East will have to give up the lead when drawing trumps, he has to eliminate at least one loser first. Careful play can result in the elimination of two losers. After winning the first diamond trick, East plays the ♣A, the ♣K, and then the ♥Q followed by the ♥3 to dummy's ♥K (or ♥A). Declarer is in dummy and plays the last heart on which he discards a low diamond from his hand. On the ♣Q he can discard his other diamond loser. Now he can lead trumps, losing only to the ♠A and ♠K.

Notes

Two East-West pairs made only nine tricks in their spade contract. If East leads trumps right away, before eliminating his losers, that is what might happen. If he concentrates on making the contract and not on getting an overtrick, he might take only 10 tricks after discarding one of his losers on dummy's extra heart winner. If he wants to do well, however, he has to concentrate on not just making the contract but taking as many tricks as possible. Those pairs scoring 450 for taking 11 tricks have a good result. How did Pair #6 E-W manage to take 12 tricks missing the ♠A and ♠K? Perhaps East led the ♠Q from his hand, after eliminating his other losers, and South played the ♠K on it, an unfortunate choice when North had to put the ♠A on the same trick. Sometimes losers disappear as though by magic!

BOARD #3

Dealer: South
Vulnerable: East-West

NORTH
♠ A 10 8 7 5
♥ Q J 3
♦ 9 3
♣ Q 9 7

WEST
♠ Q 4
♥ A K 10 8 6
♦ 7 6
♣ A 4 3 2

EAST
♠ K 9 3 2
♥ 9 4
♦ 10 8 4
♣ J 10 6 5

SOUTH
♠ J 6
♥ 7 5 2
♦ A K Q J 5 2
♣ K 8

ACBL SHORT TRAVELING SCORE
(Mitchell or Howell)

Board No. 3

N-S Pair No.	Contract	By	Made	Down	SCORE N-S	SCORE E-W	N-S Match-points	E-W Pair No.	E-W Match-points
1	2 H X	W		1	200			6	
2	2 D	S	2		90			2	
3	1 NT	S	2		120			4	
4	2 D	S	3		110			1	
5	2 H	W	2			110		3	
6	3 D	S		1		50		5	
7									
8									

Suggested Bidding

WEST	NORTH	EAST	SOUTH
			1 ♦
1 ♥	1 ♠	Pass	2 ♦
Pass	Pass	Pass	

South opens his long suit and rebids it after hearing North's response. South might also consider rebidding 1 NT, although with two doubletons he does not have a balanced hand, and he does not have a control in the heart suit (West's suit). West might consider bidding again, but since his partner could not bid after he overcalled, he has probably done enough.

Suggested Play

West will likely start by leading one of his high hearts. The defenders must then be careful to take all the tricks to which they are entitled. East should play the ♥9, an encouraging signal. If West interprets this correctly, he will continue with another high heart and then lead the suit again so that East can trump dummy's ♥Q. The defenders can get a spade trick and a club trick to hold South to exactly eight tricks. If they take their ♣A too quickly, however, declarer may be able to discard his spade loser on dummy's ♣Q.

Notes

This is a typical partscore hand, and anything might happen at the table. For example, West might be tempted to compete with a bid of 2 ♥ rather than let the opponents play in 2 ♦. This contract might make, as happened when Pair #3 E-W played the board. They scored 110 points, giving them the top result so far on the board. Pair #6 E-W were not so lucky. They were doubled in their 2 ♥ contract and defeated one trick. Because East-West are vulnerable, this cost them 200 points, giving them a bottom result, and Pair #1 N-S a top.

Partscore contracts often lead to more interesting results than games. With the points fairly evenly divided between the partnerships, either side may get the contract. A lot of matchpoints may depend on how well the contract is played or defended.

BOARD #4

Dealer: West
Vulnerable: Both

NORTH
♠ 642
♥ 10984
♦ 872
♣ Q 10 3

WEST
♠ A K J
♥ J 76
♦ A Q 6
♣ K 975

EAST
♠ Q 73
♥ K Q 5
♦ K 10 3
♣ A J 84

SOUTH
♠ 10985
♥ A 32
♦ J 954
♣ 62

ACBL SHORT TRAVELING SCORE (Mitchell or Howell)									

Board No. | 4

N-S Pair No.	Contract	By	M a d e	D o w n	SCORE N-S	SCORE E-W	N-S Match-points	E-W Pair No.	E-W Match-points
1	3 NT	W	6			690		6	
2	6 NT	W		1	100			2	
3	6 NT	W	6			1440		4	
4	4 NT	W	5			660		1	
5	6 NT	W	6			1440		3	
6	3 NT	W	6			690		5	
7									
8									

Suggested Bidding

WEST	NORTH	EAST	SOUTH
1NT	Pass	4NT	Pass
6NT	Pass	Pass	Pass

After a 1NT opening bid, a response of 4NT, one level beyond game, invites opener to carry on to slam. With a minimum opening 1NT bid, opener should pass, declining the invitation. With a maximum, opener should accept. On this hand, West has 18 points, the most he could have, so he accepts the invitation and bids 6NT.

Suggested Play

North will probably lead the ♥10 and South will take the first trick with the ♥A. West will have to take all the remaining tricks to make the slam. With only three spade tricks, two heart tricks and three diamond tricks, declarer will need to take all four club tricks. Missing the ♣Q, the general guideline is "eight ever, nine never," implying that you should take a finesse when you hold eight cards, rather than play the ace and king. If declarer plays the ♣K and then leads a low club toward dummy, planning to finesse the ♣J if the ♣Q has not appeared, he will make the contract. If declarer plays the ♣A and ♣K instead, hoping the ♣Q will appear, he will go down.

Notes

Hands where a slam can be bid and made are always exciting. As can be seen from the scoreslip, some pairs will bid the slam while others may stop in a safe game contract. Unless there are an easy 12 or 13 tricks to take, some players who bid the slam will make it while others will go down. Whatever the result, there will be lots to talk about after the game.

If a pair bids and makes a slam against you, as happened to Pair #3 N-S and Pair #5 N-S, you might count yourself unlucky. The luck evens out, however. You will get your own chances to bid and make slams — and perhaps the opponents will bid a slam and go down, as happened against the lucky Pair #2 N-S.

BOARD #5

Dealer: North
Vulnerable: North-South

```
                 NORTH
                 ♠ 9 8 7
                 ♥ 9 4
                 ♦ A 5 4 3
                 ♣ 8 6 5 2

WEST                          EAST
♠ 6 4 2                       ♠ J 3
♥ K J 7 5                     ♥ A Q 10 8 3
♦ 8 7                         ♦ K J 10
♣ A Q J 3                     ♣ K 10 7

                 SOUTH
                 ♠ A K Q 10 5
                 ♥ 6 2
                 ♦ Q 9 6 2
                 ♣ 9 4
```

ACBL SHORT TRAVELING SCORE
(Mitchell or Howell)

Board No. | 5

N-S Pair No.	Contract	By	Made	Down	SCORE		N-S Match-points	E-W Pair No.	E-W Match-points
					N-S	E-W			
1	4 H	E		1	50			5	
2	3 H	E	4			170		1	
3	4 H	E	4			420		3	
4	3 S	S		1		100		6	
5	3 H	E	3			140		2	
6	4 H	E	4			420		4	
7									
8									

Suggested Bidding

WEST	NORTH	EAST	SOUTH
	Pass	1 ♥	1 ♠
3 ♥ *	Pass	4 ♥	Pass
Pass	Pass		

West has a hand worth 12 points — 11 HCPs and 1 dummy point for the doubleton diamond. Since that is too much to raise to 2 ♥, West bids 3 ♥, showing 11–12 points and inviting partner to bid game.* East's hand is worth 15 points, so he accepts the invitation by bidding 4 ♥.

Suggested Play

South wins the first two spade tricks and may lead another spade, which declarer will trump. Declarer can afford only one more loser. There are two potential losers in the diamond suit. After drawing trumps, declarer has to lead a low diamond from dummy toward his hand. If North plays a low diamond, second hand low, declarer will have to guess which diamond to play. If he plays the ♦K, hoping North holds the ♦A, he will make the contract. If instead he finesses the ♦J (or ♦10), hoping North has the ♦Q, he will lose two diamond tricks and go down (not fulfill the contract).

Notes

As the scoreslip shows, not all pairs will reach 4 ♥. If they do, it may seem that making 4 ♥ is a 50–50 proposition, depending on how they guess to play the diamond suit. In practice, the contract will be made more often than not. South may lead a diamond after winning the first two tricks, and declarer will not have to guess. Or North may play the ♦A when declarer leads a diamond from dummy, again making it easy for declarer. Only patient and careful defense will give North-South a chance to defeat the contract.

---

*This assumes that the partnership plays Limit Raises. If the partnership plays Forcing Raises (a jump raise shows 13 or more points), West would bid a new suit, 2 ♣, planning to bid 3 ♥ over opener's rebid, again inviting opener to game.

BOARD #6

Dealer: East
Vulnerable: East-West

NORTH
♠ J 10 4
♥ Q 8 3
♦ 10 8
♣ A K 8 4 2

WEST
♠ A Q 8 6 3
♥ 6
♦ K Q 9 4 2
♣ Q 5

EAST
♠ 7
♥ K J 9 5 2
♦ A 7 5 3
♣ 10 9 6

SOUTH
♠ K 9 5 2
♥ A 10 7 4
♦ J 6
♣ J 7 3

ACBL SHORT TRAVELING SCORE
(Mitchell or Howell)

Board No. | 6

N-S Pair No.	Contract	By	Made	Down	SCORE		N-S Match-points	E-W Pair No.	E-W Match-points
					N-S	E-W			
1	2 S	W		1	100			5	
2	2 D	W	3			110		1	
3	1 NT	E	1			90		3	
4	2 D	W	4			130		6	
5	3 C X	N		2		300		2	
6	2 NT	E		1	100			4	
7									
8									

Suggested Bidding

WEST	NORTH	EAST	SOUTH
		Pass	Pass
1♠	Pass	1 NT	Pass
2♦	Pass	Pass	Pass

With two five-card suits, West should open the bidding in the higher-ranking suit, spades. Although North has a five-card suit, he does not have enough strength to make an over-call at the two level. With only 8 HCPs plus 1 point for the five-card suit, East does not have enough to bid a new suit at the two level and should respond 1 NT, keeping the bidding open but limiting his hand to 6–10 points. When the bidding gets back to West, he can show his second suit by bidding 2♦. Since East prefers diamonds to spades, he can pass and let the auction stop safely in a partscore contract. Of course, some aggressive North-South pairs may compete and try to play with clubs as trump. If they bid too much, they are likely to get doubled for penalties.

Suggested Play

Against a diamond contract by West, North will probably start by leading the ♣A and ♣K. If North leads a third round of clubs, West can trump. In addition to the two club losers, West will have to lose a heart trick and he has some spade losers to worry about. He can trump a couple of spade losers in dummy and, when the missing spades divide 4–3, he can establish a spade trick through length. Since declarer also wants to draw trumps, he might start by leading to the ♦A and taking the spade finesse, even though there is a singleton in dummy. That way, he can draw trumps as well as ruff spades twice in dummy and avoid losing any spade tricks.

Notes

The scoreslip shows that the best result will probably go to the East-West pairs who play the contract in their nine-card diamond fit and end up losing only two club tricks and a heart trick. If East-West end up in some other contract, they are less likely to get a good result since the defenders may be able to defeat them. If North-South compete too high in clubs, East-West can double them for an excellent result.

BOARD #7

Dealer: South
Vulnerable: Both

NORTH
♠ A K J 8 6 4
♥ 10 4
♦ 9 8
♣ K 10 3

WEST
♠ 10
♥ A Q J 5 3
♦ 7 3
♣ A Q 8 6 2

EAST
♠ 5 2
♥ K 8 7
♦ K J 10 5
♣ J 9 5 4

SOUTH
♠ Q 9 7 3
♥ 9 6 2
♦ A Q 6 4 2
♣ 7

ACBL SHORT TRAVELING SCORE
(Mitchell or Howell)

Board No. | 7

N-S Pair No.	Contract	By	Made	Down	SCORE N-S	SCORE E-W	N-S Match-points	E-W Pair No.	E-W Match-points
1	4 S	N	4		620			4	
2	4 S	N		1		100		6	
3	5 H X	W		3	800			2	
4	3 S	N	3		140			5	
5	4 S X	N	4		790			1	
6	5 H	W		2	200			3	
7									
8									

Suggested Bidding

WEST	NORTH	EAST	SOUTH
			Pass
1♥	1♠	2♥	3♠
4♥	4♠	Pass	Pass
Pass			

The bidding starts off quietly with West's opening bid, North's overcall and East's raise. But then it may take off. Counting 3 dummy points for the singleton club, South has 11 points, enough to raise North's overcall to the three level. West may not have enough points to undertake a game contract but, not wanting to defend 3♠, might bid 4♥ anyway. North will probably make a similar decision. With no guarantee that he can defeat 4♥, he may carry on to 4♠. If it makes, so much the better. If not, perhaps the penalty will be less than the score East-West would get for making 4♥.

Suggested Play

Declarer will have to lose two heart tricks and a club trick. He can trump the remaining club losers in dummy, but he still has a potential diamond loser. To make the contract, North will have to play a low diamond to dummy's ♦ Q, taking a finesse and hoping that East started with the ♦ K. The favorable location of the ♦ K allows him to make the contract.

Notes

The scoreslip shows the typical results for a distributional hand of this nature. Neither side really has the values to be in a game contract, but the competitive auction will likely drive both sides into bidding game. In such situations, the side with the spade suit will usually get the contract, since spades is the higher-ranking suit. Whether or not the contract makes will depend on the location of the missing cards. It would not be unusual for the final contract to be doubled, as happened when Pair #5 N-S played the board. East-West may even push on past game to stop North-South from playing the contract, as happened when Pair #2 E-W and Pair #3 E-W played the board. Whether or not this is a good idea will depend on the number of tricks they are defeated, whether or not they are vulnerable and whether or not they get doubled.

BOARD #8

Dealer: West
Vulnerable: None

NORTH
♠ A K 7 2
♥ K 6 4 3
♦ 7 5
♣ A 8 2

WEST
♠ Q 9 4
♥ 9 2
♦ A J 8 4 3
♣ K Q 10

EAST
♠ J 8 3
♥ Q 10 8
♦ K 9 6 2
♣ 7 5 3

SOUTH
♠ 10 6 5
♥ A J 7 5
♦ Q 10
♣ J 9 6 4

ACBL SHORT TRAVELING SCORE
(Mitchell or Howell)

Board No. 8

N-S Pair No.	Contract	By	Made	Down	SCORE N-S	SCORE E-W	N-S Match-points	E-W Pair No.	E-W Match-points
1	2 H	S	2		110			4	
2	2 D	W	2			90		6	
3	3 H	S		1		50		2	
4	3 D	W		1	50			5	
5	1 NT	S	1		90			1	
6	2 H	S	3		140			3	
7									
8									

Suggested Bidding

WEST	NORTH	EAST	SOUTH
1♦	Double	2♦	2♥
Pass	Pass	Pass	

With 12 HCPs plus one point for the five-card suit, West has enough to open the bidding 1♦. With 14 HCPs, North would like to compete for the auction and, holding support for all the unbid suits, can make a takeout double. East can raise partner's suit to the two level to try to keep the opponents quiet but this should not deter South from bidding his heart suit in response to his partner's takeout double. North should realize that South's bid is only competitive, with about 6–10 points. If South had more, he could jump to 3♥ to invite game or bid game himself.

Suggested Play

South will have to play carefully to make 2♥. He has a spade loser, a heart loser, two diamond losers and three club losers to worry about. To avoid a heart loser, South should take the heart finesse, playing a small heart to dummy's ♥ K and a small heart back toward his ♥ J, trapping East's (hoped for) ♥ Q. After playing the ♥ A, picking up the last trump from East, South loses two club tricks and ruffs the last club in dummy.

Notes

As with any competitive hand, there will be people playing the hand in both directions, depending on how the auction goes and how high they push or get pushed. If North-South reach 2♥, East-West might do well by bidding to 3♦. Even if they are defeated one trick, their result is better than the one they receive for defending 2♥. They might also push North-South "overboard" to 3♥ and end up getting a plus score.

LESSON 2

The Convention Card

Introducing the Convention Card
Conventions — Constructive Bidding
Conventions — Competition
Conventions — Defensive Card Play
Summary
The Finer Points

Workshop Material
Group Activities
Sample Boards

♠ *INTRODUCING THE CONVENTION CARD* ♠

If you and your partner have played bridge together for a long time, you are familiar with your bidding style. As you start to play duplicate bridge and your circle of bridge playing friends expands, you will meet people from different backgrounds whose bidding methods may seem strange to you. In an attempt to come up with the "ultimate system" — one that will get you to the best contract in all situations — many different bidding styles have evolved. There are so many possible bridge hands that no one has been able to come up with one system that will handle all possibilities, although some very complex methods have been tried.

In practical terms, you want to use a system that gets you to the right contract as often as possible without taxing you to the point that the game ceases to be fun. So-called "standard" methods are those that have passed the test of time and are popular with a majority of players. But even among experts there is no real consensus on what is "standard" practice. Methods popular today may lose favor tomorrow. As a result, when you sit down at the duplicate table, you will continually encounter players who use methods different from yours.

You are not expected to be familiar with all the special bids used by your opponents. However, you are entitled to know what their bids mean so that you can effectively counter them with the methods you have adopted. Your opponents are equally entitled to know the meaning of any bids you may make, or even any defensive signals that you use such as playing a high card as an encouraging signal. Secret understandings between partners are not allowed.

It would be impractical to have to explain all your methods each time you meet new opponents and to have to listen to a description of the system they use. This would not only be time-consuming, but since you are going to play only a couple of hands against them, most of what you find out will not be of any value.

There is a solution to this problem.

The Convention Card

Before the start of the game, each partnership fills out a *Convention Card* describing their general style and their artificial or *conventional* bids. Writing down the conventions you and your partner play is useful in making sure that both are playing the same methods. If you are playing with an unfamiliar partner, it gives you an opportunity to discuss the methods that you will use during the game. Although each partner is expected to fill out a separate Convention Card, you cannot each use different methods. Both cards must be identical.

The purpose of the Convention Card, however, is not for your benefit but for the benefit of the opponents. When you sit down at the table, each opponent can look at your Convention Card to familiarize themselves with the methods you are using. Likewise, you can look at your opponents' Convention Card. In that way, you do not have to ask a lot of questions about the methods your opponents use. You need to look only at the information you think may be relevant. In fact, you do not have to look at their card at all until you are interested in getting some information about one of the bids they have made.

During the auction, you should not reach over to look at an opponent's convention card until it is your turn to bid although, if it is sitting in front of you, you can glance at it whenever you wish. On the other hand, you must not look at your own Convention Card during the bidding to remind yourself what you are playing. Remember, your Convention Card is really for the benefit of the opponents, not yourself.

Convention Cards come in different formats and colors, depending on the type of game in which they are being used. The most common format is the white General Convention Card which is designed to cover the widest variety of conventions. There is a green Class A Convention Card for use in games where only a very limited number of conventions are allowed. This is used for some beginner games but there are many experienced players who also like to play in games where few artificial bids are employed. There also is the ACBL Standard Yellow Card which is pre-filled with a number of popular duplicate conventions and is designed for games where everyone plays the same methods.

In this lesson we will look at a simplified form of the General Convention Card and see how you go about completing it. The complete General Convention Card contains a lot of information that is not relevant at this point. Once you are familiar with the basic layout, you will be able to fill out the full card, completing only those sections that apply to your methods. The complete card is shown in Appendix A, along with a description of the parts not included on our simplified form.

The Convention Card is normally folded in half so that there is a front and a back side. Each side is divided into a number of subsections. Those on the front side generally relate to your opening bids and responses when the opponents are not competing in the auction. The back side is more concerned with the calls you make when both sides are competing for the contract (overcalls, takeout doubles, etc.) and with your opening leads and defensive signals.

The complete card looks something like this:

STUDENT CONVENTION CARD

SPECIAL DOUBLES
(Describe)

Negative _____
_____
_____
_____
_____

DIRECT NT OVERCALLS

1NT _____ to _____ HCP
Jump to 2 NT: __ to __ HCP
Unusual for Minors □
_____
_____

Vs. Wk. □ Strong □ NT Opening
Direct □   Balance □
2♣ shows   ♣
2◇ shows   ◇
2♡ shows   ♡
2♠ shows   ♠

SIMPLE OVERCALL
__ to __ HCP (occ. light □)
New suit forcing _____

JUMP OVERCALL
Strong □ Interm □ Weak □

OVER OPP'S TAKEOUT DOUBLE
New Suit Force 1–level □ 2–level □
Jp. Shift Force □ Good □ Weak □

OPENING PREEMPTS
3–Bids
Sound   □ Vul. & Not Vul.
Light   □ Not Vul. Only

Vs. Opp's Preempts Dbl. Is
Takeout
Weak 2's   □
3 Bids   □

PSYCHICS   Never □

SLAM CONVENTIONS
Mark X if you play that 4♣
over partner's NT bid asks
for aces. If 4♣ always asks
for aces, write "WHEN OB-
VIOUS" on line.

DIRECT CUEBID
Strong Takeout: Minor □ Major □
Natural: ♠ □   ◇ □

Gerber □ _____   Blackwood □ _____

Names _____
General Approach _____ Pair # _____
Strong Forcing Opening: 2♣ □ 2 bids □ 1♣ □ Other _____

NOTRUMP OPENING BIDS
1NT _____ to _____ □   2NT _____ to _____ HCP
or _____ to _____ □   3NT _____ to _____ HCP
2♣ = Non-Forc. □ Stayman   1NT-3♣/3◇   Is Forcing □

MAJOR OPENINGS
1♡-1♠ Opening on 4 Cards

	Often	Seldom	Never
1st-2nd	□	□	□
3rd-4th	□	□	□

RESPONSES:
Double Raise Forcing □ Limit □

MINOR OPENINGS
Length Promised
Almost
4+   3+ Shorter
1♣   □   □   □
1◇   □   □   □

RESPONSES:
Double Raise Forcing □ Limit □
1NT over 1♣ _____ to _____ HCP

2♣ WK □ _____ to _____ HCP. Describe _____
INT □
STR □ _____ 2◇ Neg. □   2NT Neg. □

2◇ WK □ _____ to _____ HCP. Describe _____
INT □
STR □ _____ 2NT Force □   2NT Neg. □

2♡ WK □ _____ to _____ HCP. Describe _____
INT □
STR □ _____ 2NT Force □   2NT Neg. □

2♠ WK □ _____ to _____ HCP. Describe _____
INT □
STR □ _____ 2NT Force □   2NT Neg. □

FOR MORE INFORMATION:
AMERICAN CONTRACT BRIDGE LEAGUE
2990 AIRWAYS BOULEVARD
MEMPHIS, TN 38116-3847   901-332-5586

FOR LOCAL INFORMATION:

DEFENSIVE CARD PLAY

Opening lead vs. SUITS: □ 4th best   □ Other _____
Mark card led: x x x   A K x   K Q x   Q J x   J 10 x   10 9 x
K J 10 x   K 10 9 x   Q 10 9 x   x x x x x
Opening lead vs. NT: □ 4th best   □ Other _____
Mark card led: x x x   A K J x   A Q J x   A J 10 9
A 10 9 8   K Q J x   K Q 10 9   K J 10 9   K 10 9 8
Q J 10 x   Q 10 9 8   J 10 9 x   10 9 8 x   x x x x x

FORM #0496   REVISION DATE 6/90

Printed in USA by ACBL   © Copyright 1989

Let's take it step by step and see how you would fill out a Convention Card with your partner.

♠ *CONVENTIONS — CONSTRUCTIVE BIDDING* ♠

The first part of the Convention Card deals with your bidding methods when the opponents do not intervene, leaving you and your partner free to have a *constructive* auction to try to reach your best contract. It covers your opening bids and the responses to them. The card does not have enough room to go into a lot of detail about all the possible bidding sequences that may arise. Instead, it provides a brief description that hits the highlights of your methods. Your opponents will generally be able to read between the lines once they know the basic style you are using, and they can always ask for clarification of anything they do not understand.

Names and General Approach

In the top right-hand corner is space to identify the partnership and their general bidding method.

> Names _____ Ely & Jo Culbertson _____
>
> General Approach __Standard__ Pair # _3NS_

The names of both partners are entered. In an informal game, first names are usually sufficient but, at a tournament, surnames are required. If you lose or misplace your card during the game, having your name on it will make it easier to return to you. Many players are interested in the names of the people they are playing against. After all, they may be playing against one of the bridge celebrities whose name they have heard but have never seen in person.

There is a space to fill in your partnership's *"General Approach."* For now, you can simply fill this in as "BASIC" or "STANDARD," indicating that all your opening bids, responses and rebids are natural and conform to the generally accepted practices in duplicate bridge. As your circle of bridge playing friends expands, you are likely to encounter a variety of bidding systems: Kaplan-Sheinwold (K-S), Precision Club, Eastern Scientific. Players in each area tend to gravitate toward a style that is popular with the local "experts." After a short time, you will become familiar with the major variations and whatever the approach indicated, it is explained in more detail in other sections of the convention card.

There is a space for you to enter your Pair Number, assigned to you at the beginning of the game. Having your Pair Number on the card is a useful reminder when it comes time to enter the result on the scoreslip. If you plan to use the same convention card over and over again, rather than making out a new card each time you play, leave the Pair Number blank and keep track of it in your head.

Notrump Opening Bids and Responses

We will skip over the section marked "Strong Forcing Opening" for a moment and take a look at the section on "NOTRUMP OPENING BIDS":

NOTRUMP OPENING BIDS
1NT *16* to *18*   2NT *22* to *24*
                                   3NT *25* to *27*
2♣   ☒ Stayman

Here you can write down the strength you show when you open the bidding 1 NT, 2 NT or 3 NT. Those who have taken the earlier lessons in this series will recall that a 1 NT opening bid is made with a balanced hand of 16–18 points, 2 NT is opened with a balanced hand of 22–24 points and 3 NT with a balanced hand of 25–27 points. While these are the classic ranges, you will encounter many variations among the players you meet. Some bidding systems, such as Kaplan-Sheinwold, use a weak notrump opening bid of 12–14 points. As you will see in the next lesson, a very popular style with duplicate players is to use a range of 15–17 points. Whatever range you end up playing, this is where you fill it in.

The rest of this section deals with the responses to opening notrump bids. In this abbreviated version of the card, there is only one choice indicated. Beside the 2♣ response is a box to indicate whether or not you play the Stayman convention. From the *Diamond Series* you may recall that a response of 2♣ to an opening 1 NT bid can be used to ask opener if he has a four-card or longer major suit. If he does, he bids it. Otherwise, opener rebids 2♦. If you and your partner have agreed to use this convention, you mark the box beside 2♣ with an "X". Otherwise, leave the box blank.

One-Level Major Suit Opening Bids and Responses

The section marked "MAJOR OPENINGS" is used for the opening bids of 1♥ and 1♠ and the responses to these bids:

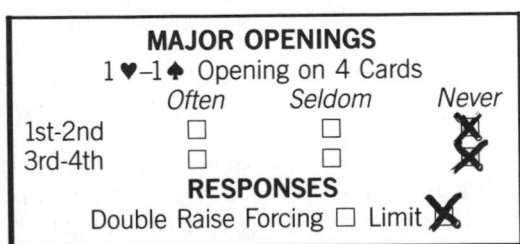

MAJOR OPENINGS
1♥–1♠ Opening on 4 Cards

	Often	*Seldom*	*Never*
1st-2nd	☐	☐	☒
3rd-4th	☐	☐	☒

RESPONSES
Double Raise Forcing ☐ Limit ☒

The primary consideration here is whether an opening bid of 1♥ or 1♠ can be on a four-card suit, or whether your partnership agreement is that you need a five-card or longer major suit to bid 1   or 1♠. You are asked whether you open with a four-card major suit

"Often," "Seldom" or "Never." The approach adopted in the *Club Series* was Five-Card Majors, the most common style among duplicate bridge players in North America. If you and your partner have adopted this approach, mark an "X" in the box under "Never." If your partnership prefers to open the bidding 1 ♥ or 1 ♠ with a four-card or longer major suit, mark an "X" in the box under "Often." Some players open 1 ♥ or 1 ♠ with a four-card suit only under certain conditions, perhaps requiring the suit to contain a minimum number of points or high cards, or perhaps only when they have both four hearts and four spades. They would mark the box under "Seldom."

There is a further option when opening the bidding 1 ♥ or 1 ♠. The partnership may agree to vary its style depending on whether the opening bid is in 1st or 2nd chair or whether it is in 3rd or 4th chair. Some players may open "light" — with less than the normal strength for an opening bid — in 3rd or 4th chair to try to get a small plus score, so some players might stick to the Five-Card Major approach when they are the dealer or the second player to bid but switch to a Four-Card Major approach when their partner has already passed. If your partnership does not play any such variations, mark an "X" in the same box on both lines.

The section under "RESPONSES" deals with responses to opening bids of 1 ♥ or 1 ♠. The initial consideration is whether a *double raise* (*jump raise*) of partner's major suit (*e.g.,* 1 ♥ — 3 ♥) is a *Forcing Raise* or a *Limit Raise*. If your jump raise is a forcing bid, showing 13 or more points and requiring opener to bid again, then mark an "X" in the box beside "Forcing." If your jump raise is an invitational bid, showing fewer than 13 points and allowing opener to pass with a minimum hand, mark an "X" in the box beside "Limit."

Minor Suit Opening Bids and Responses

The section marked "MINOR OPENINGS" is used for the opening bids of 1 ♣ and 1 ♦ and the responses to these bids:

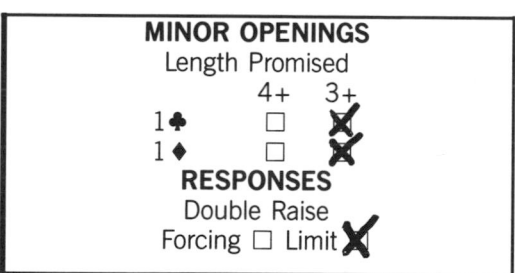

Again, the primary consideration is the length promised by the opening bid. Partnerships that play a Five-Card Major style will sometimes have to open the bidding on a three-card minor suit when they have only four cards in one or both majors. They would mark an "X" under the "3+" column for both 1 ♣ and 1 ♦ opening bids. Partnerships playing Four-Card Majors will usually have at least four cards in the minor suit when they open the bidding 1 ♣ or 1 ♦ and would mark the card accordingly. Some partnerships may adopt a style whereby an opening bid of 1♦ guarantees at least a four-card suit but 1♣ could be opened on a three-card suit or even less. Partnerships where 1♣ can be opened on fewer than three cards (*e.g.*, the "Short Club") should take a look at the full General Convention Card in the Appendix.

As with the major suit openings, the main consideration under responses is whether a jump raise (*e.g.*, 1♦ — 3♦) is a Forcing Raise or a Limit Raise. An "X" is placed in the appropriate box.

Opening Two-Level Suit Bids and Responses

There are two sections on the right-hand side of the card that relate to opening suit bids at the two level (2♣, 2♦, 2♥ and 2♠):

Strong Forcing Opening:	2 bids X

2♣ STR X	22 to + HCP.	2NT Neg. X
2♦ STR X	22 to + HCP.	2NT Neg. X
2♥ STR X	22 to + HCP.	2NT Neg. X
2♠ STR X	22 to + HCP.	2NT Neg. X

The classic approach is to use opening suit bids at the two level to show hands too strong to open the bidding at the one level — usually hands worth about 22 or more points. These are called *Strong Two-Bids*. If your partnership plays this style, then place an "X" in the box beside "2 bids" in the line for "Strong Forcing Opening" near the top of the card and put an "X" in the box marked "STR" (strong) beside the 2♣, 2♦, 2♥ and 2♠ opening bids on the lower right half of the convention card.

Playing Strong Two Bids, you cannot pass when your partner opens the bidding 2♣, 2♦, 2♥ or 2♠ since that is a forcing bid. A response of 2NT is usually used as the conventional response to indicate a very weak (*negative*) hand of about 0–5 points. You would therefore put an "X" in the box beside "2NT Neg." for each of the opening two-bids, indicating that 2NT is your negative (weak) response.

Other Conventional Calls

The remaining section on the right-hand side of the convention card provides space for "OTHER CONVENTIONAL CALLS." Until your partnership adopts conventions not covered elsewhere on the card, you can leave this space blank.

Opening Bids in a Suit at the Three Level

Opening suit bids at the three level or higher are covered in the section marked "OPEN-ING PREEMPTS" on the left-hand side of the Convention Card:

As explained in the *Diamond Series*, an opening suit bid at the three level (*e.g.*, 3♥) is normally made on a seven-card or longer suit, with three of the top five cards in the suit, and less than the point count values for an opening bid. Played in this fashion, you would mark an "X" in the box under "Sound" beside "3-bids."

Many duplicate players like to lower the requirements somewhat, leading to a friskier (and riskier) bidding style. They may open at the three level with fewer than three of the top five cards in the suit or, perhaps, with only a six-card suit. They would put an "X" in the box under "Light."

Slam Conventions

Another section on the left-hand side of the convention card which contains useful information about constructive bidding is the section marked "SLAM CONVENTIONS":

Both the *Blackwood convention* and the *Gerber convention* were mentioned briefly in the *Diamond Series*. They are used when you are interested in playing in a slam contract but first want to find out how many aces your partner has — after all, you do not want to get to a small slam missing two aces or a grand slam missing an ace.

The Blackwood convention is used when you have determined the denomination in which you plan to play. A bid of 4NT now asks partner how many aces he has and he responds 5♣ if he has no aces (or all four), 5♦ if he has one ace, 5♥ with two aces or 5♠ with three aces. If your side has all the aces and you are interested in a grand slam, you can now bid 5NT to ask partner how many kings he has and he will respond in a similar fashion.

The Gerber convention is normally used when partner opens the bidding 1NT or 2NT and you want to know how many aces he has. Since a raise to 4NT, one level beyond game, is usually played as an invitational raise rather than Blackwood (inviting partner to bid 6NT with a maximum, otherwise pass), many players use a jump to 4♣ to ask partner how many aces he has. Partner will bid 4♦ with none (or all four), 4♥ with one, 4♠ with two and 4NT with three. As with the Blackwood convention, you can now bid 5♣ to ask partner how many kings he has.

If you and partner have agreed to play either or both of these conventions, put an "X" in the appropriate box(es). Notice that the line beside each box can be used for clarification. Some players prefer to use 4♣ to always ask for aces, rather than 4NT. This saves some room on the Bidding Scale, but makes life difficult when you want to bid 4♣ as a natural bid, showing clubs. In the above example, you have clarified that you only use 4♣ as the Gerber convention directly over opening bids of 1NT or 2NT.

♠ *CONVENTIONS — COMPETITION* ♠

Having covered your constructive opening bids and responses — those bids made without interference from the opponents — it is time to take a look at the agreements and conventions that your partnership uses in competitive situations.

Special Doubles

In the top left-hand corner of the card is a section with the title "SPECIAL DOUBLES":

> ### SPECIAL DOUBLES (Describe)
> _____
> _____

You are unlikely to need to mark anything in this section at this point in time. You have only encountered the two natural uses of the double. You can make a *penalty double* when the opponents reach a game contract that you do not think they can make or when they compete to a partscore contract you do not think they can make after your side has opened the bidding or overcalled. Alternatively, if the opponents have opened the bidding, you can make a *takeout double* at your first opportunity to bid, asking partner to bid a suit. Both these types of doubles are considered standard practice for all players and need not be mentioned on the Convention Card. As you play in more and more duplicate games, you will inevitably encounter other special uses of the double since duplicate players have found this bid to be a useful tool in a number of bidding situations.

Notrump Overcalls

The section headed "DIRECT NT OVERCALLS" is used to describe your overcall of 1 NT or a jump to 2 NT when the opponents open the bidding at the one level in a suit:

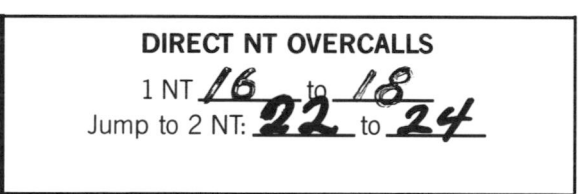

> ### DIRECT NT OVERCALLS
> 1 NT *16* to *18*
> Jump to 2 NT: *22* to *24*

Most players use an overcall of 1 NT to show exactly the same type of hand as a 1 NT opening bid: a balanced hand of about 16–18 points. Even players who open 1 NT with 15–17 points often prefer to have about 16–18 points when they overcall since the opponent on their right has already shown the values for an opening bid and so partner could have very few points. A jump to 2 NT can similarly be used to show the same strength as required for a 2 NT opening bid.

Simple Overcalls

The section headed "SIMPLE OVERCALL" is used to describe the strength required when you or your partner overcall in a suit at the cheapest available level and the meaning of your responses:

The standard range for an overcall is about 10–16 HCPs. You can make an overcall with less than the values for an opening bid, especially if your side is not vulnerable and you can bid at the one level. With more than 16 HCPs, many players prefer to start with a takeout double and then bid their suit. If you or your partner sometimes overcall with less strength than your normal range, you can mark an "X" in the box beside "occ. light" (occasionally lighter than the stated minimum HCPs).

Many partnerships respond to an overcall in a similar fashion as when responding to an opening bid — a new suit in response to an overcall is a forcing bid. If this is your partnership style, you would put an "X" in the appropriate box.

Some players play a new suit as forcing only if their partner did not pass originally, so you may see cryptic comments such as "Only by UPH" written beside the New Suit Forcing box (*i.e.,* Only forcing by an **u**n-**p**assed **h**and). The idea is to explain your particular bidding style as accurately as possible within the space available.

When the Opponents Open 1 NT

The next section is used to describe the meaning of your overcalls when the opponents open the bidding 1 NT:

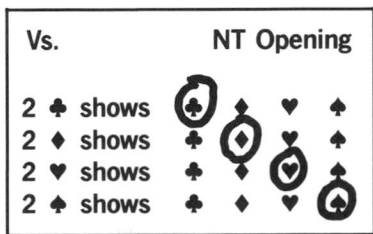

If you filled in nothing in this section, it would be assumed that your overcalls were all natural. That is, if you overcall 2♦, you are showing a five-card or longer diamond suit. Most players usually fill out this section anyway, by circling the suits shown by the various overcalls.

It may seem strange to have such an elaborate-looking section for overcalls when the opponets open the bidding 1NT, but duplicate players have come up with many fancy conventions to compete over an opponet's opening notrump bid. One of the common variations you will encounter is to use an overcall of 2♣ to show both major suits (somewhat like the Stayman convention), asking partner to choose between heats and spades. This is technically called the *Landy convention*.

Jump Overcalls

The section headed "JUMP OVERCALLS" is used when the opponents open the bidding in a suit and you, or your partner, make an overcall jumping over one of the available levels. For example, if an opponent opened the bidding 1+, you would be making a jump overcall if you bid 2♠, rather than 1♠.

JUMP OVERCALL

Strong ☐   Interm ☐   Preempt ☐

Some partnerships use such bids to show strong hands, usually with a six-card or longer suit and 17 or more HCPs. Other players use a jump overcall to show an intermediate strength hand (Interm), usually a six-card or longer suit with about 12–16 HCPs. The final alternative is to use this type of bid to show a long suit with a weak hand, less than the values for an opening bid. This is similar to a preemptive opening bid (Preempt), designed to make the auction more difficult for the opponents. Unless you have a firm agreement with your partner, you can leave this section of the card blank — and avoid making any jump overcalls!

When an Opponent Doubles for Takeout

The section headed "OVER OPP'S TAKEOUT DOUBLE" covers the situation where your side opens the bidding at the one level in a suit and the next opponent doubles for takeout:

OVER OPP'S TAKEOUT DOUBLE

New Suit Force 1–level ☒ 2–level ☒

The simplest style is to ignore the opponent's double and respond to partner's opening bid as you would if there had been no double. This means a new suit by responder is still forcing, whether it is bid at the one level or the two level.

When an Opponent Preempts

If one of your opponents opens the bidding in a suit at the three level (a *preemptive opening bid* showing a weak hand with a long suit) or at the two level with a *Weak Two-Bid* (similar to a preemptive opening bid at the three level), your partnership needs to agree on the meaning of an immediate double. This is put down in the section under "Vs. Opp's Preempts Dbl. is" (*i.e.*, versus an opponent's preemptive opening bid, the meaning of a direct double is . . .):

Vs. Opp's Preempts Dbl. Is		
Takeout	*Opt.*	*Penalty*
Wk. 2's ✘	☐	☐
3 Bids ✘	☐	☐

The most common defense to an opponent's opening suit bid at the two level or three level is to use a double for takeout, asking partner to bid a suit. This is identical to the takeout double used when an opponent opens the bidding at the one level, although, the higher the level at which you ask partner to bid, the more strength you should have.

Some players treat the double as optional (Opt.), meaning that their partner can either take it out to a new suit or pass for penalties. This would imply that they only doubled with considerable high card strength, including high cards in the opponent's suit. Other players prefer to treat the double as strictly for penalties, only doubling when they have both length and strength in the opponent's suit and not implying any support for the other suits if partner were to decide to bid.

Psychics

The section headed "PSYCHICS" has nothing to do with people who can see through the backs of other people's cards or tell what someone is going to bid before he has opened his mouth. Instead, it is used for a competitive tactic of opening the bidding when you have much less than the strength normally expected and, perhaps, when you do not even have much length in the suit you choose to bid. The idea is bluff the opponents (psyche them out) into thinking you have more strength than you do or a longer suit than you have. Perhaps they will misjudge the auction and miss an easy game contract or end up playing in the wrong suit. Of course, while such a bid may fool the opponents, it will also mislead your partner. So, when you are starting out, you should probably never use such tactics and can mark your Convention Card appropriately:

PSYCHICS			
Never	Rare	Occ.	Frequent
✘	☐	☐	☐

As you gain experience, you may want to try such a bid once or twice a year (**Rare**) or, perhaps, once or twice a month (**Occasional**). If you and your partner end up using such a tactic once or twice in every game you play (**Frequent**), you may find yourselves becoming an unwelcome sight to the more traditional players. You will also have to be careful that you and your partner do not come to "expect" such psychic bids. This would give you an unfair advantage over your opponents.

Bidding the Opponent's Suit

When an opponent opens the bidding in a suit, what does it mean if you overcall in the same suit? This is covered in the section headed "DIRECT CUEBID":

DIRECT CUEBID		
Strong Takeout:	Minor ☐	Major ☐
Natural: ♣ ☐	◇ ☐	

When an opponent bids 1♣ and you bid 2♣, the same suit, the technical name for such a bid is a *cuebid* of the opponent's suit. Since it is unlikely that you want to play in the same trump suit that your opponent wants to play in, the classical use of the direct cuebid is to show a very strong hand, one too strong for even a takeout double. It would be the type of hand that you would have opened a Strong Two-Bid if the opponent had not bid first. Nowadays, with partnerships that play five-card majors and sometimes open 1♣ or 1♦ on a three-card suit, or that play artificial systems in which the 1♣ or 1♦ could be made with even fewer cards, many players prefer to treat the overcall as natural, show-ing five or more cards in the suit.

In this section of the card you would mark an "X" beside "**Strong Takeout**" if you use the direct cuebid in the classic sense of showing a very strong hand. You have a further choice of whether you play this way only over 1♣ and 1♦ (Minor), or only over 1♥ and 1♠ (Major), or over both minor and major suits (*i.e.*, mark an "X" in both boxes).

If, instead, you play a direct cuebid as a natural overcall over one or both minor suits, you would mark an "X" beside the appropriate box(es) on the "**Natural:**" line. That is, you would check the box beside "♣" if you played a direct bid of 2♣ over the opponent's 1♣ opening bid to show a long club suit. You would check the box beside "♦" if you played a direct bid of 2♦ over the opponent's 1♦ bid to show a long diamond suit.

♠ *CONVENTIONS — DEFENSIVE CARD PLAY* ♠

The last section of the Convention Card deals with the cards you lead and play when defending a hand. When you are declarer, you are free to choose which card you play from dummy or your hand. As a defender, the card you play may have a special meaning to your partner. Declarer is entitled to know about any agreements that you have.

Opening Leads

The focus of the section headed "DEFENSIVE CARD PLAY" is on the specific card you would lead from a suit when leading against a notrump contract or a suit contract:

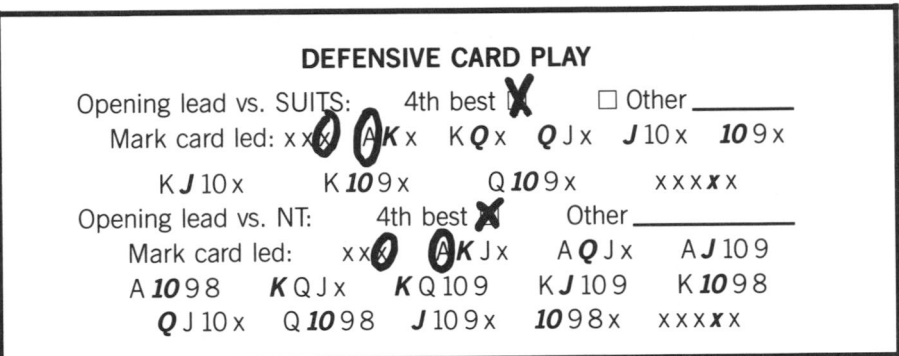

Starting with the opening lead against suit contracts (**Opening lead vs. SUITS**), you can mark an "X" beside "4th best" if you would normally lead your fourth highest card from a suit containing four or more cards headed by an honor other than the ace (*e.g.*, the 4 from K 8 6 4 2). This is the standard practice when you have a long suit that is not headed by touching high cards. If you always lead your lowest card, you would put an "X" in the box beside "Other" and add a description such as "Low."

You are then asked to mark the card you would lead from other specific holdings in a suit such as K Q x, where the "x" indicates any low card (*i.e.*, 2 through 9). To make things easier, the standard leads from most combinations are already highlighted on the card (*e.g.*, **K** Q x). Only if, for example, you do not lead the top of touching high cards, would you need to mark a different card.

The only combinations which are left entirely to your discretion are the card you would lead from three small cards (x x x) or a suit headed by both the ace and king (A K x). Some players lead low from three small cards, consistent with their leads from a three-card suit headed by an honor. Others prefer to lead the top card ("top of nothing") or the middle card. Circle or underline whichever card your partnership tends to lead. Some players lead the ace from a suit headed by the ace and king, consistent with the leads from other touching honor combinations. Others prefer to lead the king, leaving the lead of the ace to specifically deny holding the king. Again, you circle or underline the appropriate card.

You now move on to the opening leads against notrump contracts (**Opening lead vs. NT**). If you normally lead your fourth highest card against suit contracts, you probably do the same against notrump contracts and would mark an "X" in the box beside "4th best." Of course, you will tend to do this even from suits headed by the ace or by touching high cards when defending a notrump contract — something you would not likely do when leading against a suit contract.

Again, the standard leads from most other combinations are already highlighted, although you will still have to mark the card you lead from three small cards. You might note that the standard lead from a long suit headed by the ace, king and jack is the king. This is to differentiate this holding from a suit headed by the ace and king without the jack. If you still prefer to lead the ace, you would mark the card appropriately.

Defensive Signals

This section of the card is also used for any defensive signals you might use during the play of the hand. If you use only the standard methods for giving *attitude*, *count* and *suit preference* signals, there is no need to mark anything special in this section. The standard way to give an attitude signal is to play a high card if you like the suit (encouraging) and a low card if you dislike the suit (discouraging). The standard way to give a count signal is to play a high card followed by a low card to show an even number of cards (high-low) and a low card followed by a high card to show an odd number of cards in the suit (low-high). Suit preference signals are used when attitude or count signals are not needed. A high card shows preference for the higher-ranking suit and a low card for the lower-ranking suit. Defensive signals are discussed in more detail in the *Heart Series*.

♠ SUMMARY ♠

Before you start playing in a duplicate game, you and your partner must each complete a *Convention Card* which describes your basic bidding style along with any artificial conventions that you use. Filling out the card ensures that both you and your partner have the same understanding about what your various bids mean. When you sit down to play against new opponents, they can examine your card, both before you start to play and during the auction, to avoid having to ask a lot of questions about your methods. Similarly, you can look at the opponent's convention card to see what their bids mean. If there is anything you do not understand, you can ask about it when it is your turn to bid.

♠ *THE FINER POINTS* ♠

ACBL has developed a classification system for all the conventional bids that players are likely to want to use. The purpose of classifying conventions is to allow some events to be restricted to a subset of all the possible conventions. In this way, the more inexperienced players do not have to play against very complex systems and conventions which would put them at a distinct disadvantage. For example, some games for beginners are restricted to only those conventions in *Class A*, which includes such favorites as Stayman, Blackwood and Gerber. As players become more familiar with handling a wider variety of conventions, they can move into games with fewer and fewer restrictions. Only in the last stages of some National Championships are the restrictions lifted to permit virtually all of the recognized conventions.

While the format provided by the full General Convention Card can be used at virtually any level of competition (provided you only put allowable conventions on it!), several other formats have been designed for use in specific situations. Two of the most common formats you may encounter are outlined here.

The Class A Convention Card

Since many games for beginners are restricted to Class A conventions only, this abbreviated form of the General Convention Card, colored green, is sometimes available at local clubs. Since many experienced players also like to play in games in which very few conventional bids are allowed, events restricted to Class A conventions only are sometimes scheduled at major tournaments and this card is used there.

Filling out the card is very straightforward for anyone already familiar with the General Convention Card and a card completed by someone who is familiar with the methods discussed in the *Club Series*, *Diamond Series* and *Heart Series* lessons is shown on the next page.

STUDENT CONVENTION CARD

Names *John Smith & Jane Doe*
General Approach *Standard* **Pair #** *3*

Strong Forcing Opening: 2♣ ☐ 2 bids ☒ 1♣ ☐ Other _____

SPECIAL DOUBLES (Describe)

Negative _____
_____
_____
_____
_____

DIRECT NT OVERCALLS

1NT *16* to *18* HCP
Jump to 2 NT: *22* to *24* HCP
Unusual for Minors ☐

NOTRUMP OPENING BIDS

1NT *16* to *18* ☐   2NT *22* to *24* HCP
or ___ to ___ ☐   3NT *25* to *27* HCP
2♣ = Non-Forc. ☒ Stayman   1NT-3♣/3◇ Is Forcing ☐

Vs. Wk. ☐ Strong ☐ NT Opening

Direct ☐   Balance ☐
2♣ shows ④
2◇ shows ⑤
2♥ shows ⑥
2♠ shows ⑦

SIMPLE OVERCALL

10 to *16* HCP (occ. light ☐)
New suit forcing ___ X

MAJOR OPENINGS

1♥-1♠ Opening on 4 Cards
Almost

	Often	Seldom	Never
1st-2nd	☐	☐	☒
3rd-4th	☐	☐	☒

RESPONSES:
Double Raise Forcing ☐ Limit ☒

MINOR OPENINGS

Length Promised

	4+	3+	Shorter
1♣	☐	☒	☐
1◇	☐	☒	☐

RESPONSES:
Double Raise Forcing ☐ Limit ☒
1NT over 1♣ ___ to ___ HCP

JUMP OVERCALL

Strong ☐ Interm ☐ Weak ☒

OVER OPP'S TAKEOUT DOUBLE

New Suit Force 1-level ☒ 2-level ☒
Jp. Shift Force ☐ Good ☐ Weak ☐

OPENING PREEMPTS

3-Bids
Sound ☒ Vul. & Not Vul.
Light ☐ Not Vul. Only

PSYCHICS Never ☒

Vs. Opp's Preempts Dbl. Is

Takeout
Weak 2's ☒
3 Bids ☒

2♣ WK ☐ INT ☐ STR ☒ ___ to ___ HCP. Describe ___ 2◇ Neg. ☐ 2NT Neg. ☒

2◇ WK ☐ INT ☐ STR ☒ ___ to ___ HCP. Describe ___ 2NT Force ☐ 2NT Neg. ☒

2♥ WK ☐ INT ☐ STR ☒ ___ to ___ HCP. Describe ___ 2NT Force ☐ 2NT Neg. ☒

2♠ WK ☐ INT ☐ STR ☒ ___ to ___ HCP. Describe ___ 2NT Force ☐ 2NT Neg. ☒

SLAM CONVENTIONS

Mark X if you play that 4♣ over partner's NT bid asks for aces. If 4♣ always asks for aces, write "WHEN OBVIOUS" on line.

Gerber ☒ ___ Blackwood ☒ ___

DIRECT CUEBID

Strong Takeout: Minor ☐ Major ☐
Natural: ♠ ☐ ◇ ☐

FOR MORE INFORMATION:

AMERICAN CONTRACT BRIDGE LEAGUE
2990 AIRWAYS BOULEVARD
MEMPHIS, TN 38116-3847   901-332-5586

FOR LOCAL INFORMATION:

DEFENSIVE CARD PLAY

Opening lead vs. SUITS: ☒ 4th best ☐ Other___
Mark card led: x x☒ⒶKx KQx QJx J10x 10 9x
K J 10 x K 10 9 x Q 10 9 x x x x x x
Opening lead vs. NT: ☒ 4th best ☐ Other___
Mark card led: x x☒ⒶKJx AQJx AJ10 9
A 10 9 8 KQJx KQ 10 9 KJ 10 9 K 10 9 8
Q J 10 x Q 10 9 8 J 10 9 x 10 9 8 x x x x x x

FORM #0496   REVISION DATE 6/90

ACBL Standard Yellow Card

ACBL has also developed a pre-filled convention card containing the "standard" conventions used by a large percentage of the ACBL membership. This *ACBL Standard Yellow Card* is designed to be used in events where players are all playing exactly the same conventions. The players must play the conventions marked on the card and are limited to playing only those conventions.

Since some of these conventions will likely be unfamiliar to you, the contents of the card are not be discussed in this text. The *Notrump Series*, which follows this series, contains descriptions of the conventions familiar to most duplicate players and covers all those on the ACBL Standard Yellow Card.

♠ *GROUP ACTIVITIES* ♠

Exercise One — The Convention Card: Constructive Bids

Examine the layout of the Convention Card and, with the help of your partner, fill out the various sections concerned with constructive bidding (opening bids and responses). Use the following list to guide you, although you can modify it for any variations agreed upon by you and your partner.

- Fill in your names and general approach (*e.g.,* Standard).
- Fill in the range of opening notrump bids (1NT=16–18; 2NT=22–24; 3NT=25–27).
- Check off that you play:
  - The Stayman convention.
  - Five-card majors in all positions.
  - Limit raises in response to opening bids of 1♥ and 1♠.
  - Opening 1♣ and 1♦ bids on as few as three cards in the suit.
  - Limit raises in response to opening bids of 1♣ and 1♦.
  - All two-level opening suit bids as strong and forcing.
  - 2NT as the negative response (fewer than 6 points) to opening two-bids
  - Sound opening preempts (three-bids).
  - The Blackwood (4NT) and Gerber (4♣) conventions.

Exercise Two — The Convention Card: Competitive Bids

Find the various sections on the Convention Card concerned with competitive bidding (overcalls, takeout doubles) and fill them out, using the following list to guide you.

- Fill in the range of your notrump overcalls (1NT = 16–18; 2NT = 22–24).
- Fill in the range of your simple overcalls (10–16) and check off that you play a new suit as forcing in response to an overcall.
- Circle the suit symbols to indicate that when the opponents open the bidding 1NT you play overcalls as natural (showing the suit you bid).

- Check off that you play:
  - A new suit as forcing, at both the one level and the two level, when an opponent makes a takeout double.
  - A double is for takeout when an opponent opens the bidding with a preempt at the two level (Weak-two) or the three level (three-bid).
  - No psychic bids (bids showing a suit or strength that you do not have).

Exercise Three — The Convention Card: Defensive Card Play

In the section on the Convention Card for Defensive Card Play, indicate the agreements you have with your partner, using the following guidelines:

- Check off that you normally lead fourth highest (4th best) against both suit and notrump contracts when you have a four-card or longer suit.
- Indicate which card you lead from three low cards (x x x) against both notrump and suit contracts (the low card if you have no other agreement with partner).
- Indicate that you lead the ace from suits headed by both the ace and the king against both suit and notrump contracts.

♠ SAMPLE BOARDS ♠

BOARD #1

Dealer: North
Vulnerable: None

NORTH
♠ Q 9 2
♥ J 8 4
♦ K 10 3
♣ Q 10 8 6

WEST
♠ 8 7 6
♥ A 9 2
♦ 9 2
♣ J 7 5 4 2

EAST
♠ 10 4 3
♥ 6 3
♦ A Q 8 7 4
♣ K 9 3

SOUTH
♠ A K J 5
♥ K Q 10 7 5
♦ J 6 5
♣ A

ACBL SHORT TRAVELING SCORE
(Mitchell or Howell)

Board No. | 1

N-S Pair No.	Contract	By	Made	Down	SCORE N-S	SCORE E-W	N-S Match-points	E-W Pair No.	E-W Match-points
1	4 H	S		1		50		1	
2	4 H	S		2		100		3	
3	4 H	S	4		420			5	
4	4 H	S		1		50		2	
5	3 NT	N		1		50		4	
6	4 H	S		1		50		6	
7									

Suggested Bidding

WEST	NORTH	EAST	SOUTH
	Pass	Pass	1♥
Pass	2♥	Pass	4♥
Pass	Pass	Pass	

South opens 1♥ with a very strong hand. Playing five-card majors, North can raise to the two level with three-card support and 8 HCPs. Knowing there is an eight-card fit, South can jump right to game with his maximum strength hand.

Suggested Play

West has an interesting decision with his opening lead. With only a doubleton diamond, he should consider leading his short suit to try to get a ruff with one of his low trumps. Holding the ace of the trump suit, he is sure to get the lead again before trumps are drawn — this improves his chances of getting an extra trump trick for the defense. West should lead the ♦ 9, top of a doubleton. East will need to cooperate if the defense is to succeed. After winning the first diamond trick, East will have to recognize that West is leading from a short suit and continue leading diamonds. If East stops leading diamonds after winning the first two tricks, West will never get his ruff. Even if West does not lead a diamond in-itially, he will get a second chance when he wins a trick with the ♥ A. If he doesn't get his ruff this time, declarer will draw trumps and make the contract.

Notes

The scoreslip indicates that it is important for East-West to defeat the contract to get a good result. In a reasonably strong game, most pairs will find this defense. Notice also that the North-South pairs do not get a very bad result for being defeated in 4♥. It is a normal contract and it is unlucky that it can be defeated. They can take solace in having lots of company. They lose out only to the one pair that was allowed to make the contract when East-West failed to find the winning defense.

BOARD #2

Dealer: East
Vulnerable: North-South

NORTH
♠ 10
♥ 10 4 2
♦ 9 5 4 3
♣ K J 8 4 2

WEST
♠ A Q 8 3
♥ A K 7 5
♦ A 10 8 2
♣ 6

EAST
♠ K J 7 5 2
♥ Q J 8
♦ K Q 6
♣ Q 9

SOUTH
♠ 9 6 4
♥ 9 6 3
♦ J 7
♣ A 10 7 5 3

	ACBL SHORT TRAVELING SCORE (Mitchell or Howell)							Board No.	2

N-S Pair No.	Contract	By	Made	Down	SCORE N-S	SCORE E-W	N-S Match-points	E-W Pair No.	E-W Match-points
1	6 S	E	6			980		1	
2	6 S	E	7			1010		3	
3	4 S	E	6			480		5	
4	6 S	E	7			1010		2	
5	5 S	E	7			510		4	
6	6 S	E	6			980		6	
7									

Suggested Bidding

WEST	NORTH	EAST	SOUTH
		1♠	Pass
4NT	Pass	5♣	Pass
6♠	Pass	Pass	Pass

As soon as East opens 1♠, West should be interested in a slam contract. With 17 HCPs plus 3 dummy points for the singleton club, there should be at least 33 points in the combined hands. West could jump directly to 6♠. Since there might be a grand slam if there are no missing aces, West might start by using the Blackwood convention instead. A direct jump to 4NT over partner's opening 1♠ bid implies that spades will be the trump suit and asks opener how many aces he holds. The 5♣ response shows zero (or all four) and now West knows an ace is missing. He can settle on 6♠, confident there is not enough for a grand slam.

Suggested Play

If South leads the ♣A, East is held to 12 tricks. His remaining club loser can be trumped in dummy or discarded on one of dummy's extra winners. On the other hand, if South leads something other than a club, declarer can win the trick, draw trumps and then discard both club losers on dummy's extra winners. One is discarded on the extra heart winner and the other goes on dummy's ♦10 after the ♦J appears when declarer takes the ♦K and ♦Q.

Notes

While most pairs will bid the slam, the top result will go to the East-West pairs who make an overtrick when South does not lead a club. At duplicate bridge, when the opponents bid quickly and confidently to slam, it is usually a good idea to lead an ace, if you have one. If declarer has the king, you will establish it as a trick but, if partner has the king, you may be able to take two quick tricks before declarer has a chance to discard his losers. On boards such as this one, the ♣A lead will prevent declarer from ending up with an overtrick.

BOARD #3

Dealer: South
Vulnerable: East-West

NORTH
♠ J 10 9 7 3
♥ Q 10 4
♦ K J 3
♣ K 10

WEST
♠ K Q 6
♥ A K 7 2
♦ 8 4 2
♣ A J 8

EAST
♠ A 8
♥ 9 3
♦ A 10 7 6 5
♣ 9 6 4 2

SOUTH
♠ 5 4 2
♥ J 8 6 5
♦ Q 9
♣ Q 7 5 3

ACBL SHORT TRAVELING SCORE
(Mitchell or Howell)

Board No.   3

N-S Pair No.	Contract	By	M a d e	D o w n	SCORE N-S	SCORE E-W	N-S Match-points	E-W Pair No.	E-W Match-points
1	2NT	W	2			120		6	
2	3NT	W		1	100			2	
3	2NT	W	3			150		4	
4	3NT	W	3			600		1	
5	3NT	W		1	100			3	
6	3 D	E	3			110		5	
7									
8									

Suggested Bidding

WEST	NORTH	EAST	SOUTH
			Pass
1NT	Pass	2NT	Pass
3NT	Pass	Pass	Pass

The bidding will probably be the same whether you are playing a 1NT opening bid to show 15-17 or 16–18 points. With 8 HCPs and an extra point for the five-card diamond suit, East has enough to invite and, with 17 HCPs, West has enough to accept the invitation.

Suggested Play

North will likely lead the ♠J, top of a sequence in his longest suit. Declarer starts with three spade tricks, two heart tricks, one diamond trick and one club trick, for a total of seven. To make nine tricks, declarer's best chance is to try to establish two extra tricks in the diamond suit. This can be done if declarer gives up two diamond tricks to the opponents and the missing diamonds divide 3–2. However, declarer must be careful to keep an entry to dummy so that he can take the established diamond tricks. If the opponents continue to lead spades when declarer loses the diamond tricks, dummy's ♠A will soon disappear. The only remaining entry is dummy's ♦A. So declarer will have to *duck* the first two diamond tricks, losing them to the opponents. Only on the third round of diamonds can declarer afford to play dummy's ♦A. Now declarer is in dummy and can take the two established diamond tricks.

Notes

Although the bidding and play look relatively straightforward when you see the entire deal, it is not always so easy when you are actually at the table. Some pairs may not bid to game, and even if they do get there, not all declarers will find the way to get nine tricks. Any pair who bids and makes 3NT will receive a good score.

BOARD #4

Dealer: West
Vulnerable: Both

NORTH
♠ K J 7 3
♥ 7 6
♦ K 10 8
♣ A Q 8 2

WEST
♠ 8 4
♥ J 9 4
♦ A 9 5 4
♣ K 10 6 5

EAST
♠ Q 9 5
♥ A 10 8 2
♦ Q 7 6 2
♣ 9 4

SOUTH
♠ A 10 6 2
♥ K Q 5 3
♦ J 3
♣ J 7 3

ACBL SHORT TRAVELING SCORE
(Mitchell or Howell)

Board No. 4

N-S Pair No.	Contract	By	Made	Down	SCORE		N-S Match-points	E-W Pair No.	E-W Match-points
					N-S	E-W			
1	2 S	N	2		110			6	
2	4 S	N	4		620			2	
3	4 S	N		1		100		4	
4	3 S	N	3		140			1	
5	3 S	N		1		100		3	
6	2 D X	E		2	500			5	
7									
8									

Suggested Bidding

WEST	NORTH	EAST	SOUTH
Pass	1♣	Pass	1♥
Pass	1♠	Pass	3♠
Pass	Pass	Pass	

With no five-card major suit, North opens 1♣. South responds 1♥, bidding his suits up the line. North rebids 1♠, continuing the search for a major suit fit. Now South knows the partnership has a Golden Fit in spades. With 11 HCPs plus 1 dummy point for the doubleton diamond, South invites opener to game by jumping to 3♠. With a minimum opening bid, North should decline the invitation and settle for partscore.

Suggested Play

North can make anywhere from 8 to 10 tricks, depending on how he guesses the location of the opponents' cards. There is a potential spade loser since the ♠Q is missing. Holding both the ♠J and ♠10, declarer can finesse either opponent for the missing ♠Q, or he might play the ♠A and ♠K, hoping the ♠Q is doubleton. The general advice when missing the queen is "eight ever, nine never," meaning you should finesse with only eight cards in the suit and play the ace and king when you have nine. The only declarers to avoid a trump loser will be those who play the ♠K first and then lead a low spade to dummy's ♠10, hoping East started with the ♠Q. Missing both the ♦A and ♦Q, declarer needs to guess what to do in the diamond suit to avoid two losers. If he leads a diamond from dummy toward his hand and West follows with a low card, he will have to decide whether to play the ♦K, hoping West has the ♦A, or take a finesse against the ♦Q. Even if declarer guesses what to do in diamonds, he will still have to lose the ♥A and a trick to the ♣K. In the meantime, the defense must be careful not to make life easy for declarer by playing their high cards too soon. There's lots of scope for both sides on this hand.

Notes

The best North-South results will go to those pairs who stop in partscore and make nine or 10 tricks. East-West will get a good result if North-South get too high or don't make enough tricks.

BOARD #5

NORTH

Dealer: North
Vulnerable: North-South

NORTH
♠ K Q 7 3
♥ Q 5 2
♦ A K 8 4
♣ 7 4

WEST
♠ A 8
♥ K 10 8 6
♦ J 6
♣ J 10 9 8 3

EAST
♠ J 10 5 2
♥ A 7
♦ 10 9 7 3 2
♣ K 5

SOUTH
♠ 9 6 4
♥ J 9 4 3
♦ Q 5
♣ A Q 6 2

ACBL SHORT TRAVELING SCORE
(Mitchell or Howell)

Board No. 5

N-S Pair No.	Contract	By	Made	Down	SCORE N-S	SCORE E-W	N-S Match-points	E-W Pair No.	E-W Match-points
1	1NT	S	1		90			5	
2	2NT	S		1		100		1	
3	1NT	S		1		100		3	
4	2 D	E		2	100			6	
5	2 H	S		1		100		2	
6	1NT	N	2		120			4	
7									

Suggested Bidding

WEST	NORTH	EAST	SOUTH
	1 ♦	Pass	1 ♥
Pass	1 ♠	Pass	1 NT
Pass	Pass	Pass	

After North's 1 ♦ opening, South has room to show his heart suit at the one level. North can now show his four-card spade suit and South, not caring for either of North's suits, can rebid 1 NT. With a minimum hand, North has no reason to get the partnership any higher.

Suggested Play

Against a notrump contract, West will probably lead the ♣ J, top of his sequence. East should play the ♣ K on partner's ♣ J, in case West is leading from an interior sequence such as ♣ A J 10 9 3. On the actual hand, South will get two club tricks with the ♣ A and ♣ Q no matter what West does. South also has three diamond tricks and needs to develop two more tricks to make the contract. The best chance is in the spade suit, where South can plan to lead twice toward the dummy, hoping that West has the ♠ A. Playing this way, declarer will get tricks with both the ♠ K and the ♠ Q. The defenders should end up with a spade trick, two heart tricks and three club tricks.

Notes

This is a typical partscore deal. The normal result is for North-South to end up in a partscore of 1 NT and make exactly seven tricks. Nonetheless, there will be a variety of results since it is easier to see what should happen after the deal is over, rather than at the table. North-South may reach the wrong contract or may get too high. East-West may find a way into the auction or misdefend against North-South's contract.

BOARD #6

NORTH
Dealer: East   ♠ Q J 8 7 5 2
Vulnerable: East-West ♥ 6 3
                       ♦ 8 4
                       ♣ 8 6 5

WEST   EAST
♠ 9 4 3   ♠ A K
♥ 9 4 2   ♥ K J 10 8 7
♦ K 10 3   ♦ Q J 6 2
♣ Q 10 9 7   ♣ 4 2

SOUTH
♠ 10 6
♥ A Q 5
♦ A 9 7 5
♣ A K J 3

	ACBL SHORT TRAVELING SCORE (Mitchell or Howell)								

					Board No.		6		

N-S Pair No.	Contract	By	M a d e	D o w n	SCORE		N-S Match-points	E-W Pair No.	E-W Match-points
					N-S	E-W			
1	2 S	N	3		140			5	
2	1 NT	S		2		100		1	
3	3 H X	E		1	200			3	
4	2 S	N	2		110			6	
5	3 H	E		1	100			2	
6	1 NT	S		1		50		4	
7									

Suggested Bidding

WEST	NORTH	EAST	SOUTH
		1 ♥	1 NT
Pass	2 ♠	Pass	Pass
Pass			

After East's 1 ♥ opening bid, South can overcall 1 NT to give a perfect description of his hand. South has a balanced hand with 18 HCPs and strength (stoppers) in the opponent's suit. This does not leave West with much to do, although some adventuresome types might raise to 2 ♥. The focus now falls on North. With only 3 HCPs, he knows the partnership has enough combined strength for only a partscore contract. With a six-card suit, however, North knows that the partnership has at least eight spades in the combined hands. So North should bid 2 ♠. This should be a better contract than 1 NT. The auction should end at that point, provided South recognizes North's bid as a signoff bid, not an invitational or forcing bid. If South bids again, the partnership will probably get too high.

Suggested Play

In a 2 ♠ contract, North is missing the ♠A and ♠K and has to worry about a heart loser, a diamond loser and a club loser. Although North can afford five losers, he wants to make as many tricks as possible to try and beat the scores of the other North-South pairs. He can try taking both the heart finesse and the club finesse when he has the opportunity. The club finesse fails but the heart finesse works and North should end up with an overtrick.

If South is left to play in 1 NT, he will have a difficult time. With the ♥ K on his right, he will probably get two heart tricks, a diamond trick and two club tricks, but additional tricks will be hard to come by. Even if he can establish dummy's spade suit, there is no entry to the North hand. That is one of the disadvantages of playing in a notrump contract rather than a spade contract.

Notes

North-South will do well if they can reach the "par" contract of 2 ♠. If East-West compete any higher, they should be defeated and may even get doubled. If North-South languish in a notrump partscore, they are unlikely to get many matchpoints.

BOARD #7

Dealer: South
Vulnerable: Both

NORTH
♠ Q 8 3
♥ 8 7 2
♦ 5 4 3
♣ A 8 7 3

WEST
♠ 4 2
♥ A 9 6 5
♦ A 9 7
♣ K Q 10 5

EAST
♠ K 7 6
♥ Q J 10 3
♦ K 6 2
♣ 9 4 2

SOUTH
♠ A J 10 9 5
♥ K 4
♦ Q J 10 8
♣ J 6

ACBL SHORT TRAVELING SCORE
(Mitchell or Howell)

Board No. | 7

N-S Pair No.	Contract	By	M a d e	D o w n	SCORE		N-S Match- points	E-W Pair No.	E-W Match- points
					N-S	E-W			
1	3 H	E	3			140		4	
2	2 S	S	2		110			6	
3	4 H	E		2	200			2	
4	3 S	S	1			100		5	
5	3 H	E	3			140		1	
6	2 H	E	4			170		3	
7									

Suggested Bidding

WEST	NORTH	EAST	SOUTH
			1♠
Double	2♠	3♥	Pass
Pass	Pass		

After West's takeout double, North should raise to 2♠ to make it more difficult for the opponents to buy the contract. This should not deter East from competing with 3♥, however. If East does not bid, North-South will get a good result. West should not continue on to 4♥. Even though East has bid at the three level, West should realize that he is only competing. The opponent's 2♠ bid did not leave room for East to bid at the two level.

Suggested Play

If South leads the ♦Q, the defenders should end up with two spade tricks, a diamond trick and a club trick, holding declarer to nine tricks. Declarer avoids losing a trump trick by leading the ♥Q (or ♥J or ♥10) and trapping South's ♥K.

If North-South push on to 3♠, West should lead the ♣K and the defense should end up with two heart tricks (by trapping declarer's ♥K), two diamond tricks and a club trick. If a trick gets away, South will end up making 3♠.

Notes

East-West will get a good result for bidding and making 3♥. If they get to 4♥ and are defeated, they will get a poor result since most pairs in their direction will end up with a plus score. North-South will get a very good result if they are allowed to play in 2♠. Even if they bid on to 3♠ and are defeated one trick, losing 100 points, that will be better than letting East-West get 140 points for making 3♥. Of course, since they are vulnerable, they risk getting doubled and being defeated one trick. Then they will lose 200 points and get a bottom board.

BOARD #8

Dealer: West
Vulnerable: None

NORTH
- ♠ J 10 9 6 3
- ♥ 10 6
- ♦ A 10 7 2
- ♣ J 3

WEST
- ♠ Q 8
- ♥ A Q 8 4 2
- ♦ 9 6 4
- ♣ K Q 5

EAST
- ♠ 7 4 2
- ♥ K J 7 3
- ♦ K Q 8 5
- ♣ A 8

SOUTH
- ♠ A K 5
- ♥ 9 5
- ♦ J 3
- ♣ 10 9 7 6 4 2

ACBL SHORT TRAVELING SCORE
(Mitchell or Howell)

Board No.: **8**

N-S Pair No.	Contract	By	Made	Down	SCORE N-S	SCORE E-W	N-S Match-points	E-W Pair No.	E-W Match-points
1	4 H	W	4			420		4	
2	4 H	W	4			420		6	
3	4 H	W	4			420		2	
4	4 H	W	4			420		5	
5	4 H	W	4			420		1	
6	4 H	W	4			420		3	
7									

Suggested Bidding

WEST	NORTH	EAST	SOUTH
1♥	Pass	2♦	Pass
2NT	Pass	4♥	Pass
Pass	Pass		

This is how the auction would go if East and West are playing limit raises. East is too strong to make a limit raise and so makes a temporizing response of 2♦, forcing. After West finishes describing his minimum balanced hand with the 2NT rebid, East can jump directly to game in the known fit. If the partnership plays forcing raises, the auction would be more straightforward:

WEST	NORTH	EAST	SOUTH
1♥	Pass	3♥	Pass
4♥	Pass	Pass	Pass

Suggested Play

If North leads the ♠J, the defenders will take the first two spade tricks. Declarer will have to be careful not to lose two diamond tricks as well. He should plan to lead twice toward dummy's ♦K and ♦Q, hoping North has the ♦A. He will have to draw trumps before leading diamonds twice or else South will be able to ruff an established winner.

Notes

Almost all the East-West pairs should reach 4♥ and make it. If everyone gets the same result, the board is said to be *flat*. Each pair gets the same number of matchpoints on the board.

LESSON 3

The Mitchell Movement

Organizing the Game
The Mitchell Movement
The Director
Laws of the Game
Summary

Workshop Material
Group Activities
Sample Boards

In the previous lessons you have learned how to bid, play and score — duplicate style — each deal that you play against another pair. You have also seen how the scoreslip is completed at the end of each hand and can be used to compare your result with the results at other tables. So far, however, the boards you played were all played against the same pair. In this lesson we'll look at how duplicate bridge is organized so that you play against more than one pair.

♠ *ORGANIZING THE GAME* ♠

In a duplicate game you play against a number of different opponents. It requires some careful organization to ensure that you do not play the same boards more than once and, at the same time, you meet new opponents every few boards. Let's take a look at how the game is organized, starting with the moment you walk in, ready for a pleasant session of bridge.

The Entry

When you first arrive, the person organizing the game will introduce you to a suitable player if you came without a partner. You and your partner then buy an *entry form* from the bridge organizer. Although the entry fee varies from one part of the country to another, it is usually about the same price as going to a movie.

The entry form you are given will look something like this:

DUPLICATE BRIDGE PAIR ENTRY

Name _____

Street _____

City/State/Zip _____

Phone _____ ACBL No. _____

Name _____

Street _____

City/State/Zip _____

Phone _____ ACBL No. _____

Pair Number _____

N–S _____ E–W _____

Section _____

American Contract Bridge League
P.O. Box 161192
Memphis, TN 38186

Form 112 PE (Rev. 91)

Printed in USA by ACBL
Copyright • ACBL 1983

The first piece of important information is the table number and direction. On the above entry form, you are assigned to Table #5, North-South. This is your starting position. Each of the tables will have a guide card indicating the table number and compass directions. You and your partner would find Table #5 and one of you would sit in the North direction and the other in the South direction. You are free to choose which one of you sits in which chair but you might keep in mind that the North player is responsible for putting the result on the scoreslip at the end of each deal. If neither you nor your partner is familiar with how to keep score, you might ask to play East-West until you become more familiar with the scoring.

On arriving at your table, complete the entry form by filling in your name, address and perhaps your telephone number. If you are a member of the American Contract Bridge League (ACBL), you will have been sent an official *ACBL membership number* and can fill this in on the form. In a local club game, you do not have to complete anything other than your names once you become a regular. At a tournament you must complete the entire form.

Having completed the entry form, you and your partner can then fill out your Convention Cards if you have not already done so. Now you are ready to play.

The Different Types of Games

Several different formats are used for playing duplicate bridge. The most common is the *pair game*, where you and your partner play together throughout the event and your results are compared to those of the other pairs sitting in the same direction as you. There are two ways that a pair game can be organized. The most common is called the *Mitchell movement*, which is organized so that the North-South pairs remain stationary at their starting tables throughout the game and the East-West pairs move from table to table. When there are not many pairs playing, the *Howell movement* is sometimes used. In this movement, the pairs change direction from time to time, playing both North-South and East-West. In a complete movement each pair meets each other pair throughout the game. Another type of game is the *individual*, in which you play with a different partner every couple of boards. In these forms of the game, the players' scores are determined by matchpointing the results on each board. Duplicate players often refer to these types of games as *playing matchpoints*.

It is also possible to play a *team game*, where two partnerships form a team-of-four and play against other teams. In later lessons, we will look at the team format, as well as the Howell and Individual movements. For now, let's focus our attention on the most popular format, the Mitchell movement.

♠ *THE MITCHELL MOVEMENT* ♠

The Basic Movement

In the basic Mitchell movement all of the North-South pairs remain at their starting table throughout the game. The East-West pairs move from one table to the next, going in a **higher** direction. Pairs from Table #2 go to Table #3, from Table #3 to Table #4, and so on. When they get to the highest-numbered table, they move on to Table #1. The East-West pairs play a *set* of two or three boards (sometimes more) against each North-South pair before moving to the next table. Each set of boards is called a *round*. You may meet only some or all of the pairs sitting in the other direction depending on the length of the game and the number of boards you play each round.

At the end of each round, the North player is responsible for passing the boards to another table. So that the East-West pair that just played the boards do not play the same hands again at the next table, the boards are passed in the opposite direction to that in which the East-West players move. As the players move to the next higher-numbered table, the boards move to the next **lower** numbered table. North at Table #4 passes the boards to Table #3, North at Table #3 passes the boards to Table #2, and so on. The boards from Table #1 are passed to the highest-numbered table. To make it easy for the players and boards to move, the tables are usually laid out in rows so that the highest-numbered table eventually meets back with Table #1. For example, if there are eight tables in play, they would ideally be laid out in this fashion:

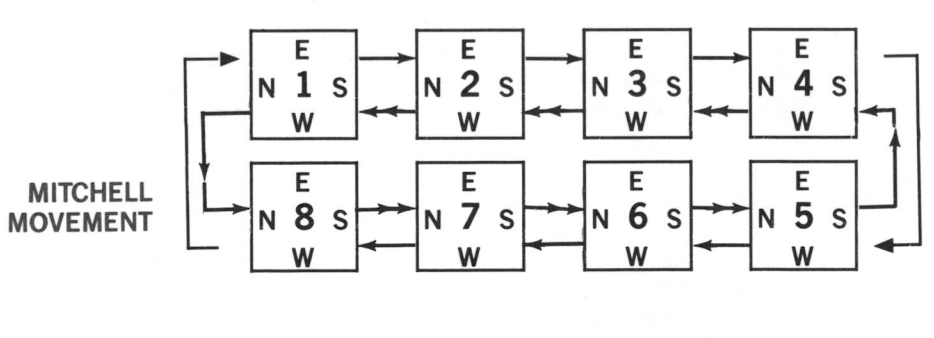

MITCHELL MOVEMENT

EW Pair Movement   **Board Movement**

Of course, the actual dimensions of the playing area will dictate how the tables have to be laid out. In a large game it may be impossible to even fit them all into the same room! An East-West pair may find itself with a long walk to the next table. The North-South pair will direct them to the location of the next table if its location is not obvious. When there is more than one section of tables in play, the East-West pairs must be careful not to wander into a different section than the one they started in.

The Skip and the Relay

If there is an odd number of tables in your section, the same boards and players will never meet again. They will pass each other midway through the game, traveling in opposite directions. If there is an even number of tables, the East-West players would meet the same boards about half way through the game. The director solves this problem in one of two ways.

One method is to have the East-West players *skip* a table just when they are about to meet the same boards again. At the end of one of the rounds, the person organizing the game will make an announcement something like this: "On the next round, would the East-West pairs please skip a table?" The East-West pair at Table #5, for example, would move to Table #7 rather than Table #6. This means they would never play against the North-South pair at Table #6. This may be disappointing if you were looking forward to playing against this particular pair. On the other hand, you might be quite happy not to have to play against them.

To avoid having the East-West pairs skip a table, another method is sometimes used. In this format, two of the tables share the same set of boards each round. This is referred to as a *relay*. For example, suppose you are sitting at Table #1 and are instructed to relay boards with Table #8. If you are playing two boards each round, you would start off playing the first board while Table #8 plays the second board. When both tables are finished, they exchange boards and you play the second board while Table #8 plays the first board. To make this movement work properly, one set of boards is left sitting out each round. This is called a *bye-stand*. These boards are moved back into play at the end of each round while a new set of boards sits out on the bye-stand. The mechanics may seem a little complicated, but once the game gets under way, the movement runs quite smoothly and there is no need for the East-West pairs to skip a table.

Sit-Outs

If there is an odd number of pairs in the game, it is not possible to have all of the pairs play at the same time. One of the pairs will have to sit out each round. One way to arrange this is to have no North-South pair at the highest-numbered table. When an East-West pair reaches this table, it sits out for the round. This is called an *East-West sit-out*. The alternative is to have one of the North-South pairs assigned as a *rover*. They sit out the first round and then *bump* out a different North-South pair each round.

♠ *THE DIRECTOR* ♠

Although the Mitchell movement may seem quite complex, the players do not have to be concerned. The responsibility for running the game is put into the hands of someone who is experienced with the various formats and who can help ensure that the game runs smoothly.

The Director

The person in charge of running the game is called the *director*. The director selects the format of the game and organizes the players and the boards so that everything is coordinated correctly — at the right time, at the right speed, in the right direction.

Let's look at what a session of bridge entails for a typical director.

Before the Game

The director is often the same person who arranges the partnerships and sells the entry forms. He will lay out the guide cards for the expected number of tables. Even while selling the entries, the director keeps an eye on the clock. If the game has been announced to start at 8 o'clock, for example, it is the director's responsibility to get the players in their places by that time. Using a microphone, or finding a position in the room where he can be heard, the director announces, "Game time, everyone. Please take your places," shortly before it is time to start.

Since there could be anywhere from two or three tables up to 20 or more at a duplicate game, it is up to the director to select the appropriate format to ensure that everyone will have an enjoyable time while meeting as many other pairs as possible. He decides how many hands will be played during the game, how many will be played on each round and where the boards should be positioned for the first round. Once he has placed the appropriate number of boards on each table, he tells the players to shuffle, deal and play.

The cards are shuffled and dealt only once during a session. Sometimes no shuffling and dealing is necessary because pre-dealt boards or printed hand records of the boards are furnished.

During the Game

A standard time allowed for each board has been established by ACBL and the director moves the players along so they are on time for each round. It is important that each pair complete the round in the allotted time. If a pair is late finishing, they not only hold up the game for the East-West pair waiting to come to the table but also for the North-South pair waiting at the next table.

In a regular duplicate game, the players are expected to complete each board in about seven and a half minutes. If there are two boards in a round, for example, the director will call the round every 15 minutes. In a student or beginner game, the director will usually allow about 10 minutes for each board. At the completion of each round, the director will say something such as "All move for the next round. East-West pairs to the next higher-numbered table. Pass the boards to the next lower-numbered table."

In an open game you would normally play from 24 to 28 boards in a session, which would take about three and a half hours. A student game should last only a couple of hours, with only 12 to 15 boards being played. Each partnership must continue to play until the game is over — otherwise the movement would be spoiled for the remaining pairs.

Another major function of the director during the game is to give rulings pertaining to the Laws of Duplicate Contract Bridge (see Exercise Three). In order for the conditions of a game to be fair, everyone has to follow the same rules. The director is familiar with these rules and is responsible for seeing that they are correctly applied. Let's consider a typical example. Although all the players know that they must *follow suit* on every trick (play a card of the same denomination as the one led, if they have one), there are times when even the best players in the world *revoke* (fail to follow suit when they could have). When this is discovered, the director is called to the table to give an appropriate ruling so that the game can continue smoothly. If the director is looking in your direction, you can raise your hand to get his attention. Otherwise, you can get his attention by calling out "Director," loudly enough for him to hear but not so loudly that it disturbs the other players. The director will listen to what happened and explain to the players any penalty that may apply or any other options they may have.

After the Game

Once the game is over, it is the director's responsibility to determine the matchpoints on each board. He records all the results and totals them up to find the winner. We'll see how he does that in the next lesson.

♠ *LAWS OF THE GAME* ♠

Since each pair is supposed to play the same deals under similar conditions, the rules are there to make the game fair. The rules are contained in a book called *The Laws of Duplicate Contract Bridge*. While the players are expected to have some familiarity with the Laws, it is the director's responsibility to see that they are properly applied during the game. The rules usually provide the director with a number of choices when the players call him to the table after an irregularity has occurred. He may be able to determine that no harm has been done and the players can continue with the bidding or play as though nothing occurred. He may have to explain the options available to one of the players, or adjust the result — *e.g.*, give one pair an extra trick and take away a trick from the other pair, or even change the contract.

Let's look at some common situations where the director is called to the table to give a ruling.

Incorrect or Incomplete Hands

In a duplicate game there are number of things that can go wrong, even before the auction and play commence. Each player is originally dealt 13 cards, but during the game, in the excitement of putting the cards back in the board after a hand is played, a card may get lost and find its way onto the floor or into the wrong pocket of a board. A player may take the wrong hand out of one of the pockets of the board. A pair may move to the wrong table and start to bid and play the boards. The wrong set of boards may have been passed to the table.

In all of these situations, the director must be called to the table to help correct the problem. Whenever possible, the director tries to remedy the situation so that the game can continue as though nothing had happened. In some situations, however, the director may need to assess a penalty or adjust a result.

For example, at the beginning of each round, the players are expected to remove the cards from their pocket and count them, face down. If a player has too few or too many cards, the director is called. Any player, whether or not he is the player who has the wrong number of cards, can call the director. Since none of the players has seen their cards, the director will decide that no harm has been done and will merely try to correct the problem. He usually does this by asking players who previously played the board to try and reconstruct it correctly. In some cases, the original layout of the board has been recorded and it is a simple matter to correct the problem. Play can then resume.

If all the players did not count their cards before the bidding started, an incorrect hand might not be noticed until near the end of the play. Perhaps one player started with 14 cards and another with 12. Now the error cannot be corrected so easily. It would not be fair, for example, to let the result stand when one player had the advantage of holding 14 cards. The director may have to adjust the result, after determining who was at fault and what impact the missing or extra cards had on the way the board was played.

Bidding Irregularities

Problems can arise during the auction in a number of ways. A player might drop a card face up on the table or make a lead before the auction is finished. A player may make a *bid out of turn*, bidding when it is his partner's or an opponent's turn to bid. Someone may make an *insufficient bid*, bidding at the one level, for example, when the auction is already at the two level.

The director must be called to give a ruling. In order that the auction continue as normally as possible, without any damage to the non-offending side, the Laws usually provide a number of options which can be exercised at the player's discretion. The director will explain the options to the players involved.

For example, suppose you have made an insufficient bid, overcalling 1 ♥ when the opponent on your right opened the bidding 1 ♠. First, the opponent on your left is given the option of accepting the bid and continuing the auction from that point. If he does not elect to exercise that option, you have the option of making your bid sufficient by bidding the same suit at the correct level, 2 ♥. If you elect this option, the auction will continue normally from that point. Finally, if you do not want to make the bid sufficient, you can bid something else but your partner must now pass for the remainder of the auction whenever it is his turn to call. In addition, there might be a lead penalty if your side ends up defending.

This may seem severe, but if you change your bid in the middle of the auction, you are giving your partner more information about your hand than if you made only one bid. Your opponents, and the other pairs in the game, have been put at a disadvantage and must be provided with sufficient protection against this *unauthorized information*, even though it was unintentional.

During the Play

During the play, you may accidentally lead out of turn when you are defending or declarer may lead from the dummy when he won the previous trick in his hand. A card, or even an entire hand, might be dropped on the table. A player may revoke, failing to follow suit when he could have. Again if irregularities occur, the director is called to explain the various options available so that play can continue as normally as possible.

For example, suppose you are defending and you lead the ♠5 when it was actually your partner who won the previous trick. Declarer is presented with a number of options. He can accept the lead, and play will continue as though it were your lead. Instead, he can request that your partner lead a spade, or he can forbid your partner from leading a spade. Finally, declarer can let your partner lead whatever he wants but the ♠5 now remains face up on the table as a *penalty card*. A penalty card must be played at the first opportunity to do so — either in following suit, when discarding on another suit or when leading to a new trick.

Score Adjustments

The director has a number of ways to adjust the scores and assess penalties where necessary. In a typical situation, where neither side is particularly at fault but the board cannot be played completely because of an irregularity, he may award an *average* result to both the North-South and East-West pairs. Awarding an average result means that each pair receives exactly half the available matchpoints on the board. For example, if the board is played 11 times during the game, then 10 is the top score possible on the board (some pair beats all the other pairs in their direction). Average would then be 5, half the maximum.

If one pair was at fault while the other pair was not at fault, the director might award an *average minus* to the offending pair and an *average plus* to the non-offending pair. Average minus is 40% of the maximum on a board and average plus is 60% of the maximum. In an example where 10 is top, the pair at fault would receive 4 matchpoints (40% of 10), while the innocent pair would end up with 6 matchpoints (60% of 10). If both pairs are clearly at fault, the director can award each of them an average minus on the board.

Committees

If there is a dispute about the facts or one of the pairs does not agree with the ruling given by the director, the director can arrange for an *appeals committee* at the end of the game. The committee is usually composed of three or more of the pair's peers with one of them acting as chairman. The director explains the facts as he understands them and the relevant rulings. Each player involved gives the committee his description of what happened, along with any other relevant information. The committee then makes a ruling, either confirming the ruling made by the director or making their own adjustment.

Committees are not needed very often. Most rulings are clear-cut, and even when they are not, the director's decision is usually happily accepted by the players. If, however, you are asked to appear at a committee hearing, it is part of the game and you should not see this action as anything unusual.

♠ SUMMARY ♠

The most common type of duplicate game is the pair game, commonly referred to as "matchpoints." The usual format is the Mitchell movement, in which the North-South pairs remain at their starting tables throughout the game while the East-West pairs move from table to table at the end of each round. The East-West pairs move to the next higher-numbered table while the set of boards they have just played is passed to the next lower-numbered table.

A director is in charge of selecting the format that will be used and will ensure that the movement proceeds smoothly throughout the game. The director is also responsible for scoring the game at the end of the session.

Since the conditions at each table must be duplicated as much as possible, all the players have to adhere to the same set of rules. If there is an irregularity at the table, the director is called to help out. The director will explain the various options and see that the laws are properly applied. His main objective is to make the game as fair as possible for all the players involved, while ensuring that everyone has an enjoyable time.

♠ GROUP ACTIVITIES ♠

Exercise One — The Mitchell Movement

You are playing in a nine-table game and are assigned to start at Table #5 E-W. A Mitchell movement is being used and it is the end of the first round.

- Which table number will you move to next?
- To which table will the set of boards you just played be sent?
- Who is responsible for moving the boards?
- Which pair number will you be following throughout the session?
- Which table will you go to after you have played at Table #9?

Exercise Two — The Director

What are two of the functions a director might perform before a game starts? What are two functions he might perform during the game? What two functions might he perform at the end of the game?

Exercise Three — The Laws

The auction is over and you make an opening lead of the ♥5 face up on the table. Your partner points out that you should not be leading since the declarer is on your left, not your right. What should you do? What will the director do when he comes to the table? How might you have avoided the problem?

♠ *SAMPLE BOARDS* ♠

BOARD #1

Dealer: North
Vulnerable: None

NORTH
♠ A J 8
♥ J 4
♦ Q 10 8 3 2
♣ A J 2

WEST
♠ 9 6 4
♥ K 9 6 3
♦ A 6
♣ K 9 8 5

EAST
♠ Q 10 7 3
♥ A 7 5
♦ 9 4
♣ Q 7 6 4

SOUTH
♠ K 5 2
♥ Q 10 8 2
♦ K J 7 5
♣ 10 3

ACBL SHORT TRAVELING SCORE (Mitchell or Howell)									
							Board No.	1	

N-S Pair No.	Contract	By	M a d e	D o w n	SCORE		N-S Match-points	E-W Pair No.	E-W Match-points
					N-S	E-W			
1	2 D	N	3		110			1	
2	1 NT	N	2		120			3	
3	1 NT	N	3		150			5	
4	3 D	N	3		110			2	
5	2 NT	N	2		120			4	
6	1 NT	N	3		150			6	
7									

Suggested Bidding

WEST	NORTH	EAST	SOUTH
	1 ♦	Pass	1 ♥
Pass	1 NT	Pass	Pass
Pass			

North should rebid 1 NT to show his balanced distribution and minimum strength instead of rebidding his five-card suit. South knows there is probably not enough combined strength for game and so he wants to settle for the best partscore. Playing duplicate, a 1 NT contract is likely to score better than a 2 ♦ contract if declarer can make any overtricks, so South should pass rather than support partner's diamonds.

Suggested Play

Against 1 NT, East will probably lead a spade and North will end up with three spade tricks. North can establish four winners in the diamond suit by driving out the ♦A and will also get a trick with the ♣A. He should end up with at least eight tricks for a score of 120 points. If North plays in a contract of 2 ♦, he will probably lose at least two heart tricks, one diamond trick and one club trick. Even making nine tricks will give North-South a score of only 110 points.

Notes

As the scoreslip shows, it is very important to play in notrump rather than a minor suit whenever possible. Pairs playing in notrump scored at least 120 points and a couple got 150 points by making two overtricks. Both pairs playing in diamonds received a poor matchpoint result. When you play duplicate bridge, you must remember that your true opponents are the other pairs sitting in your direction. You are trying to outscore them at every opportunity and you have to adjust your bidding tactics accordingly.

BOARD #2

Dealer: East
Vulnerable: North-South

NORTH
♠ Q 10 3
♥ A 6
♦ 8 5 2
♣ J 10 9 6 3

WEST
♠ A K 9 5
♥ Q 10 5
♦ A 7 4
♣ A 7 4

EAST
♠ 7 4 2
♥ K J 7 4 3
♦ K J 9
♣ 8 5

SOUTH
♠ J 8 6
♥ 9 8 2
♦ Q 10 6 3
♣ K Q 2

ACBL SHORT TRAVELING SCORE
(Mitchell or Howell)

Board No. 2

N-S Pair No.	Contract	By	Made	Down	SCORE		N-S Match-points	E-W Pair No.	E-W Match-points
					N-S	E-W			
1	4H	E		1	50			1	
2	4H	W		1	50			3	
3	4H	W	4			420		5	
4	3NT	W		1	50			2	
5	4H	E	4			420		4	
6	3NT	W		2	100			6	
7									

Suggested Bidding

WEST	NORTH	EAST	SOUTH
		Pass	Pass
1 NT	Pass	2♣	Pass
2♠	Pass	3♥	Pass
4♥	Pass	Pass	Pass

After the 1 NT opening bid, East has to bid carefully to get the partnership to the best contract. With 8 HCPs plus 1 point for the five-card suit, East is too strong to settle for partscore but not strong enough to force the partnership to game. East wants to issue an invitational sequence. In addition, East wants to investigate whether the partnership belongs in hearts or notrump. He is, therefore, too strong to bid 2 ♥, a signoff bid, but not strong enough to bid 3 ♥, a forcing bid.

East can make use of the Stayman convention to deal with the situation. He starts by bidding 2♣, supposedly asking West if he has a four-card major suit. After opener shows his four-card spade suit, East invites to game by bidding his heart suit. This is invitational because West could have bid 2 ♥ immediately, if he wanted to stop in partscore, or 3 ♥ immediately if he wanted to show a five-card suit and force opener to choose a game level contract. With 17 HCPs and three hearts, opener accepts the invitation by raising to 4 ♥.

The Play

Declarer has to lose a spade trick, a heart trick and a club trick. The secret to making the contract is to avoid losing a diamond trick as well. There is the possibility of taking the diamond finesse, hoping North has the ♦Q, but a better line of play is to first see how the missing spades are divided. After drawing trumps, declarer can play the ♠A, ♠K and then another round of spades. When the opponents' spades turn out to be divided 3–3, West's remaining spade is a winner. This can be used to provide the discard of a diamond from the East hand. If the spades do not divide evenly, declarer has to fall back on the diamond finesse as his last hope.

Notes

Since both the bidding and play are complicated, any pair that makes 4 ♥ will get a very fine result.

BOARD #3

Dealer: South
Vulnerable: East-West

NORTH
♠ A 10 7 3
♥ K J 6 4
♦ K Q 8
♣ 7 5

WEST
♠ K J 8 2
♥ A 10
♦ 9 4 3
♣ K Q 9 3

EAST
♠ Q 6
♥ 9 7 2
♦ 10 6 2
♣ A 10 8 4 2

SOUTH
♠ 9 5 4
♥ Q 8 5 3
♦ A J 7 5
♣ J 6

ACBL SHORT TRAVELING SCORE
(Mitchell or Howell)

Board No. 3

N-S Pair No.	Contract	By	Made	Down	SCORE		N-S Match-points	E-W Pair No.	E-W Match-points
					N-S	E-W			
1	2H	S	2		110			6	
2	2C	W	2			90		2	
3	3C	W		1	100			4	
4	3H	S		1		50		1	
5	3CX	W		1	200			3	
6	2H	S	2		110			5	
7									

Suggested Bidding

WEST	NORTH	EAST	SOUTH
			Pass
1♣	Double	2♣	2♥
Pass	Pass	Pass	

North should make a takeout double to compete over the 1♣ opening bid. This should not stop East from raising to 2♣ (or even bidding 1 NT). Now South does not have to bid, but with 8 HCPs he should take some action since North wants to compete for the contract. With a choice of bidding the four-card heart suit or the four-card diamond suit, South should prefer the major. Not only is it worth more in the scoring, but North's takeout double almost always promises good support for the unbid major suits, whereas his support for the unbid minor suits may not be quite as good. After South's 2♥ bid, the other players may compete further, although any higher contract is likely to be defeated.

Suggested Play

South has only two spade losers, a heart loser and two club losers. He should easily end up with eight tricks. It is difficult to make any more without some help from the opponents — any North-South pair that climbs to 3♥ will probably be defeated. If East-West compete to 3♣, they should lose a spade trick, a heart trick and three diamond tricks, going down one — unless the defenders are careless.

Notes

This deal illustrates the delicate choices that take place during a competitive auction. If North-South bid no higher than 2♥, they get a plus score, either for making that contract or defeating the opponents' 3♣ contract. If they double 3♣, they can collect 200 points for a top board, since East-West are vulnerable. On the other hand, the best East-West can do after North-South bid to 2♥ is pass and defend or risk bidding 3♣ in the hope that they do not get doubled or that the opponents push on to 3♥. An East-West pair that is allowed to play in 2♣, when the opponents are too timid to compete, will get an excellent result.

BOARD #4

Dealer: West
Vulnerable: Both

NORTH
♠ A 10 7 3
♥ 9 2
♦ 9 4 2
♣ K 6 4 3

WEST
♠ Q 6
♥ A Q 10 8 6
♦ Q J 7 5
♣ Q 8

EAST
♠ 9 8 5
♥ K J 7 3
♦ A K 8
♣ 10 7 5

SOUTH
♠ K J 4 2
♥ 5 4
♦ 10 6 3
♣ A J 9 2

ACBL SHORT TRAVELING SCORE
(Mitchell or Howell)

Board No. | 4

N-S Pair No.	Contract	By	M a d e	D o w n	SCORE N-S	SCORE E-W	N-S Match-points	E-W Pair No.	E-W Match-points
1	3H	W	3			140		6	
2	4H	W		1	100			2	
3	4H	W		2	200			4	
4	3H	W	3			140		1	
5	4H	W		1	100			3	
6	3H	W	4			170		5	
7									

Suggested Bidding

WEST	NORTH	EAST	SOUTH
1♥	Pass	3♥	Pass
Pass	Pass		

This is how the auction should go if East-West are playing limit raises. East will invite opener to game and West, with a minimum opening bid, should decline. Notice that East has an interesting problem if the partnership is playing forcing raises. Now he is not strong enough to raise to 3♥, which would be forcing to game, but will have to temporize by bidding a new suit. The auction might go:

WEST	NORTH	EAST	SOUTH
1♥	Pass	2♦	Pass
3♦	Pass	3♥	Pass
Pass	Pass		

A more complex auction is necessary to end up in the same spot as those playing limit raises. East has to bid a three-card suit since he has no four-card suit other than hearts. East-West will have to be careful not to get too high when the auction starts this way.

Suggested Play

There should not be much to the play. West has to lose two spade tricks and two club tricks, and it will be difficult for the defenders to fail to take their tricks, no matter which card North leads. But then anything can happen at the bridge table — and usually does.

Notes

It is unlikely that North-South will find their way into the auction, so the result hinges on where the East-West pair ends up. Those pairs that stop in partscore will be well rewarded, while those pairs that overbid to the game level will get a poor result. The matchpoint score that North-South receive is really in the hands of their East-West opponents. Some will get lucky when their opponents bid too much. Others will get a below average result even though they did nothing wrong!

BOARD #5

Dealer: North
Vulnerable: North-South

NORTH
♠ A 9 5 4
♥ K 10 5 2
♦ 9 5 4
♣ 9 6

WEST
♠ J 8
♥ 7 6 4
♦ A Q J 10 3
♣ Q 7 4

EAST
♠ 10 7 3
♥ A J 8 3
♦ K 6
♣ A K 10 2

SOUTH
♠ K Q 6 2
♥ Q 9
♦ 8 7 2
♣ J 8 5 3

ACBL SHORT TRAVELING SCORE (Mitchell or Howell)									
							Board No.	5	

N-S Pair No.	Contract	By	Made	Down	SCORE		N-S Match-points	E-W Pair No.	E-W Match-points
					N-S	E-W			
1	2NT	W	3			150		5	
2	3NT	E	4			430		1	
3	2NT	E	3			150		3	
4	3NT	E	3			400		6	
5	3NT	W	3			400		2	
6	3NT	E	3			400		4	
7									

Suggested Bidding

WEST	NORTH	EAST	SOUTH
	Pass	1♣	Pass
1♦	Pass	1♥	Pass
2NT	Pass	3NT	Pass
Pass	Pass		

If East were to open the bidding 1NT with only 15 HCPs, the auction would be very straightforward since West would raise directly to 3NT. If the partnership uses a range of 16–18 HCPs for a 1NT opening, the auction is a little more complicated. East opens the bidding 1♣ and rebids 1♥ over partner's 1♦ response. Now, West has a difficult choice of rebids. With 10 HCPs plus 1 point for the five-card diamond suit, he has enough to invite game by jumping to 2NT or, perhaps, 3♦. With 15 points, West will accept the invitation.

Suggested Play

If the defenders lead a spade, they can take their four tricks and then declarer will take the rest. Declarer has a heart trick, five diamond tricks and three club tricks. If the defenders do not take their spade tricks right away, South will have to be careful to hold on to all his clubs to prevent declarer from making an overtrick.

Notes

Since it is not always as easy to get to game as it looks, pairs reaching 3NT will get an above average result. The top East-West result will likely go to any pair that makes an overtrick when the opponents do not lead spades and South discards a club when declarer takes his diamond winners. The best North-South can do is take their tricks when they have the opportunity.

BOARD #6

Dealer: East
Vulnerable: East-West

NORTH
♠ A J 10 7 4 2
♥ 7 3
♦ K J 6 2
♣ 4

WEST
♠ K 9 6
♥ A 6 4
♦ 10 8 4
♣ J 10 3 2

EAST
♠ Q 3
♥ Q J 10 5
♦ 9 5 3
♣ Q 9 7 6

SOUTH
♠ 8 5
♥ K 9 8 2
♦ A Q 7
♣ A K 8 5

ACBL SHORT TRAVELING SCORE
(Mitchell or Howell)

Board No. | 6

N-S Pair No.	Contract	By	Made	Down	SCORE		N-S Match-points	E-W Pair No.	E-W Match-points
					N-S	E-W			
1	4S	N		1		50		5	
2	4S	N	4		420			1	
3	4S	N	4		420			3	
4	3NT	S		1		50		6	
5	4S	N		1		50		2	
6	3NT	S	3		400			4	
7									

Suggested Bidding

WEST	NORTH	EAST	SOUTH
		Pass	1 NT
Pass	4♠	Pass	Pass
Pass			

With 9 HCPs and a six-card suit, North wants to be in game once South opens the bidding 1 NT. With a six-card major suit, North jumps directly to game in the known fit.

Suggested Play

While it is not difficult to get to 4♠ on this deal, it is not as easy to make the contract. East will probably start off by leading the ♥ Q, top of a sequence, and South's ♥ K will be trapped. No matter what declarer does, he will lose two heart tricks and have to play carefully from this point on to avoid losing two trump tricks.

If North simply plays the ♠ A and another spade, the defenders will get tricks with both the ♠ K and the ♠ Q. Instead, North should start by leading one of dummy's small spades toward his hand. Assuming West plays a small spade, North should finesse the ♠ 10 (or ♠ J). On the actual deal, this loses to East's ♠ Q. When North regains the lead, however, he should lead the remaining small spade from dummy and, when West plays another small spade, he should finesse the ♠ J. The second finesse works and North can play the ♠ A to draw West's remaining ♠ K. By taking the two spade finesses, North restricts his spade losers to one.

Notes

Most pairs should reach the 4♠ contract, but the majority of the matchpoints will go to the pairs who actually make the contract. In an expert game, most declarers will have no trouble taking 10 tricks, but if the players are less experienced, most will not be familiar with the best technique for handling the trump suit.

BOARD #7

Dealer: South
Vulnerable: Both

NORTH
♠ 1052
♥ A K J 2
♦ A 7
♣ J 9 7 3

WEST
♠ K 9 4
♥ 8 5 4 3
♦ K J 5 3
♣ 8 5

EAST
♠ A Q J 8 3
♥ 10 7 6
♦ 10 9 4
♣ A 6

SOUTH
♠ 7 6
♥ Q 9
♦ Q 8 6 2
♣ K Q 10 4 2

ACBL SHORT TRAVELING SCORE
(Mitchell or Howell)

Board No. | 7

N-S Pair No.	Contract	By	Made	Down	SCORE N-S	SCORE E-W	N-S Match-points	E-W Pair No.	E-W Match-points
1	3SX	E		1	200			4	
2	3C	N	3		110			6	
3	2S	E	2			110		2	
4	3S	E		1	100			5	
5	2C	N	3		110			1	
6	2NT	N		1		100		3	
7									

Suggested Bidding

WEST	NORTH	EAST	SOUTH
			Pass
Pass	1♣	1♠	2♣
2♠	Pass	Pass	3♣
Pass	Pass	Pass	

Both sides are competing for a partscore and both sides are vulnerable. It is reasonable for South to push on to 3♣ with 9 HCPs and five-card support for partner's suit rather than defend 2♠. It would be somewhat aggressive for either East or West to compete to 3♠.

Suggested Play

East might lead the ♠A from the suit bid and supported by the partnership. If he does, West can encourage with the ♠9 and the defense should take the first two tricks. They should later get a club trick and a diamond trick, provided West does not lead a diamond away from his ♦K.

If East chooses to lead something other than a spade, perhaps hoping to trap the ♠K if North has it, declarer will have a good opportunity to make an overtrick. Before drawing trumps, he can play the ♥Q and then a heart back to his hand. He can play another high heart and discard a spade from the dummy. Now, when the defenders get the lead with their ♣A, they will be able to take only one spade trick.

Notes

In a competitive situation where both sides are vulnerable, both sides must be careful not to get too high and risk losing 200 points. On this deal, for example, if East-West bid on to 3♠, they risk being doubled and getting a bottom board when they cannot make their contract.

BOARD #8

Dealer: West
Vulnerable: None

NORTH
♠ 8 4
♥ J 10 9 6
♦ 9 6 3
♣ K Q 10 8

WEST
♠ A K 10 3
♥ K 7 2
♦ K Q 8
♣ J 6 3

EAST
♠ Q J 6 5
♥ A 8
♦ A 7 5
♣ 7 5 4 2

SOUTH
♠ 9 7 2
♥ Q 5 4 3
♦ J 10 4 2
♣ A 9

ACBL SHORT TRAVELING SCORE
(Mitchell or Howell)

Board No. | 8

N-S Pair No.	Contract	By	Made	Down	SCORE N-S	SCORE E-W	N-S Match-points	E-W Pair No.	E-W Match-points
1	4S	W	4			420		4	
2	4S	W	4			420		6	
3	4S	W	4			420		2	
4	3NT	W	3			400		5	
5	3NT	W	3			400		1	
6	4S	W	4			420		3	
7									

Suggested Bidding

WEST	NORTH	EAST	SOUTH
1 NT	Pass	2♣	Pass
2♠	Pass	4♠	Pass
Pass	Pass		

When West opens the bidding 1 NT, East should make use of the Stayman convention to look for a Golden Fit. When West shows his four-card spade suit, East can put the partnership in game.

Suggested Play

Declarer can trump his heart loser in the dummy and so loses only three club tricks.

If West ends up playing in 3 NT, the defenders can take the first four club tricks. If North leads the ♣K, South should overtake with the ♣A to *unblock* the suit. He can then lead back the ♣9 and North will take three more club tricks, provided he is careful to overtake the ♣9 with his ♣10.

Notes

Although a notrump contract is worth more than playing in a major suit when both contracts yield the same number of tricks, playing in the suit contract will usually provide at least one extra trick. On this deal, declarer gets an extra trick by trumping a heart loser in the dummy. This is not possible in a notrump contract. It is usually best to explore for a major suit fit before settling in a notrump contract.

BOARD #9

Dealer: North
Vulnerable: East-West

NORTH
♠ Q 10 5
♥ Q 10 7 5
♦ 9 8 6 4
♣ Q 7

WEST
♠ 7 3
♥ 9 4 2
♦ A Q 10 7 2
♣ 9 5 4

EAST
♠ A K 8
♥ A K 6
♦ J 5
♣ A 10 8 6 3

SOUTH
♠ J 9 6 4 2
♥ J 8 3
♦ K 3
♣ K J 2

ACBL SHORT TRAVELING SCORE
(Mitchell or Howell)

Board No.: 9

N-S Pair No.	Contract	By	Made	Down	SCORE		N-S Match-points	E-W Pair No.	E-W Match-points
					N-S	E-W			
1	3NT	E	4			630		3	
2	2NT	E	2			120		5	
3	3NT	E	3			600		1	
4	3NT	E		1	100			4	
5	1NT	E	4			180		6	
6	3NT	E		1	100			2	
7									

Suggested Bidding

WEST	NORTH	EAST	SOUTH
	Pass	1♣	Pass
1♦	Pass	2NT	Pass
3NT	Pass	Pass	Pass

East is too strong to open 1 NT and so starts the bidding with 1♣, intending to show the strength of the hand with his rebid. After West's 1♦ response, East describes his hand with a jump to 2NT and West carries on to game.

Suggested Play

South will probably lead a spade and East must determine the best way to take nine tricks. He has six sure tricks with aces and kings and the diamond suit looks as though it could provide three or four more tricks. If East leads the ♦J, planning to finesse, the number of tricks he ends up with will depend on what South does and what East does next.

Suppose South plays his low diamond, East will play a low diamond from dummy and the ♦J will win the trick. When East leads his remaining diamond, South's ♦K appears and East ends up with all five diamond tricks — making an overtrick. Instead of playing a low diamond, South should play the ♦K on declarer's ♦J, covering an honor with an honor. Declarer can win the trick with dummy's ♦A and take the ♦Q and ♦10, but will now have to lose a trick to North's ♦9. With no entry to dummy's last diamond, declarer ends up with only eight tricks — down one. Can declarer make the contract if South covers the ♦J? Yes, by playing a low diamond from dummy, just as he would if South had played a low diamond. By giving up one trick to the opponents, he still has a low diamond left to get over to dummy's ♦A, ♦Q, ♦10 and ♦7. This gives him exactly nine tricks.

Notes

This deal provides a good battle of wits between declarer and the defenders. Even though most of the E-W pairs will end up in 3NT, the result depends on the skill of both declarer and the defenders. East will end up making anywhere from eight to 10 tricks.

BOARD #10

Dealer: East
Vulnerable: Both

NORTH
♠ A Q 6
♥ 3 2
♦ K 7 5
♣ A J 10 7 3

WEST
♠ K 8 2
♥ K 9
♦ Q 10 9 2
♣ 8 5 4 2

EAST
♠ J 9 7 5 4
♥ 10 8 7 5
♦ 8 4
♣ K 6

SOUTH
♠ 10 3
♥ A Q J 6 4
♦ A J 6 3
♣ Q 9

ACBL SHORT TRAVELING SCORE
(Mitchell or Howell)

Board No. | 10

N-S Pair No.	Contract	By	M a d e	D o w n	SCORE		N-S Match-points	E-W Pair No.	E-W Match-points
					N-S	E-W			
1	4H	S		1		100		3	
2	3NT	N	3		600			5	
3	3NT	N	3		600			1	
4	3NT	N		1		100		4	
5	3NT	N	4		630			6	
6	3NT	N		2		200		2	
7									

Suggested Bidding

WEST	NORTH	EAST	SOUTH
		Pass	1 ♥
Pass	2 ♣	Pass	2 ♦
Pass	3 NT	Pass	Pass
Pass			

Although South has a minimum opening bid, he can show his second suit with his rebid since it is lower ranking than his original suit. North wants to be in a game, and when South describes a hand with hearts and diamonds, North can judge that the partnership belongs in notrump.

Suggested Play

East will probably lead his fourth best spade and West will play the ♠ K, third hand high. On this deal, North can count six winners once he sees the ♠ K — two spades, one heart, two diamonds and a club. He needs three more. Looking at the dummy, the heart suit seems to present a good opportunity to develop the three extra tricks. But if declarer takes the heart finesse, he may go down on this board. The finesse loses and West leads another spade, driving out declarer's remaining high spade. When the missing hearts divide 4 2, declarer can take only two heart tricks. If he leads another heart to develop a ninth trick, East will win and take enough spade tricks to defeat the contract. If declarer tries the club finesse, that also does not work. In fact, declarer may now be defeated two tricks, losing three spade tricks, two heart tricks and a club trick.

The heart suit is an optical illusion. Declarer must be careful to examine all the alternatives before deciding how to play the deal. The club suit offers a sure way to make the contract. Because the ♣ K is the only missing high card, declarer can establish three extra club tricks whether or not the club finesse works. The club finesse loses, but declarer still has two spade tricks, a heart trick, two diamond tricks and four club tricks, enough to make the contract. He may even make an overtrick by establishing an extra heart winner, provided he is careful enough to hold up one of his spade winners so that West has no spades left when he wins a trick with the ♥ K.

Notes

Careful technique rewards declarer. Less careful play will lead to a good result for the East-West pair.

LESSON 4

Winning the Game

Determining a Winner
Masterpoints
Bridge Etiquette
Skip Bid Warning
Summary

Workshop Material
Group Activities
Sample Boards

Part of the excitement of any game is seeing who won. In duplicate bridge, you and your partner are testing your skill against the skills of other players sitting in the same direction. The reward in duplicate is the feeling of satisfaction for a job well done, some honor and glory, and the awards given out by the American Contract Bridge League. First let's see how the winner is decided.

♠ DETERMINING A WINNER ♠

The traveling scoreslip lets you know how you did on each individual board during the game. Since you play many boards throughout the game, the results on the individual boards have to be totaled together to determine the winner.

The Recap Sheet

At the end of the game, the director gathers the scoreslips and determines the matchpoints for each board. He then enters the results on a large sheet called a *recap* sheet (recapitulation sheet). A typical recap sheet would look like this:

MATCHPOINT RECAPITULATION

EVENT _____ MOVEMENT _____ AVERAGE _____

SESSION _____ DATE _____ SECTION _____

No.	North and South	Rank	Total	1	2	3	4	5	6	7	8	9	10	11

At the top is the name of the event, the type of movement, the average total score, the date and, in the case of multiple sections, a section identifier. The average total score is average on a single board (½ of top) times the number of boards played. Down the left-hand column are the pair numbers: first the North-South pairs (North-South *field*) and then the East-West pairs (East-West *field*). Beside each pair number is a space for the players' names. Next comes a column for the total number of matchpoints scored by each of the pairs, derived by adding up the matchpoints for each board they played, and a column for the rankings. The remainder of the sheet contains the matchpoints for each board.

In a typical Mitchell movement, there will be separate rankings for both the North-South and East-West pairs. Approximately the top third of the pairs are ranked. If there are 11 tables, for example, there will be North-South rankings of first through fourth and also East-West rankings of first through fourth.

In some clubs and at most tournaments, the recap sheets are prepared by computer. Regardless of the format of the recap sheet, at the end of the game players crowd around to see their results. The director may announce the names of the winners as soon as they are known. He then will post the final results and matchpointing so that everyone can see how they did. If a player discovers an error, he can inform the director who will then make the appropriate correction after confirming the result with the pairs involved.

Negative Scoring

When a North-South pair get a top on a board, the East-West pair who were their opponents get a bottom. Similarly, if the North-South pair score a bottom, the East-West pair score a top. Essentially, the matchpoints awarded in one direction are the complement of those awarded in the other. For example, if 12 is top on a board and the North-South pair get 8, the opposing East-West pair get 4 (8 + 4 = 12).

Matchpointing each board twice, once for the North-South pairs and once for the East-West pairs, is very time-consuming, especially when all the pairs are anxious to see how they did. Fortunately, there is a form of scoring to make life easier for the director and to give the players the results more quickly. Instead of matchpointing the North-South and East-West results separately, the director matchpoints the board from only the North-South point of view and then awards the identical number of matchpoints to the opposing East-West pair. For example, if North-South Pair #3 played East-West Pair #5 and scored 11 matchpoints on a board, East-West Pair #5 is also given 11 matchpoints for the board. This means that a large number of matchpoints in the East-West direction represents a poor result on a board while a small number of matchpoints represents a good score on the board. Since the lower your score the better your result when sitting East-West, this is referred to as *negative scoring*.

The East-West pair with the lowest overall total will win in their direction when negative scoring is used. This is similar to score tallies in golf, where the lower the score the better the result. When you look for your score on the recap sheet, it is important to remember your direction so that you know whether you are looking for a high or low score as a good result.

When the game is scored by a computer, however, the computer is fast enough to do the matchpointing in both directions. There is no need for negative scoring and the high score in each direction wins.

Selecting an Overall Winner

In club championship events and tournaments, where there might be a trophy at stake, there is a need to determine an overall winner in addition to the winners in each direction.

In order to come up with one winning pair, the total matchpoints for the pairs in both directions have to be compared. For example, if the best North-South total is 180 matchpoints and one of the East-West pairs scored 185 matchpoints, the East-West pair is the overall winner. When negative scoring is used, the East-West results will first have to be converted to their proper positive score.

When computer scoring is used, the total matchpoint result of each pair is usually converted into a percentage. The pair with the highest percentage is the overall winner. A percentage result is determined by dividing the total number of matchpoints received by the total number available and multiplying by 100. For example, if there are 13 tables in play, the best result you can get on any one board is to beat every pair in the room. If you beat all 12 pairs, you get 12 matchpoints, top on the board. If there were 26 boards in play, a perfect score would be 312 (12 × 26). Suppose you scored 156 matchpoints. This would be a 50% game ($\frac{156}{312}$ × 100 = 50). Another way of describing your game is to say it was *average* — you got exactly half the available matchpoints. If you scored 187 matchpoints in total you would have about a 60% game ($\frac{187}{312}$ × 100 = 59.94).

If negative scoring is used, convert your score to a positive one before calculating the percentage. For example, if you scored 140 matchpoints out of a possible 312, this is equivalent to 172 matchpoints in the North-South direction (312 − 140 = 172), a 55% game ($\frac{172}{312}$ × 100 = 55.13).

In a single session, a score of 60% to 65% is very good and usually will win, although pairs have been known to score more than 80%! When a game is played over a number of sessions, the scores tend to even out and the overall winner may be in the 55% to 60% range. You do not have to be much above average to have a chance of being in the overall rankings!

♠ *MASTERPOINTS* ♠

When you play in a game organized through the American Contract Bridge League, you receive *masterpoints* (not to be confused with matchpoints) each time you are in the winning circle. The total number of masterpoints you win throughout your bridge career is a measure of how well you have played and how often you have played. If you are a member of ACBL, the masterpoints you win are recorded on a central computer at ACBL's headquarters in Memphis, Tennessee, and you receive a regular feedback on your accumulated total.

How Masterpoints Are Awarded

The size of the masterpoint awards you win when you are ranked in the top third of the field depends on the size and caliber of the game. If you are playing in a beginner game and there are six tables in play, you would expect to earn far fewer masterpoints than for winning in the final of a North American Bridge Championship (NABC) which started out with several hundred tables.

In club games, the director gives the winners a *club masterpoint slip*, which is a record of how many masterpoints have been awarded. A club masterpoint point slip looks like this:

For ACBL Sanctioned Clubs Only
AMERICAN CONTRACT BRIDGE LEAGUE • P.O. BOX 161284, MEMPHIS, TENNESSEE 38186-1284

CLUB MASTERPOINT CERTIFICATE
TO RECORD YOUR CERTIFICATES SEND THEM TO THE ABOVE ADDRESS

PLAYER'S
NAME _____ DATE _____
(PLEASE PRINT)

(CHECK ONE) CLUB _____ CLUB# _____

OVERALL ☐   SECTION ☐   CITY _____ STATE _____
TABLES _____   RANKING _____

_____ BDS, MATCHES WON _____

CLUB CHAMP. ☐   CHARITY CHAMP. ☐   AUTHORIZED SIGNATURE

CHECK MOVEMENT   Individual ☐   Handicap ☐   Stratified ☐   Team ☐   Howell ☐   Mitchell ☒

CLASSIFICATION (Circle One) 1 - 2 - 3 - 4   BONUS FACTORS (Circle One) 0 - 1 - 2 - 3 - 4 - 5 - 6

B 1597201

NOTE: Please add your certificates and provide a total. If participating in any of the Masterpoint contests, you must provide separate totals for points earned this year and points earned in previous years.

PLAYER'S NUMBER

RP7-9/89 Printed in U.S.A. Copyright ACBL 1989

J2560

In most club games, you receive only a fraction of a full masterpoint for winning. The number shown on the slip, 24, represents $^{24}/_{100}$ (.24) of a masterpoint. These points are called *fractionals*. If you play often enough in a club, you will soon collect over 100 fractional masterpoints, representing your first full masterpoint.

There is other information on the club masterpoint slip. It shows the number of tables in play and where you finished (2nd). It shows the rating of the game (open, invitational or novice) and what bonus factors the game claims (whether the game was run by a certified or qualified director; whether the club runs a teaching program and games for novices, etc.). Higher rating and more bonus factors determine the award charts to be used. There is an incentive for the club to meet these requirements so that its participants can qualify for the highest possible awards.

When you become a member of ACBL, you receive a membership number which is used when recording your points. You can collect your club masterpoint slips and send them to Memphis, along with your membership number, whenever you have 100 fractionals (1 full masterpoint) or more. Masterpoints won at tournaments are automatically recorded for you by the tournament directors.

Ranks of Achievement

Most sports have their own ways of measuring achievement. There are four distinct colors of masterpoints which you can collect. The points won at a club game are usually *black points*. In order to become a *Life Master*, you have to show that you can be among the winners of tournament games, which are more competitive than club games. *Silver points* can be earned by winning at *sectional tournaments*, which are held frequently during the year in many cities and towns across the country. *Red and gold points* can be won at the next step up, the *regional tournaments*, which are held about once a year in major cities. Finally, *red and gold points* can also be won at one of the three North American Bridge Championships held each year, which are attended by players from all across the continent and from other parts of the world.

The various levels that can be achieved by accumulating masterpoints are:

Rookie	Less than 5 points of any color
Junior Master	5 or more points of any color
Club Master	20 or more points of any color
Sectional Master	50 or more points, including 5 silver points
Regional Master	100 or more points, including 15 silver and 5 red or gold points
NABC Master	200 or more points, including 5 gold, 15 red or gold, and 25 silver points
Life Master	300 or more points, including 25 gold, 25 red or gold, and 50 silver points

After Life Master, there are additional levels of achievement that can be reached:

Bronze Life Master	500 points
Silver Life Master	1,000 points
Gold Life Master	2,500 points
Diamond Life Master	5,000 points
Grand Life Master	10,000 points

Only a handful of players have ever become Grand Life Masters, but many players have reached the Life Master level through participation in club games and at tournaments.

Flighted Events

Some events are open only to players holding a certain number of master points. For example, the Life Master Pairs event, held at one of the North American Bridge Championships, is open only to players who are Life Masters. It works the other way around as well. A 99er event, for example, is restricted to players with less than 100 masterpoints and a beginner game may be restricted to players with less than 5 masterpoints. At a tournament, many of the events are *flighted*. For example, there may be a section for players with less than 50 points, one for players with less than 300 points and an unlimited section. In this way, people can play in a game suited to their level of experience, moving up to the next level only when they feel confident enough.

♠ *BRIDGE ETIQUETTE* ♠

When you move into duplicate bridge the code of conduct is more formal than what you may have been used to while playing in student games or in your own home. Of course, in all situations, you are expected to behave in a friendly manner toward your partner and your opponents. Nevertheless, you should be aware of some of the differences when you sit down to play duplicate in a club or at a tournament.

Bidding

A bid consists of a number from one to seven and a denomination (clubs, diamonds, hearts, spades or notrump) or "pass", "double" or "redouble". These are the only permissible words. In an informal game, a player might add his feelings about the bid he is making by sighing, "I never get any high cards! I guess I'll have to pass again." The implication to everyone at the table is that this player has a very weak hand. If he said only the word "pass," everyone could infer that he has fewer than 13 points but no one would know whether he has 0 or 12.

As another example, a player might say, "I don't think you can make 3♥, I'm going to double you." This leaves no doubt that the subsequent double is for penalties, rather than a takeout double. If only the word "double" had been used, it would be up to the player's partner and the opponents to interpret the meaning in the given situation. In duplicate bridge, the only calls allowed are those without any qualifying comment.

Gestures, such as frowning, raising your eyebrows or stamping your foot, are also against the rules. For example, you cannot make a bid and then fold up your cards, placing them face down on the table, to make it clear to your partner that he is not expected to bid again. The tone and speed of your bidding must be consistent, so that you give partner information based only on the bids you make, not the way you make them.

You might be thinking that you cannot be expected to bid at the same tempo all the time since some hands are more difficult than others. It is not always easy. For example, suppose you hold the following hand:

♠ A J 5
♥ Q 7 3
♦ Q 6 2
♣ 10 9 5 2

Partner opens the bidding 1♦ and you are considering what you are going to respond, probably 1 NT, when the opponent on your right bids 3♥. This is a typical type of problem with which you will be faced at the table. There is no right answer. Perhaps you should double or perhaps you should pass. The longer it takes you to decide what you are going to do, the clearer it becomes to everyone at the table, especially your partner, that you must have some strength or you would not have a problem. Suppose you eventually pass, your left-hand opponent passes and your partner holds this hand:

♠ K 7
♥ 10 5 2
♦ A K J 7 5
♣ A K 6

Your partner also has a problem. If you have taken a long time to pass, indicating some strength, he knows it is safe to keep bidding, perhaps risking 3NT or doubling. If you had passed very quickly, signifying you had nothing, he would know it was dangerous for him to bid again. Your hesitation, then, has given your partner information to which he is not entitled.

This is an awkward situation. Because you have passed information to your partner with your hesitation, your opponents have been put at a disadvantage. The slow pass sent the message, "I have a problem, partner." Your partner is obligated not to take advantage of such *unauthorized information*, information given through means other than the actual bid.

Unfortunately, you cannot read another person's mind. Your partner may well have intended to bid again if you had passed in tempo, but no one can ever know for sure — including your partner. You want to avoid any undue hesitations in the bidding whenever possible.

You might be surprised if the opponents called the director to the table when you took a long time before making your bid. Nonetheless, this is perfectly normal. All they are doing is protecting their right not to be put at a disadvantage compared to the other pairs in the field. They want to ensure that your partner bids only on the legitimate information he has — his own hand and a pass from you. The director will warn your partner to bid exactly as if there had been no hesitation.

Beginner games are fairly informal, and it is unlikely that the director would be called after a hesitation most of the time. As you move from beginner games to more advanced games, you will encounter these bidding situations more frequently and you are expected to become more fluent and more consistent in your tempo.

Play

As with the bidding, the play of the cards must follow the standard rules of etiquette. You must not pass information to your partner by the manner in which you play your cards. For example, if you like the card your partner has led, you cannot show your enthusiasm by smiling, or leaning slightly forward in anticipation of another lead of the same suit. If you do not like the card your partner has led, you must not slap or snap your card on the table, frown, or slump down in your chair. Partner is expected to work out which card to play through legitimate signals — high cards to encourage and low cards to discourage, for example.

Suppose you lead a singleton against a suit contract, hoping for a ruff. If you lead very quickly and look expectantly across the table, it becomes clear to partner that you want him to return the suit. You must lead your card in the same tempo that you lead any other card, hoping partner can work out that you want the suit returned without the help of gestures or other unauthorized information.

Another part of the rules is that you must not deliberately attempt to mislead your opponents through the way in which you play your cards. For example, suppose declarer leads the jack toward dummy in the following layout:

DUMMY
K 10 9

YOU
8 7 3

DECLARER
J

Holding only low cards, you have no problem about what to play and should be able to play a card in tempo. It is unethical for you to take a long time considering which card to play, trying to persuade declarer that you have one of the missing high cards. Of course, declarer takes any inference from your hesitation at his own risk and, if he guesses incorrectly, has no one but himself to blame.

Asking Questions

Although you have every intention of paying attention during the game, there are times when you cannot remember either the auction or one of the cards that have been played. Or you may want an explanation of a bid. Here is how you go about getting the information you need.

If you want to review the auction, do so only when it is your turn to call, but if you did not hear a call, you can ask immediately that it be repeated. When the auction is over, you can ask whether or not you are on opening lead. If it is not your lead, you can ask for a review only after your partner has chosen his opening lead. A review of the auction is given by your opponents and includes everything that was originally said. Although you can no longer ask for a review of the entire auction once the first trick has been completed, you can still ask for an explanation of a specific bid that the opponents made during the auction.

During the play, you can ask to see the cards played to a trick as long as both you and your partner have not turned your cards face down. If all four cards to a trick have been turned over, then none of the players can ask to see the cards again. You can look at your own last card, but you cannot show it to anyone else. At the end of a hand, you can look at all of the tricks, especially if you think that one of the opponents revoked (did not follow suit on a trick).

Claims

During the play, you are not to express your feeling about whether or not the contract can be made, using such comments as, "I think I can take the rest of the tricks, but we'll see." Nevertheless, at any point in the hand you can make a formal *claim* by saying, "The rest of the tricks are mine," or a *concession* such as, "You get only one more trick." In making a claim, unless it is obvious to everyone at the table, you have to show your cards and state exactly the order in which they will be played. If the opponents dispute your claim, play ceases and the director is called. He will have to adjudicate the result.

If you make a claim or concession as a defender, you are doing it for both you and your partner. If you say, "I get one more trick," you are, in effect, saying that the partnership can take only one more trick, unless your partner immediately objects. Until you are quite experienced, avoid making a claim or concession. Even expert players sometimes make a mistake when trying to bring the hand to a rapid conclusion.

More About Etiquette

The rationale behind the proprieties is to make the conditions the same at all tables. If, at one table, dummy gets up and looks at everyone's hand, the conditions may become inequitable. Dummy's facial expression or comment may tell declarer or the opponents something about the board which was not available to the players at other tables. In general, you should handle only your own cards during the bidding and play of the board.

Another objective of the proprieties is to make the game more enjoyable for everyone. Have you ever been playing as declarer and had one of the defenders pull a card out of his hand before you decided what you were going to play? Most players find this annoying. It is as though the play is so simple that your opponent knows what you should do before you can figure it out yourself. What other actions bother most players? Most of us do not like being stared at, especially by an opponent. You would also expect people to take an interest in what is going on at the table and not be reading a newspaper at the same time that they are defending a board.

The Laws

The rules governing the game are contained in *The Laws of Duplicate Contract Bridge*. Here is a summary from the section on propriety:

Breaches of Propriety

1. Using different designations for the same call.
2. Indicating approval or disapproval of a call or play.
3. Indicating the expectation or intention of winning or losing a trick that has not been completed.
4. Commenting or acting during the auction or play so as to call attention to a significant occurrence, or to the number of tricks still required for success.
5. Looking intently at any other player during the auction and play, or at another player's hand as for the purpose of seeing his cards or of observing the place from which he draws a card.
6. Showing an obvious lack of further interest in a deal (as by folding one's cards).
7. Varying the normal tempo of bidding or play for the purpose of disconcerting an opponent.
8. Leaving the table needlessly before the round is called.

♠ *SKIP BID WARNINGS* ♠

We saw earlier that the opponents can make it difficult for us to exchange information when they are competing in the auction. This is especially true when an opponent jumps or *skips* more than one level of bidding. To avoid the problems associated with hesitations, when anyone is planning to skip a level of bidding they can issue a *skip bid warning*. Let's look at what this means and why such a warning is useful.

The Skip Bid Announcement

Whenever you are about to make a bid that skips one or more levels on the Bidding Scale, you can announce, "I am about to make a skip bid, please wait." After you make your bid, the opponent on your left is expected to look at his hand intently for approximately 10 seconds before making his call.

The purpose of making this announcement, warning your opponent and asking him to deliberately wait before making his call, is to avoid the difficult problems associated with hesitations. Since your opponent has to wait about 10 seconds before bidding — which should give him enough time to decide on a call even with a difficult hand — his partner will not be given any unauthorized information through the tempo in which the call is made.

For example, suppose the opponent on your right says, "I am about to make a skip bid, please wait. 3♥," and this is your hand:

♠ J 9 7 5
♥ 10 9 4
♦ Q 7 6
♣ J 10 5

You are certainly not planning to bid anything starting at the three level or higher but, before saying pass, you must wait for 10 seconds. There is a difference between this hesitation, with no bidding problem, and the hesitation described earlier in the lesson. This time, the hesitation is at the request of your opponent. While you are waiting for 10 seconds, you are not to do anything which would indicate you have nothing to think about. After all, you might have held this hand:

♠ K 10 7 5 2
♥ J 3
♦ A 9 6
♣ K J 5

It may not be clear-cut whether you should bid or pass and you might take longer to pass than you did with the previous hand. If you hesitate with both of the above hands, your partner does not know which type of hand you have.

When to Use the Skip Bid

You do not have to give a skip bid warning, but you must be consistent. You cannot use the warning when you skip a level holding a weak hand — before a preemptive 3♥ opening, for example — but not when you have a strong hand — before opening with a strong 2♦, for example. In general, it is good practice to make the skip bid warning all the time, because it prevents the opponents from inadvertently giving unauthorized information.

♠ *SUMMARY* ♠

At the end of the game, the director puts the matchpoints for each board on a recap sheet. The matchpoints for each pair are then added up and the pair with the highest total wins in each direction. (If negative scoring is used, the East-West pair with the lowest total will be the winners in their direction.)

Masterpoints are awarded to all pairs who finish in the top third of the field. The size of the masterpoint award depends on the number of pairs competing and the caliber of the game. Fractional points are usually awarded in club games and issued on club master-point slips which can be sent to ACBL for recording once you become a member. At tournaments, you can also win silver, red and gold points, which are needed to reach the rank of Life Master.

The etiquette for duplicate bridge is based on the premise that you want to make the game as comfortable and as pleasant as possible for all the players while making sure, as much as possible, that the boards are played under the same conditions at each table. The proprieties are laid out in the *Laws of Duplicate Contract Bridge* and the director is responsible for ensuring that everyone adheres to them.

When a player is going to skip one or more levels of bidding, he can give a skip bid warning: "I am about to make a skip bid, please wait." His left-hand opponent is then expected to wait about 10 seconds before calling.

♠ *GROUP ACTIVITIES* ♠

Exercise One — The Recap Sheet

You are Pair #3 N-S, playing in a five-table game. Two of your friends are Pair #4 N-S. After the game, the director adds up the results and posts the following recap sheet:

	MATCHPOINT RECAPITULATION													

EVENT _STUDENT DUPLICATE_   **MOVEMENT** _MITCHELL_   **AVERAGE** _20_
SESSION _ONLY_   **DATE** _JAN. 30/1990_   **SECTION** _A_

No.	North and South	Rank	Total	1	2	3	4	5	6	7	8	9	10	11
1	ROMEO AND JULIET		15	4	0	-	0	1	3	0	1	4	1-	
2	ELMER AND BUGS	1	23-	1	4	-	3-	4	3	1	3	2	1-	
3	YOU AND YOUR PARTNER		20-	3	2	2	2	3	-	2-	2	2	1-	
4	YOUR NEW BRIDGE FRIENDS		19	2	1	4	1	0	3	2-	4	0	1-	
5	FRANKIE AND JOHNNY	2	22	0	3	3	3-	2	-	4	0	2	4	
6														

- In what position did you finish?
- Which pair won in the North-South direction?
- What was the average score?
- Were you above or below average?
- How many matchpoints did you get on Board #5?
- Did you do better or worse than your friends (Pair #4 N-S) on Board #8?
- Did you do better or worse than your friends overall?

Exercise Two — Masterpoints

Here is a club masterpoint slip that you receive at the end of a game in your local club:

For ACBL Sanctioned Clubs Only
AMERICAN CONTRACT BRIDGE LEAGUE • P.O. BOX 161284, MEMPHIS, TENNESSEE 38186–1284

CLUB MASTERPOINT CERTIFICATE
TO RECORD YOUR CERTIFICATES SEND THEM TO THE ABOVE ADDRESS

PLAYER'S NAME _____ DATE _____
(PLEASE PRINT)

(CHECK ONE)   CLUB _____   CLUB# _____

OVERALL ☐   *9*   SECTION ☐   *2*   CITY _____   STATE _____

TABLES ____*1*____   RANKING _____

_____ BDS, MATCHES WON _____

CLUB CHAMP. ☐   CHARITY CHAMP. ☐   AUTHORIZED SIGNATURE

CHECK MOVEMENT   Individual ☐   Handicap ☐   Stratified ☐   Team ☐   Howell ☐   Mitchell ☒

CLASSIFICATION (Circle One) 1 - 2 - 3 - 4   BONUS FACTORS (Circle One) 0 - 1 - 2 - 3 - 4 - 5 - 6

B 1597202

PLAYER'S NUMBER

NOTE: Please add your certificates and provide a total. If participating in any of the Masterpoint contests, you must provide separate totals for points earned this year and points earned in previous years.

18

RP7-9/89 Printed in U.S.A. **Copyright ACBL 1989**   J2560

- How many fractional points did you collect?
- How many more fractional points will you need for a full masterpoint?
- In what place did you finish in your direction?
- How many tables were in play?
- How many other pairs in your direction will be awarded masterpoints?

Exercise Three — Bridge Etiquette

Together with the other players at your table, make a list of five things which you consider would be in poor taste at the bridge table.

Exercise Four — Skip Bid Warning

You decide to open the bidding 3♣. Exactly what would you say at the table? What advantage would there be in asking your opponent to wait before calling?

♠ *SAMPLE BOARDS* ♠

BOARD #1

Dealer: North
Vulnerable: None

NORTH
♠ 9
♥ A K J 10 5 3
♦ A K 5
♣ J 8 3

WEST
♠ K 10 8 4 2
♥ Q 8 7 2
♦ J 6
♣ A 6

EAST
♠ J 6 3
♥ 4
♦ 9 7 4 3
♣ K Q 10 7 5

SOUTH
♠ A Q 7 5
♥ 9 6
♦ Q 10 8 2
♣ 9 4 2

ACBL SHORT TRAVELING SCORE (Mitchell or Howell)									

Board No. **1**

N-S Pair No.	Contract	By	M a d e	D o w n	SCORE		N-S Match-points	E-W Pair No.	E-W Match-points
					N-S	E-W			
1	4H	N	5		450			1	
2	4H	N		1		50		3	
3	4H	N		1		50		5	
4	3NT	S		2		100		2	
5	4H	N	4		420			4	
6	4H	N	4		420			6	
7									
8									

Suggested Bidding

WEST	NORTH	EAST	SOUTH
	1♥	Pass	1♠
Pass	3♥	Pass	4♥
Pass	Pass	Pass	

Opener's rebid of 3♥ shows a medium strength hand (17–18 points) with at least six hearts. With 8 HCPs, responder has a close decision. With a doubleton heart, he knows there is a Golden Fit. Most players will probably carry on to game.

Suggested Play

East's opening lead will most likely be the ♣K. With only a doubleton club, West should overtake the ♣K with the ♣A, to unblock the suit, and lead back a club. In this way, the defenders can take the first three tricks in clubs. If West does not overtake the ♣K, then the second trick is won with the ♣A and West has to find another suit to lead. Declarer may then be able to discard his remaining club loser on dummy's extra diamond winner after trumps are drawn.

If the defenders take the first three club tricks, declarer will have to avoid a trump loser. He can do this by going over to dummy's ♠A (or ♦Q) and leading the ♥9. If West plays low, declarer can take the finesse by playing a low heart from his hand. He is then still in dummy and can repeat the finesse by leading dummy's ♥6 to his ♥10 (or ♥J). Note what happens if declarer plays the ♥A or ♥K before taking the first finesse. That would leave dummy with only one heart and declarer would be unable to repeat the finesse after it works. Since West started with four trumps, he would end up winning a trick with the ♥Q.

Notes

As the scoreslip shows, some players will not make the contract when they play the ♥A and ♥K rather than take the heart finesse for the missing ♥Q. As pointed out above, they also will not make the contract if they play one high heart before taking the finesse since, unfortunately, the missing hearts are divided 4–1, even though the ♥Q is with West. One declarer made an overtrick when the defenders did not take their three club tricks, and he was able to discard one of his losers after correctly drawing trumps.

BOARD #2

NORTH
♠ 10 7 5
♥ K 9 3
♦ J 8
♣ 9 6 4 3 2

Dealer: East
Vulnerable: North-South

WEST
♠ J 8 4 3
♥ 8 6
♦ A 10 7 4
♣ 10 8 7

EAST
♠ Q 9 6 2
♥ 4 2
♦ Q 6 3 2
♣ A J 5

SOUTH
♠ A K
♥ A Q J 10 7 5
♦ K 9 5
♣ K Q

ACBL SHORT TRAVELING SCORE
(Mitchell or Howell)

Board No. | 2

N-S Pair No.	Contract	By	Made	Down	SCORE N-S	SCORE E-W	N-S Match-points	E-W Pair No.	E-W Match-points
1	1H	S	5		200			1	
2	4H	S	4		620			3	
3	4H	S	5		650			5	
4	5H	S		1		100		2	
5	4H	S	5		650			4	
6	3H	S	4		170			6	
7									
8									

Suggested Bidding

WEST	NORTH	EAST	SOUTH
		Pass	2♥
Pass	2NT	Pass	3♥
Pass	4♥	Pass	Pass
Pass			

South has 22 HCPs plus 2 points for the six-card heart suit. This is too much to start the bidding with 1 ♥, since North might pass with only 3 or 4 points and the partnership would miss a game. North should give a skip bid warning before bidding 2 ♥. In response to South's 2 ♥ bid, North should make a negative 2NT response to show a weak hand. South shows the extra length in hearts by rebidding the suit, giving North a chance to choose the final contract or show a suit of his own. North should not pass the 3 ♥ bid since the opening 2 ♥ bid is forcing to the game level. With good support for partner's suit, he should happily carry on to game in that suit.

Suggested Play

Declarer has three potential losers in diamonds as well as a club loser. He can eliminate one of the diamond losers by planning to trump it in dummy while there are still some hearts left. He may consider going over to dummy's ♥K to lead toward the ♦K, hoping East started with the ♦A. That does not work on this deal, but declarer can still trump a diamond loser in dummy. The defenders may make it easy for declarer if they take their ♦A early. Now declarer will make an overtrick.

Notes

Most pairs will reach the 4♥ contract, and the top North-South result will go to those declarers who make an overtrick. (Declarer can make the overtrick even if West does not lead the ♦A by establishing two extra tricks in dummy's club suit. Most declarers will not find this line of play.)

BOARD #3

Dealer: South
Vulnerable: East-West

NORTH
♠ 9 5
♥ J 6 4
♦ K 6 5 3
♣ Q 9 7 3

WEST
♠ K 6
♥ A Q 7 5
♦ A 9 8 2
♣ K 10 5

EAST
♠ J 8
♥ K 10 9 2
♦ Q J 7 4
♣ A J 2

SOUTH
♠ A Q 10 7 4 3 2
♥ 8 3
♦ 10
♣ 8 6 4

ACBL SHORT TRAVELING SCORE
(Mitchell or Howell)

Board No. | 3

N-S Pair No.	Contract	By	M a d e	D o w n	SCORE N-S	SCORE E-W	N-S Match-points	E-W Pair No.	E-W Match-points
1	3SX	S		3		500		6	
2	4H	E	5			650		2	
3	3S	S		3		150		4	
4	4H	E	5			650		1	
5	3H	E	5			200		3	
6	4H	E	4			620		5	
7									
8									

Suggested Bidding

WEST	NORTH	EAST	SOUTH
			3♠
Double	Pass	4♥	Pass
Pass	Pass		

With a good seven-card spade suit but only 6 HCPs, South should start the bidding with a preemptive 3♠. This takes a lot of bidding room away from the opponents and they may make a mistake when judging what to do at a high level. The bid is less risky than it seems, since even if the opponents double, the penalty may be less than the value of the contract they could make. South should announce a skip bid before bidding 3♠.

West has the right type of hand to make a takeout double of the 3♠ bid, although he is probably forcing the partnership to bid at the game level. He cannot afford to pass and let South "steal" the contract. East should bid 4♥, preferring the major suit to the minor suit.

Suggested Play

If South is on lead and leads his singleton ♦10, East will have to be careful. He can guess that South is leading from a short suit, not from a sequence of touching cards, since he can see the ♦9 in dummy. He should win the ♦A, draw trumps and then drive out the ♦K. Declarer can lead toward dummy's ♣K and guess the location of the ♣Q to make an overtrick. If declarer plays a low diamond on the first trick, North can win the ♦K and lead the suit again, giving partner a ruff. Declarer will now be held to 10 tricks (nine if he misguesses the ♣Q).

Notes

As the scoreslip illustrates, an opening 3♠ bid may prevent some of the East-West pairs from reaching game. Most declarers will make 11 tricks although, as pointed out above, one or two declarers may let their opponents get a trump trick.

BOARD #4

Dealer: West
Vulnerable: Both

NORTH
♠ K Q 5
♥ A J 3
♦ Q 4
♣ A K J 7 5

WEST
♠ 8 3 2
♥ 1 0 9 7 4
♦ K 8 3
♣ 9 4 2

EAST
♠ J 10 9 7
♥ Q 6 2
♦ J 9 5
♣ 10 8 6

SOUTH
♠ A 6 4
♥ K 8 5
♦ A 10 7 6 2
♣ Q 3

ACBL SHORT TRAVELING SCORE
(Mitchell or Howell)

Board No. | 4

N-S Pair No.	Contract	By	Made	Down	SCORE N-S	SCORE E-W	N-S Match-points	E-W Pair No.	E-W Match-points
1	3NT	N	6		690			6	
2	6NT	N	6		1440			2	
3	4NT	N	5		660			4	
4	6NT	N		1		100		1	
5	6NT	S		1		100		3	
6	3NT	S	5		660			5	
7									
8									

Suggested Bidding

WEST	NORTH	EAST	SOUTH
Pass	1♣	Pass	1♦
Pass	2NT	Pass	6NT
Pass	Pass	Pass	

With a balanced hand of 20 HCPs and a five-card suit, North is too strong to open the bidding 1NT but not strong enough to open 2NT. Instead, North starts the bidding with 1♣. After South responds 1♦, North can show his distribution and strength by making a jump rebid of 2NT. Since this shows a balanced hand of about 19–21 points, South knows there should be enough combined strength for a slam and can bid directly to what should be the best contract.

Suggested Play

Declarer has three spade tricks, two heart tricks. one diamond trick and five club tricks (assuming the missing clubs are not divided 5–0). He needs one more trick to make the contract. There are two possibilities. He can play the ♥K and lead toward the ♥J, taking a finesse and hoping West started with the ♥Q, or he can lead a low diamond toward the ♦Q, hoping West started with the ♦K. It may seem like a guess, but one choice is much better than the other. If declarer tries the heart finesse first and it does not work (as in the actual hand), it is too late to lead toward the ♦Q. West will take the ♦K and that will be the second trick for the defenders. If declarer leads toward the ♦Q first and it turns out that East has the ♦K, there is still the second chance that the heart finesse will work. Playing toward the ♦Q first gives you two chances, rather than one.

Notes

Any pair that bids the slam and applies the proper technique in the play is well rewarded on this hand. Even pairs who do not bid the slam will score well if they manage to take 12 tricks.

BOARD #5

Dealer: North
Vulnerable: North-South

NORTH
♠ J 4 2
♥ A 6 4
♦ 10 8 7
♣ K J 8 6

WEST
♠ K Q 10 7 3
♥ K 9 5
♦ K 6 2
♣ 7 5

EAST
♠ 8 6 5
♥ Q 2
♦ A 9 5 3
♣ Q 10 4 2

SOUTH
♠ A 9
♥ J 10 8 7 3
♦ Q J 4
♣ A 9 3

ACBL SHORT TRAVELING SCORE
(Mitchell or Howell)

Board No. | 5

N-S Pair No.	Contract	By	Made	Down	SCORE N-S	SCORE E-W	N-S Match-points	E-W Pair No.	E-W Match-points
1	2H	S		1		100		5	
2	3S	W	3			140		1	
3	2S	W		1	50			3	
4	2H	S	2		110			6	
5	3H	S		2		200		2	
6	2S	W	2			110		4	
7									
8									

Suggested Bidding

WEST	NORTH	EAST	SOUTH
	Pass	Pass	1♥
1♠	2♥	2♠	Pass
Pass	Pass		

West has only 11 HCPs and a five-card suit, but after South's 1♥ opening bid, he should make an overcall at the one level, especially since his side is not vulnerable. North has enough to raise partner to the two level and, similarly, East has enough to raise his partner's overcall. The bidding will probably die at 2♠, although North-South may want to compete further. Although they have the majority of the high card strength, they must be careful not to get overboard since they are vulnerable, and it could prove expensive if they are defeated. Sometimes, it is better to go quietly.

Suggested Play

If West declares 2♠, he should make it with careful play. He should plan to lead spades twice toward his hand in order to limit his losers in that suit to one whenever South has the ♠A. If the defenders lead the ♥A, West will have only one loser in that suit; if not, West should plan to trump one of his losers in the dummy. There are also two club losers and a diamond loser. If the defenders are slow to lead diamonds, West may be able to avoid losing the diamond trick by leading twice toward dummy's clubs, planning to finesse the ♣10 if North plays low.

If South declares a heart contract, his potential losers are a spade trick, two heart tricks, two diamond tricks and a club trick. If West leads the ♠K, however, South can win the ♠A and lead toward dummy's ♠J to establish a winner on which to discard his club loser.

Notes

In a rubber bridge game, this would probably be a boring hand. In a duplicate game it can be much more interesting, as both sides struggle to get a plus score. When the points are fairly evenly divided, whichever side ends up with a plus score is likely to get a good matchpoint result.

BOARD #6

Dealer: East
Vulnerable: East-West

NORTH
♠ —
♥ 9 8 4 3 2
♦ 1 0 6 5 3
♣ J 1 0 4 2

WEST
♠ K 6 5 2
♥ J 6
♦ Q 8 7
♣ K Q 9 5

EAST
♠ A 8 7 4 3
♥ Q 1 0 7 5
♦ A K J
♣ 7

SOUTH
♠ Q J 1 0 9
♥ A K
♦ 9 4 2
♣ A 8 6 3

ACBL SHORT TRAVELING SCORE
(Mitchell or Howell)

Board No. 6

N-S Pair No.	Contract	By	M a d e	D o w n	SCORE		N-S Match-points	E-W Pair No.	E-W Match-points
					N-S	E-W			
1	4S	E		2	200			5	
2	4SX	E		2	500			1	
3	4SX	E		2	500			3	
4	4S	E		3	300			6	
5	3S	E		1	100			2	
6	3H	N	3			150		4	
7									
8									

Suggested Bidding

WEST	NORTH	EAST	SOUTH
		1♠	Pass
3♠	Pass	4♠	Double
Pass	Pass	Pass	

This is how the auction is likely to go if East-West are playing limit raises. East has enough to accept West's invitation. Playing forcing raises, the auction might go like this:

WEST	NORTH	EAST	SOUTH
		1♠	Pass
2♣	Pass	2♥	Pass
3♠	Pass	4♠	Double
Pass	Pass	Pass	

In either case, South can make a penalty double of the final contract. It looks as though he has two sure spade tricks, two heart tricks and a probable club trick.

Suggested Play

Since the trumps divide 4–0, declarer has to lose two trump tricks, two heart tricks and the ♣A.

Notes

Declarer will be disappointed to be defeated two tricks in a perfectly reasonable contract. However, he should have lots of company. After all, 4♠ would make if the missing spades were divided 2–2. Since all the East-West pairs will be going down, North-South will actually get a below average result for defeating the contract two tricks if they do not double. If they double, they collect 500 points to tie for a top result on the board. You do not often get an opportunity to double the opponents for penalties when they freely bid to a game contract, so South should not miss the opportunity when it comes along.

BOARD #7

Dealer: South
Vulnerable: Both

NORTH
♠ K J 9 4 3
♥ 8 5 2
♦ 6 2
♣ Q 9 7

WEST
♠ A 8 6
♥ A 9 6 3
♦ J 4
♣ A K 8 5

EAST
♠ 10 5
♥ K J 7
♦ K Q 10 7 5
♣ J 6 2

SOUTH
♠ Q 7 2
♥ Q 10 4
♦ A 9 8 3
♣ 10 4 3

| | | ACBL SHORT TRAVELING SCORE (Mitchell or Howell) | | | | | | | |

| | | | | | | | Board No. | 7 | |

N-S Pair No.	Contract	By	M a d e	D o w n	SCORE		N-S Match-points	E-W Pair No.	E-W Match-points
					N-S	E-W			
1	3NT	W		1	100			4	
2	2NT	W	2			120		6	
3	3NT	W	3			600		2	
4	3D	E	3			110		5	
5	3NT	W	3			600		1	
6	3NT	W	4			630		3	
7									
8									

Suggested Bidding

WEST	NORTH	EAST	SOUTH
			Pass
1 NT	Pass	3 NT	Pass
Pass	Pass		

The bidding is quite straightforward on this hand. All the East-West pairs should get to 3 NT.

Suggested Play

North should lead the ♠4, fourth highest, and South should play the ♠Q, third hand high. If West wins the first trick with the ♠A, he will end up going down. He has only one sure trick in spades, two in hearts and two in clubs. He will have to promote some diamond winners and, when South wins the ♦A, he will return a spade to North's four winners. To prevent this from happening, declarer must *hold up* the ♠A until the third round of the suit. Now, when South wins with the ♦A, he has no spades left to lead back to his partner. Declarer must also be careful to start the diamond suit by leading the ♦J, high card from the short side. If he plays the ♦4 first, South can defeat the contract by holding up the ♦A for two rounds.

Notes

While all the East-West pairs should reach 3 NT, there may still be a variety of scores. North-South have a chance to defeat the contract if declarer does not hold up or does not handle the diamond suit correctly. Declarer should come to nine tricks with careful play and may make 10 tricks if North discards a club toward the end of the board.

BOARD #8

Dealer: West
Vulnerable: None

NORTH
♠ Q 9 7
♥ 10 9 8 3 2
♦ A 6 4
♣ Q 9

WEST
♠ A J
♥ J 5
♦ K Q
♣ K J 10 8 7 5 4

EAST
♠ K 8 6 4 2
♥ K 7 4
♦ J 8 3
♣ 6 2

SOUTH
♠ 10 5 3
♥ A Q 6
♦ 10 9 7 5 2
♣ A 3

ACBL SHORT TRAVELING SCORE
(Mitchell or Howell)

Board No. 8

N-S Pair No.	Contract	By	Made	Down	SCORE		N-S Match-points	E-W Pair No.	E-W Match-points
					N-S	E-W			
1	3C	W		1	50			4	
2	3S	E		1	50			6	
3	3C	W	3			110		2	
4	3NT	E		2	100			5	
5	3H	N		2		100		1	
6	2C	W	3			110		3	
7									
8									

Suggested Bidding

WEST	NORTH	EAST	SOUTH
1♣	Pass	1♠	Pass
3♣	Pass	Pass	Pass

West has 15 HCPs plus 3 points for the seven-card club suit. After opening the bidding 1♣, he makes a jump rebid of 3♣ over partner's 1♠ response to show both his strength and distribution. Since 3♣ is only an invitational rebid, East, holding only 7 HCPs, should pass and settle for a partscore contract.

Suggested Play

If West plays in 3♣, North will probably lead the ♥10, top of his sequence. This traps East's ♥K and South will get two heart tricks. The defenders also have the ♦A and so West will have to hold his trump losers to one if he is going to make the contract. Missing both the ♣A and ♣Q, West should plan to lead clubs toward his hand. This is easier said than done since there is only one entry to the dummy. West will have to overtake the ♦J with dummy's ♦K to get to the dummy. When he then leads a club, South should be prepared to play second hand low, leaving declarer to guess whether to finesse the ♣10 (or ♣J) or play the ♣K. If South plays the ♣A, or hesitates a while before playing low, declarer will probably guess correctly. If South plays his ♣3 smoothly, West may play the ♣10 and end up with two club losers.

Notes

Most East-West pairs should get to a partscore contract in clubs, although some will find other contracts or get too high. Some North-South pairs may find their way into the auction but must be careful not to get too high. Whichever pair ends up with a plus score should get most of the matchpoints.

BOARD #9

Dealer: North
Vulnerable: East-West

NORTH
♠ 10 7 4 3
♥ K 6 2
♦ K J
♣ A Q 9 5

WEST
♠ A Q
♥ 9 3
♦ 8 7 6 4 3
♣ J 7 3 2

EAST
♠ 6 5
♥ A J 10 8 5
♦ A 9 5
♣ K 8 4

SOUTH
♠ K J 9 8 2
♥ Q 7 4
♦ Q 10 2
♣ 10 6

ACBL SHORT TRAVELING SCORE
(Mitchell or Howell)

Board No. | 9

N-S Pair No.	Contract	By	Made	Down	SCORE N-S	SCORE E-W	N-S Match-points	E-W Pair No.	E-W Match-points
1	2H	E		1	100			3	
2	2S	S		1		50		5	
3	3D	W		2	200			1	
4	2S	S	2			110		4	
5	2S	S	2			110		6	
6	2S	S		1		50		2	
7									
8									

Suggested Bidding

WEST	NORTH	EAST	SOUTH
	1♣	1♥	1♠
Pass	2♠	Pass	Pass
Pass			

Although he is vulnerable, East should overcall 1♥ after North's opening bid of 1♣. East-West may be able to compete for the contract or the bid might help partner during the defense of the hand. South can still make his natural response of 1♠, and North should raise to 2♠ to show his support and the minimum strength of his hand. With only 8 HCPs and 1 for the five-card suit, South should go no further.

Suggested Play

If the defenders are careful, they can defeat 2♠. West should lead the ♥9, top of his doubleton, and if declarer plays a low heart from dummy, East should not play the ♥A. Instead, he should let South win the first trick with the ♥Q, keeping dummy's ♥K trapped. If East does that, South will eventually lose two spade tricks, two heart tricks, a diamond trick and a club trick. If East plays the ♥A on the first trick, declarer will end up losing only one heart, rather than two.

Notes

As seen on the scoreslip, East-West will get a good result if they can find the defense to defeat 2♠. If they let declarer make the contract, they will get a poor result and might have done better by bidding on. If they bid too much, however, they might give North-South a top result for defeating their contract by two tricks.

BOARD #10

Dealer: East
Vulnerable: Both

NORTH
♠ K Q 10 7 3
♥ J 7 4
♦ 4 3
♣ Q 10 6

WEST
♠ J 8 4
♥ 9 5 3
♦ K 10 9
♣ 8 7 3 2

EAST
♠ 9 5 2
♥ 10
♦ A Q J 7 6 5 2
♣ 9 5

SOUTH
♠ A 6
♥ A K Q 8 6 2
♦ 8
♣ A K J 4

ACBL SHORT TRAVELING SCORE
(Mitchell or Howell)

Board No. 10

N-S Pair No.	Contract	By	Made	Down	SCORE		N-S Match-points	E-W Pair No.	E-W Match-points
					N-S	E-W			
1	4H	S	6		680			3	
2	4H	S	7		710			5	
3	5DX	E		4	1100			1	
4	6H	S	6		1430			4	
5	4H	S	6		680			6	
6	6H	S	7		1460			2	
7									
8									

Suggested Bidding

WEST	NORTH	EAST	SOUTH
		3 ♦	Double
Pass	3 ♠	Pass	4 ♥
Pass	Pass	Pass	

A preemptive 3 ♦ opening will make it very difficult for North-South to reach their slam. South might jump directly to 4 ♥, making sure he reaches game with his 21 HCPs and six-card suit. Or South might double and then bid hearts, showing a hand too strong to only overcall 3 ♥. With only 8 HCPs, North will have a difficult time envisioning a possible slam contract, and it is unlikely the North-South will get beyond the game level. Without the preemptive 3 ♦ opening, the bidding might well go like this:

WEST	NORTH	EAST	SOUTH
		Pass	2 ♥
Pass	2 ♠	Pass	3 ♣
Pass	3 ♥	Pass	4 NT
Pass	5 ♣	Pass	6 ♥
Pass	Pass	Pass	

South can start with a strong two-bid, and when North shows a positive response and later supports South's heart suit, South will probably carry on to slam. He may jump directly to 6 ♥ or use the Blackwood convention (4 NT) to find out how many aces North has first. North's 5 ♣ response shows no aces, so South knows that the partnership is missing one ace.

Suggested Play

South should have no trouble taking 12 tricks and will end up taking all 13 if the opponents do not take their diamond trick right away — declarer can discard his diamond loser on the extra spade winner in dummy.

Notes

A preemptive opening bid takes bidding room away from the opponents and will often lead them to underestimate or overestimate the combined strength of their hands.

LESSON 5

The Howell Movement

The Howell Movement
Keeping a Private Score
Kibitzing
The Alert Procedure
Summary

Workshop Material

Group Activities
Sample Boards

We are past the half-way point in the lesson series and you have been introduced to the basics of duplicate bridge. You can fill in your Convention Card, understand the scoreslip, move comfortably in a Mitchell movement, be relaxed when the director is called to your table and feel confident that you know the etiquette of the game — we have come a long way. In this lesson, we will look at another type of movement for a pair game which is sometimes used. We will also discuss how you can keep your own scorecard during the game, how to act when you are a spectator, and a new use of the double.

♠ *THE HOWELL MOVEMENT* ♠

In a *Howell movement*, the partnerships may play in both the North-South and East-West directions. As in the Mitchell movement, your table number and your starting position are normally found on your entry form. Your pair number, however, does not necessarily match the table number. Your entry may start you at Table #2 E-W but you may be Pair #5. Notice that your pair number has no direction associated with it since you will be playing in both the North-South and East-West directions. Every pair will have a different pair number.

Instructions are provided for moving after the first round. Sometimes, small individual cards with instructions for moving at the end of each round are given to each pair. Usually, the instructions are in front of you on the Howell guide card on the table. It is a bit like a treasure hunt: "Go next to Table #5 N-S." When you get to Table #5, you can read your next instructions from the guide card: "Go next to Table #3 E-W." Here is a sample Howell guide card for a five-table game:

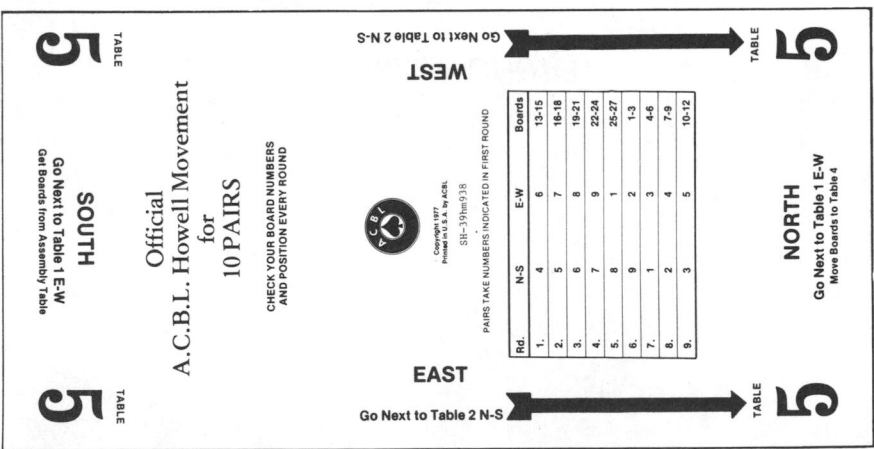

Although one or more pairs will remain stationary throughout the game, most pairs will realize after a couple of rounds that they are following the same pair around the room from table to table. It is important to remember your pair number. As in a Mitchell game, North enters the score on the scoreslip. When entering the result, North enters on the line for his pair number, and asks East-West for their pair number.

Because the movement of the boards is somewhat complex in some Howell movements, the boards are usually moved by the director. The boards you should be playing each round, however, are indicated on the Howell guide card. You should check the board numbers against the guide card before you start to play.

The Recap Sheet

At the end of the game, the director calculates the matchpoints for each board. Since the pairs have changed direction throughout the game, the boards must be matchpointed for each North-South and East-West pair so that a positive number of matchpoints can be assigned to each pair number. When the results are totaled, there will be only one overall winner, not separate East-West and North-South winners as in a Mitchell movement. The recap sheet might look like this:

MATCHPOINT RECAPITULATION

EVENT _Tuesday Pairs_ MOVEMENT _Howell_ AVERAGE _30_
SESSION _only_ DATE _Feb 14/90_ SECTION _A_

No.	Names	Rank	Total Points	1	2	3	4	5	6	7	8	9	10	11	12	13	14	15	16
1	Harry + Sally	④/5	30⁻	3⁻	0	4	1	2	1	4	0	3	1	2-⁻	3	1	4		
2	Ely + Jo	②	31⁻	-	4	0	3	2	-	2-	4	4	1	2-2	2	1	2-		
3	Lerner + Lowe	①	34	3-1	1	4	2	2	2-	1	2	3	1	4	4	1	2-		
4	Ozzie + Harriet		28-	--	3	2-	0	2	3-	1	3	-	3	0	3-	2	3	1	
5	Lucy + Dezi		27-	2	0	2-	3	2	2	0	4	-	3	1-3	1	3	0		
6	Paul + Linda	③	31	1	2	4	1	2	-	4	1	3-	0	4	0	3	1	4	
7	Stan + Ohlie		28-	3	2	1-	1	2	3-	1-	0	3-1	4	1	0	3	1-		
8	Di + Charles		29-	4	4	3	1	2	0	1-	2	0	3	1-2	1	3	1-		
9	Nancy + Ronald	④/5	30-	2	1	0	3	2	4	3	3	1	4	0	3-	0	4	0	
10	Linda + Ursula		28	0	3	1-	3	2	3	0	2	2	1	3	-	4	0	3	

Although there is only one winner, approximately as many pairs receive masterpoints in a Howell movement as in a Mitchell movement. In a six-table game, the first five pairs would get masterpoint awards. If you were playing a Mitchell Movement, the first two pairs in each direction would get awards.

Reasons for Playing a Howell

There are two reasons for using a Howell movement. If there is a small number of tables, three for example, a Mitchell movement would allow you to play only three rounds, one against each of the three pairs sitting in the opposite direction. If you wanted to play fifteen boards during the session, you would have to play five boards against each pair. The Howell movement enables you to play five rounds, one round against each of the other five pairs. You would play only three boards against each pair before moving on to the next table and would still end up playing 15 boards in total. This makes it a fairer and more interesting event.

The second reason for playing a Howell movement is when you want a single overall winner and you want to ensure that the competition has been as fair as possible. In a Mitchell movement, your real competition is against the other pairs sitting in your direction. If they are all inexperienced pairs, you will be able to do very well even if all the North-South pairs are good opponents. It will not be as easy for a North-South pair since their score on each board will have to be compared against the other experienced North-South pairs. By playing a Howell movement, any such bias is removed, since the good pairs will play in a mixture of directions. The finals of many major pairs championships usually involve a Howell movement to make sure that each pair gets to meet every other pair in the event.

♠ KEEPING A PRIVATE SCORE ♠

At the end of each board, you can look at the scoreslip and see how you are doing compared to the other pairs that have already played the board. As you become more familiar with the game, you will find that you want to keep track of your results as you are going along, since you soon forget what happened at each table. After the game, players often gather to discuss the boards. You will hear comments from your friends such as, "What did you do on Board #5?" You want to be able to refer to some record you have kept of what happened on the board — the contract and the result.

Keeping Track

You can keep track of your results on the inside of your Convention Card. It is pre-printed in a format that makes it easy to keep a private record of every board you play:

BD # PAIRS	DLR AND VUL	BD # TEAMS	VS	CONTRACT & DECLARER	PLUS	MINUS	PTS. EST.	PTS.
1	N NONE							
2	E N-S							
3	S E-W							
4	W BOTH	2		3DW⁻¹	100			
5	N N-S	2		4HS	620			
6	E E-W	2		2NTW⁺²		180		
7	S BOTH	1		4S×S⁻²		500		
8	W NONE	1		2H N	110			
9	N E-W	1		3H W⁺¹		170		
10	E BOTH							
11	S NONE							

There is a line for every board number that you might play, from 1 to 36. To help you out, the dealer and the vulnerability are already indicated for each board. There is then a column for the pair number of the people against whom you played the board (vs.), if you want to keep track of them. You might feel that they played extremely well against you and want to look them up on the recap sheet after the game to see if they did as well against everyone else or they were merely lucky against you! Then there is a column for the contract and declarer. You can use the same type of shorthand that is used on the scoreslip — 4S E for a contract of 4♠ by East — or develop a system of your own. You can then record the result in the "Plus" or "Minus" column. If you make a vulnerable 4♠ contract, you would put 620 in the plus column.

If you want to estimate how you are doing as the game progresses, there is a column to put down your estimate (Pts. Est.). If you know that 12 is top on a board, you can put down your estimate of how many matchpoints you think you got. At the end of the game, you can look at the recap sheet to compare your estimates with the actual number of matchpoints you received. There is even a column for you to record your matchpoints (Pts.). After a while, you will find you can get quite good at estimating your points — you know that the board you lost 2200 points on is going to be a zero! You might develop your own notation for estimating: perhaps "A" for average, "A+" for above average and "A−" for below average.

Reasons for Keeping a Private Score

Since this is your private scorecard, you can put down whatever you like. You might want to put an "*" or "?" beside a result, if you think you could have made another trick on a hand but are not sure. Looking at the recap sheet after the game will let you know what other players sitting in your position did with the cards. If you want to talk about a particular hand with your partner after the game, make a note on your card beside the board. You will not have much time to discuss the boards during the game — and it is certainly not the time to question partner if you think he has made a mistake!

The scorecard is also useful for comparing your results against those that appear on the recap sheet. Every now and then, a mistake will be made in the matchpointing and you can spot it if you have kept a private score. Also, the director may come over to query a result that was entered on a scoreslip. By referring to your private score, you will usually be able to confirm what happened.

Many players keep their scorecards long after the game is over, especially if they had a good game. In major events, the scorecard of the winning pair is sometimes published so that others can see what they did to win the event.

♠ *KIBITZING* ♠

There are times when you will be a spectator, or *kibitzer*, at a bridge game. You might drop by to watch a few boards at a local club or tournament, perhaps to see how one of the local experts bids and plays. At other times you will be sitting out for a round and may want to watch a board that you have already played to see what someone else does with it. Whenever you are watching a bridge deal, there is a code of conduct that must be obeyed.

The Role of the Kibitzer

The word "kibitzer," according to the *Official Encyclopedia of Bridge*, is derived from the German word for a green plover, a highly inquisitive bird. That is a much kinder description than Webster's dictionary where "kibitzer" is defined as one who looks on and often offers unwanted advice or comment, especially at a card game.

There are rules of etiquette for spectators which differ from one sport to another. Think of a wrestling match or a football game where the air is full of the crowd's opinions of how the athletes are performing. Compare this to a tennis match where, at the proper time, there are outbursts of applause from the spectators, but if the hand-clapping lasts too long, the onlookers are given a gentle reminder, "Quiet, ladies and gentlemen. Please." There are those sports, such as chess and billiards, where the spectators are so quiet you hardly know they are there. Being a kibitzer at a bridge game, however, is unusual.

Remember the 3-D movies? By putting on a pair of glasses, you were right in the middle of the action. Being a kibitzer is a little like that. You sit very close to the competitors — you could reach out and touch them. You can see the whites of their eyes — and they can see yours! Since you are so close to the action, however, you must be careful not to display any gesture which could influence what is happening.

The etiquette for the kibitzer is straightforward and clearly set out in the *Laws of Duplicate Contract Bridge*. Law 76 reads:

Spectators
  A. Conduct During Bidding or Play
   1. One Hand Only
    A spectator should not look at the cards of more than one player, except by permission.

   2. Personal Reaction
    A spectator must not display any reaction to the bidding or play while a hand is in progress.

   3. Mannerisms or Remarks
    During the round, a spectator must refrain from mannerisms or remarks of any kind (including conversation with a player).

   4. Consideration for Players
    A spectator must not in any way disturb a player.

  B. Spectator Participation
    A spectator may not call attention to any irregularity or mistake, nor speak on any question of fact or law except by request of the Director.

By following these few rules, you can be a good kibitzer and enjoy a very exciting part of the game of bridge.

♠ THE ALERT PROCEDURE ♠

Your opponents fill out their Convention Card so that you can familiarize yourself with their style of bidding and any unusual conventions that they play. Yet, since you play only a couple of boards against each opponent, you do not want to have to spend your time reading their entire Convention Card and asking questions about their special calls — which are unlikely to come up during the deals you play against them. To make things as easy as possible, ACBL has developed a procedure to warn you whenever the opponents make a call that may be unfamiliar to you. This method gives you the opportunity to ask about an unusual call in the middle of the auction.

The Alert

When someone at the table makes a call that has a special meaning for the partnership, his partner must say the word *"Alert."* This warns the opponents that the last call has been assigned some conventional message, rather than the natural meaning you might have come to expect. The player whose turn it is to bid can now ask the person who Alerted for a clarification of the special meaning of the call.

Note that it is the **partner** of the person who made the conventional call who does the Alerting and the explaining, not the player who made the call. Otherwise, you would be able to remind your partner any time you were making a special call by saying "Alert." It is up to your partner to remember your agreements — it is not up to you to remind him.

Notice also that you ask for an explanation from the partner of the player who made the conventional call, not the player who made the call. Otherwise, the player who made the bid could describe exactly what he had in his hand! It is up to his partner to explain what he **believes** to be the partnership understanding. He may well have it all wrong, but the Alert procedure is not there to give him a chance to correct any misunderstanding. If he does give the wrong explanation, his partner should say nothing and go on bidding as though the Alert never occurred.

If the player who gave the wrong explanation becomes dummy or declarer, then one of that partnership should summon the director to ensure that the opponents have not been put at a disadvantage by the mistaken explanation. If the player who gave the wrong explanation becomes a defender, then after the play of the board, the director should be summoned for the same reason.

Let's look at an example of the Alert procedure in action. Suppose your opponents have agreed to play Jacoby transfer bids in response to notrump openings and have marked this on their Convention Card. When you sit down against them, you may have no idea what this convention entails, even if you happen to notice it on their Convention Card. You do not need to ask for an explanation before you start to bid since the convention may not come up in the couple of boards you will play against this pair.

Suppose the opponent on your right opens the bidding 1 NT. That does not require an Alert since it is a natural bid, and you can look at the opponent's Convention Card to see the strength it shows (*e.g.*, 16–18), if you are interested. After you pass, opener's partner responds 2♥. The natural interpretation of a 2♥ response is that it is a weak signoff bid showing five or more hearts. Since this is not the case when the opponents are playing transfer bids, opener should say "Alert."

If your partner wants an explanation, he can ask and opener would inform him that they are playing Jacoby transfers. If partner is familiar with this convention, he can continue the auction, having the information he needs. If he has never heard of Jacoby transfers, he can ask for a further explanation. Opener would now explain that the 2♥ response asks him to bid 2♠ and that his partner might have a weak hand and be planning to pass the 2♠ response, or he might have a stronger hand and be planning to bid again.

When opener now bids 2♠, his partner will Alert since opener is merely responding to the transfer and his spades may or may not be a biddable suit. Since it is your turn to bid, you can now ask for an explanation of any of the calls made by the opponents.

Which Bids Are Alertable?

In general, natural bids are not Alertable. For example, if you open the bidding 1♥, showing a heart suit, there is no need to Alert, whether you play four-card or five-card majors. Your opponent can glance at your card, or ask, if he wants to know exactly how many hearts you are promising.

Some conventional bids do not have to be Alerted, since they are used by so many players that they are the standard use of the bid. For example, a response of 2♣ to a 1 NT opening bid is assumed to be the Stayman convention — you would Alert only if your partnership played it as a natural bid! Similarly, a bid of 4NT after a suit has been agreed on is assumed to be the Blackwood convention, asking partner how many aces he has. On the other hand, conventions such as Jacoby transfers are Alertable.

All the bidding covered in the series so far is natural. So there is no need to worry about Alerting any of your partner's calls. As you start to play duplicate, however, you may adopt some special conventions with your favorite partner and you will soon encounter opponents who use Alertable calls.

To make it easy to determine which calls are Alertable and which are not, Alertable calls are marked in **red** on the General Convention Card. There is a copy of this card in the Appendix. When filling out this Convention Card, you have only to notice which bids are filled in on the red sections to know that they are Alertable. For example, take a look at the section under NOTRUMP OPENING BIDS. You can see that Jacoby transfers are marked in red, so they must be Alerted when they are used.

NOTRUMP OPENING BIDS

1 NT _____ to _____   2 NT _____ to _____ HCP

1 NT _____ to _____   3 NT _____ to _____ HCP

2 ♣ Forc. ☐ Non-Forc. ☐ Stayman Solid Suit ☐: _____

2 ♦ Forc. ☐ No-Forc. ☐ Stayman _____

Transfers: Jacoby ☐ Texas ☐ Other ☐ _____

1 NT - 3 ♣/3 ♦ Is Invitational ☐   Preemptive ☐   Forcing ☐

Other _____

When using the Alert procedure, keep the following points in mind:

- Do not Alert your own bid.

- If your partner gives the wrong explanation of your call, don't correct him until after the bidding is completed if your side declares but after the play is over if your side defends. The Alert is for the opponents' benefit, not for the advantage of the partnership making the unusual call.

- Do not automatically offer information about the call. Simply say "Alert." If the opponents do not ask for an explanation, you do not need to give one.

- If your opponent Alerts, you do not have to ask for an explanation. However, if you want one, ask only when it is your turn to call.

Until you are very familiar with the game, you should probably take the opportunity to ask for an explanation whenever the opponents Alert — you might be surprised at the answer you get! For example, your right-hand opponent may start the bidding with 2 ♦ and your left-hand opponent might say "Alert." When you ask your left-hand opponent what the bid means you might be told it is Flannery. This means nothing to you, so you ask for a further clarification. Your opponent now explains that the 2 ♦ bid shows an opening bid of 11–16 HCPs with exactly four spades and five hearts — certainly not what you expected. You will now have to decide what to do. You may not understand why the opponents are playing this particular convention but, nonetheless, they must provide you with an explanation.

By using the Alert procedure, it will not take you long to catch on to the most common conventions used in your area, and you and your partner will be able to discuss how you want to handle them. You may still run into someone using some convention you have never heard of, but at least you will be warned if it comes up in the middle of the auction.

The Alert procedure is not required at all bridge clubs. Also some opponents you encounter may require that you *not* Alert any calls.

♠ *SUMMARY* ♠

In a *Howell movement*, each pair plays some of the hands in the North-South direction and some of the hands in the East-West direction. They will meet all, or most, of the other pairs in the game, not just those sitting in one direction. At the end of the game, there will be only one winning pair.

On the inside of the Convention Card is a place to keep track of your results during the game. You can use this to record whatever information you feel is relevant.

Spectators are expected to watch without showing any reaction to the bidding or play, thereby avoiding giving any unauthorized information to the players.

Most calls that carry some conventional or artificial meaning should be *Alerted* by the partner of the player making the call. An opponent can then ask for an explanation of the call when it is his turn to call. The bids that must be Alerted are those that are in the red areas on the General Convention Card.

♠ *GROUP ACTIVITIES* ♠

Exercise One — The Howell Movement

You and your partner are playing in a Howell Movement and have been given a starting assignment of Table #5 E-W. When you arrive, the following guide card is on the table:

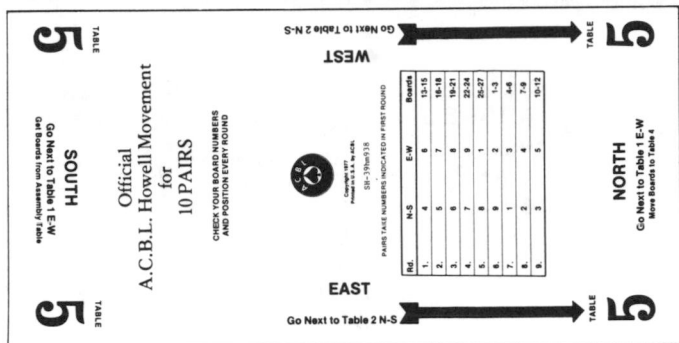

- Which table will you go to next?
- Why would you be told to move to a North-South position when you are currently sitting East-West?
- Why are you assigned as Pair #6 and the North-South pair assigned as Pair #4 when you are both starting off at Table #5?
- Which boards will you play on the first round?
- Who will enter the results on the scoreslip for each board you play at the table?

Exercise Two — Kibitzing

What conclusion might you draw in each of the following situations where you have a spectator watching a board being played at your table?

- The spectator moves from behind one player to behind another player during the auction.
- The spectator raises his eyebrows when you call for the ♦ 5 to be played from dummy.
- The spectator gets up and leaves halfway through the play of the board.

Exercise Three — The Alert

The opponent on your right opens the bidding 2 ♣ and the opponent on your right says "Alert." What should you do?

♠ *SAMPLE BOARDS* ♠

BOARD #1

Dealer: North
Vulnerable: None

NORTH
♠ J 6
♥ Q 7 5
♦ K Q J 10 8
♣ 9 6 3

WEST
♠ 10 9 8 5 2
♥ A 10 2
♦ A 5 3
♣ 5 2

EAST
♠ Q 7 4
♥ K 8 6 3
♦ 9 7 2
♣ J 7 4

SOUTH
♠ A K 3
♥ J 9 4
♦ 6 4
♣ A K Q 10 8

ACBL SHORT TRAVELING SCORE (Mitchell or Howell)									

Board No. 1

N-S Pair No.	Contract	By	Made	Down	SCORE N-S	SCORE E-W	N-S Match-points	E-W Pair No.	E-W Match-points
1	3NT	S	5		460			7	
2	3NT	S	3		400			9	
3	5 C	S		1		50		11	
4	3NT	S	5		460			8	
5	3NT	S		1		50		10	
6	3NT	S		1		50		12	
7									
8									

Suggested Bidding

WEST	NORTH	EAST	SOUTH
	Pass	Pass	1 NT
Pass	3 NT	Pass	Pass
Pass			

With 17 HCPs and a balanced hand, South can open the bidding 1 NT. North has 9 HCPs plus 1 point for the five-card suit, enough to raise directly to 3 NT.

Suggested Play

While 3 NT will be the most likely contract, the number of tricks taken by declarer will depend on how well the defenders perform. West should start by leading the ♠10, top of a sequence in his longest suit. This traps dummy's ♣J. If declarer plays dummy's ♣J, East can play the ♣Q; if declarer does not play the ♣J, East can hold on to his ♣Q. After winning one of his spade tricks, declarer can count two sure spade tricks and three sure club tricks. If he plays the ♣A and ♣K, he will find out that the missing clubs are divided 3–2 and so he has five club tricks. Needing two more tricks for the contract, South will have to play diamonds, trying to drive out the opponents' ♦A.

When South leads diamonds, the defenders have an opportunity to defeat the contract. If West wins the first diamond trick and leads back a spade, declarer makes 11 tricks — two spades, four diamonds and five clubs. Instead, West should hold up the ♦A until South has no diamonds left. Since dummy has no entry in another suit, declarer will be unable to reach dummy's established diamond winners. To defeat the contract, West should hold up his ♦A exactly one round, winning the second diamond trick. This restricts declarer to eight tricks. If West waits until the third round, declarer will have gotten two diamond tricks to go along with his seven other tricks and make the contract.

How is West to know how long to hold up? East should be giving a count signal when declarer leads diamonds, playing low-high to show an odd number (three) rather than high-low to show an even number (two). If West knows his partner has three diamonds, he can work out that declarer has only two and that he needs to hold up only one round.

Notes

The results on the scoreslip show that most North-South pairs will reach 3 NT and not all East-West pairs will find the defense to defeat the contract. Those East-West pairs that let the contract make may want to review their use of count signals on defense.

BOARD #2

Dealer: East
Vulnerable: North-South

NORTH
♠ A 4
♥ Q 8 6
♦ Q 9 5 4 2
♣ 10 7 5

WEST
♠ 9 7 5 2
♥ 7 4 2
♦ K 10 7
♣ K 4 2

EAST
♠ Q J 10 8 6 3
♥ A K 3
♦ 8
♣ A Q J

SOUTH
♠ K
♥ J 10 9 5
♦ A J 6 3
♣ 9 8 6 3

ACBL SHORT TRAVELING SCORE
(Mitchell or Howell)

Board No. 2

N-S Pair No.	Contract	By	Made	Down	SCORE N-S	SCORE E-W	N-S Match-points	E-W Pair No.	E-W Match-points
1	2 S	E	3			140		7	
2	4 S	E		1	50			9	
3	4 S	E	4			420		11	
4	4 S	E	4			420		8	
5	4 S	E		1	50			10	
6	3 S	E	4			170		12	
7									
8									

Suggested Bidding

WEST	NORTH	EAST	SOUTH
		1♠	Pass
2♠	Pass	4♠	Pass
Pass	Pass		

With 17 HCPs plus 2 points for the six-card suit, East opens the bidding 1♠. In response to East's 1♠ opening bid, West has four-card support and 6 HCPs, enough to raise to the two level. When the bidding gets back to East, he jumps directly to game with his maximum hand.

Suggested Play

South will probably start with the ♥J against the 4♠ contract. Holding the ♥Q, North should make an encouraging signal by playing the ♥8. East can win this and should count his losers. There are two trump losers, a heart loser and a diamond loser, one too many. To get rid of a loser, East should plan to lead toward dummy's ♦K, hoping South has the ♦A. This has two possibilities. First, South may not play his ♦A and East will have no diamond loser. Second, even if South does take his ♦A, East can use dummy's ♦K to discard his heart loser.

East will have to be careful to lead his diamond before starting to draw trumps. If East were to lead a spade at trick two, South could win it and, encouraged by North's ♥8, lead another heart to drive out East's remaining high card. It is now too late to lead a diamond. South can win the ♦A and take a heart winner to defeat the contract.

Notes

Most pairs should reach the 4♠ contract and the outcome will depend on whether the defenders get off to the best defense and whether declarer finds the winning line of play.

BOARD #3

Dealer: South
Vulnerable: East-West

NORTH
♠ Q 8 6
♥ Q 10 8 4 2
♦ 9 7
♣ K 5 2

WEST
♠ K 9 5
♥ 9 5
♦ J 10 6 3
♣ Q 9 7 4

EAST
♠ A 10 7 4 3
♥ J 6
♦ K 5
♣ A J 6 3

SOUTH
♠ J 2
♥ A K 7 3
♦ A Q 8 4 2
♣ 10 8

ACBL SHORT TRAVELING SCORE
(Mitchell or Howell)

Board No. | 3

N-S Pair No.	Contract	By	M a d e	D o w n	SCORE		N-S Match-points	E-W Pair No.	E-W Match-points
					N-S	E-W			
1	2 S	E	2			110		12	
2	3 S	E		2	200			8	
3	3 H	N	3		140			10	
4	2 S	E		1	100			7	
5	2 H	N	3		140			9	
6	4 H	N		1		50		11	
7									
8									

Suggested Bidding

WEST	NORTH	EAST	SOUTH
			1♦
Pass	1♥	1♠	2♥
2♠	Pass	Pass	3♥
Pass	Pass	Pass	

This hand should develop into a struggle to buy the contract. North should respond 1♥ to South's 1♦ and East will probably overcall in his five-card suit, 1♠. South should raise to 2♥ with his four-card support and West will probably compete to 2♠, holding support for his partner's overcalled suit. North, with only 7 HCPs, should pass at this point and the bidding will come back to South. Having already shown a minimum strength opening bid by raising only to 2♥, South should compete further to 3♥ rather than let the opponents play in 2♠. This should end the auction since East-West are vulnerable and cannot afford to compete too friskily.

Suggested Play

With a difficult choice of opening leads, East should probably select spades, the suit his side has bid and raised. East should lead the ♠A, rather than a small spade when defending against a suit contract. West, holding the ♠K can make an encouraging signal by playing the ♠9 and East can lead another spade. When West wins the ♠K, he can see that leading more spades will not do much good and, looking at the diamond strength and club weakness in the dummy, should lead a club. This traps North's ♣K and the defenders get two club tricks.

Having lost four tricks by the time he gets the lead, North will have to draw trumps and take the diamond finesse to avoid losing any more. Luckily for him, East holds the ♦K and declarer ends up making exactly nine tricks.

Notes

If North-South choose to defend 2♠, they will not get a good result, even if they defeat it one trick. East-West should compete to 2♠ but, being vulnerable, cannot afford to get too high or they may suffer a penalty larger than the value of the opponents' partscore.

BOARD #4

Dealer: West
Vulnerable: Both

NORTH
♠ J 10 8 5 3
♥ Q 5
♦ Q 8 6
♣ A 9 5

WEST
♠ 6
♥ A K J 10 8 6 4 2
♦ 7 4
♣ 10 3

EAST
♠ Q 9 7
♥ 7
♦ K J 9 5 3 2
♣ K Q 8

SOUTH
♠ A K 4 2
♥ 9 3
♦ A 10
♣ J 7 6 4 2

ACBL SHORT TRAVELING SCORE
(Mitchell or Howell)

Board No. 4

N-S Pair No.	Contract	By	M a d e	D o w n	SCORE		N-S Match-points	E-W Pair No.	E-W Match-points
					N-S	E-W			
1	4 H	W	4			620		12	
2	3 H	W	4			170		8	
3	4 S X	N		2		500		10	
4	4 H	W		1	100			7	
5	4 H	W		1	100			10	
6	4 H X	W	4			790		11	
7									
8									

Suggested Bidding

WEST	NORTH	EAST	SOUTH
4♥	Pass	Pass	Pass

With a good eight-card suit and not enough high-card strength to open the bidding at the one level, West should start the bidding with a preemptive opening bid. With a seven-card suit, you normally open the bidding at the three level. With an eight-card suit, the preemptive opening bid can be at the four level, making it even more difficult for the opponents to determine what to do. Neither North nor South really has enough strength to compete at the four level, although one of them may double the 4♥ contract for penalties, feeling that his side is being "robbed."

Suggested Play

North will likely lead the ♠J, top of his touching high cards and West will trump the second spade trick. With nine hearts in the combined hands, West should probably draw trumps by playing the ♥A and ♥K (hoping the ♥Q will appear) rather than taking the heart finesse. West should then lead a club toward dummy, hoping North has the ♣A so that declarer can develop a potential extra winner on which to discard one of his diamond losers. North should be careful to win the ♣A and put West to the test by leading a diamond before West can discard a loser. West will have to guess whether to play dummy's ♦K or ♦J in order to make the contract. If he plays the ♦K, South can win the ♦A and lead back a diamond to defeat the contract. If West chooses to play the ♦J (assuming North would not be brave enough, or foolhardy enough, to lead a small diamond if he held the ♦A), there is nothing the defenders can do.

Notes

West will get his side a good result if he bids 4♥ and makes the contract. If North-South compete, they may be sorry if they are doubled. The defenders potentially have a spade trick, two heart tricks, a diamond trick and two club tricks for an 800-point penalty, although they may not be able to get all their tricks. Whatever happens, the hand should prove exciting for both sides.

BOARD #5

Dealer: North
Vulnerable: North-South

NORTH
♠ Q 5 2
♥ A J 10 4
♦ 6 4 2
♣ J 7 6

WEST
♠ 8 4
♥ Q 6 3
♦ Q 10 9 8 5
♣ A 9 5

EAST
♠ A 7 6 3
♥ K 7 5 2
♦ K J
♣ K Q 2

SOUTH
♠ K J 10 9
♥ 9 8
♦ A 7 3
♣ 10 8 4 3

ACBL SHORT TRAVELING SCORE
(Mitchell or Howell)

Board No. 5

N-S Pair No.	Contract	By	Made	Down	SCORE		N-S Match-points	E-W Pair No.	E-W Match-points
					N-S	E-W			
1	2NT	E		1	50			11	
2	2NT	E	2			120		7	
3	2D	W	3			110		9	
4	3NT	E		1	50			12	
5	1NT	E	3			150		8	
6	3NT	E		2	100			10	
7									
8									

Suggested Bidding

WEST	NORTH	EAST	SOUTH
	Pass	1 NT	Pass
2 NT	Pass	Pass	Pass

East has a normal 1 NT opening bid. With 8 HCPs and 1 point for the five-card diamond suit, West should invite partner to game by raising to 2 NT. With a minimum hand, East should decline the invitation and stop in partscore.

Suggested Play

East should be able to make the 2 NT contract, but if South defends well, East will have to be careful. South may start off by leading the ♣J, top of his interior sequence. This will work well if his partner holds either the ♣A or the ♣Q. On the actual hand, North holds the ♣Q, enough to help drive out declarer's ♣A. East can count his tricks. He has one spade trick and three club tricks, so he will need four more. These can come from the diamond suit by driving out the opponents' ♦A. After winning the ♣A, East should start by leading the ♦K and then the ♦J.

South should make life difficult for declarer by refusing to win either the first or second diamond trick. If South ducks the ♦J, East will be defeated if he plays a small diamond from dummy. The diamonds will not yet be established and the only sure entry to dummy is the ♣A. Instead, East must counter South's defense by overtaking the ♦J with dummy's ♦Q so that he can lead the suit again, keeping the ♣A as an entry to the established diamonds.

Notes

Some pairs may get too high with the East-West cards and, provided North-South defend carefully, will be unable to make their contract. East-West will do well to stop in partscore and play carefully to make the contract.

BOARD #6

Dealer: East
Vulnerable: East-West

NORTH
♠ K J 10 7 5 2
♥ 7
♦ K 10 4 2
♣ 8 3

WEST
♠ 9 4
♥ A 9 6 4
♦ A 9 3
♣ K 9 6 5

EAST
♠ A Q 6
♥ Q 10 5 2
♦ 8 7 6
♣ J 4 2

SOUTH
♠ 8 3
♥ K J 8 3
♦ Q J 5
♣ A Q 10 7

ACBL SHORT TRAVELING SCORE
(Mitchell or Howell)

Board No. 6

N-S Pair No.	Contract	By	Made	Down	SCORE		N-S Match-points	E-W Pair No.	E-W Match-points
					N-S	E-W			
1	2 S	N	3		140			11	
2	3NT	S		2		100		7	
3	2 S	N	2		110			9	
4	3 H	E		2	200			12	
5	2 D	N	2		90			8	
6	4 S	N		1		50		10	
7									
8									

Suggested Bidding

WEST	NORTH	EAST	SOUTH
		Pass	1♣
Pass	1♠	Pass	1NT
Pass	2♠	Pass	Pass
Pass			

North should respond 1♠ to South's opening bid. When South describes a minimum balanced hand with his 1NT rebid, North should settle for partscore. North knows that there is not enough combined strength for game and also that the partnership has at least eight combined cards in spades. He should, therefore, rebid 2♠ rather than introduce his diamond suit. South should respect North's decision to play in 2♠.

Suggested Play

North has two spade losers, a heart loser, a diamond loser and a club loser. He can try the spade finesse, hoping that West has the ♠Q, but he will be disappointed. He might also try the club finesse, but that does not work either. If the opponents do not lead clubs initially, North may have a chance to make use of dummy's heart suit. He can lead a heart toward dummy (or East may lead a heart initially) and play the ♥J, forcing West to win the trick with the ♥A. Now, he can use dummy's ♥K to discard his club loser and avoid having to try the finesse.

Notes

The scoreslip shows that North-South will do well if they stop in the best partscore and make the maximum number of tricks. If East-West enter the auction, they will have to be careful not to get too high or they may lose 200 points or more, getting a bottom board.

BOARD #7

Dealer: South
Vulnerable: Both

NORTH
♠ A Q 6
♥ J
♦ K 10 5
♣ A K Q 9 5 3

WEST
♠ J 10 8 3
♥ 8 7 4 3
♦ 7 6 2
♣ 10 4

EAST
♠ K 9 5
♥ A 10 9 6 2
♦ 9
♣ J 8 7 6

SOUTH
♠ 7 4 2
♥ K Q 5
♦ A Q J 8 4 3
♣ 2

ACBL SHORT TRAVELING SCORE
(Mitchell or Howell)

Board No. 7

N-S Pair No.	Contract	By	Made	Down	SCORE N-S	SCORE E-W	N-S Match-points	E-W Pair No.	E-W Match-points
1	6 C	N		1		100		10	
2	6 D	S	6		1370			12	
3	3NT	S	4		630			8	
4	6 D	S	6		1370			11	
5	5 D	S	6		620			7	
6	5 C	N	5		600			9	
7									
8									

Suggested Bidding

WEST	NORTH	EAST	SOUTH
			1 ♦
Pass	3 ♣	Pass	3 ♦
Pass	4 NT	Pass	5 ♦
Pass	6 ♦	Pass	Pass
Pass			

South's opening bid of 1 ♦ should start North thinking about a slam contract. North has 19 HCPs and 2 points for the six-card suit, which, opposite the strength for even a minimum opening bid, means the partnership has at least 34 combined points. Before bidding slam, however, North needs to determine the best denomination. North could start by responding 2 ♣, which would be forcing, but he can show the strength of his hand and interest in slam by jump-shifting to 3 ♣. When South rebids his diamonds, North knows the partnership has a suitable trump suit and he can check for aces by using the Blackwood Convention. When South shows only one ace, North knows the partnership has to settle for a small slam.

Suggested Play

West will probably lead the ♠ J, top of his touching high cards in the suit, and South should resist the temptation to finesse. If the finesse loses, the defenders will also be able to take the ♥ A and defeat the contract. Instead, South should win the ♠ A, draw trumps and discard his two spade losers on dummy's extra club winners. The only trick the opponents get is the ♥ A. If the missing clubs were divided 3–3, South would also be able to discard all his hearts and make an overtrick. As the cards lie, declarer still has to lose a heart trick.

Notes

Not all pairs will reach the slam contract, and even if they do, North must be careful to steer the partnership to the best denomination. If North gets carried away with his fine club suit and ignores the diamond suit, he will be sorry. Because the missing clubs divide 4–2, he will have to lose a club trick as well as the ♥ A.

BOARD #8

Dealer: West
Vulnerable: None

NORTH
♠ 8 5
♥ A 10 4
♦ A Q 10 7 5 4
♣ K Q

WEST
♠ Q 9 4 2
♥ J 9 8 6 3
♦ J 2
♣ A 7

EAST
♠ A K J 6
♥ K Q 7 2
♦ 9
♣ J 9 4 3

SOUTH
♠ 10 7 3
♥ 5
♦ K 8 6 3
♣ 10 8 6 5 2

	ACBL SHORT TRAVELING SCORE								
	(Mitchell or Howell)								

Board No. **8**

N-S Pair No.	Contract	By	M a d e	D o w n	SCORE		N-S Match-points	E-W Pair No.	E-W Match-points
					N-S	E-W			
1	3 H	W	4			170		10	
2	4 H	W	4			420		12	
3	4 S	E		1	50			8	
4	5 D X	N		1		100		11	
5	4 H X	W	4			590		7	
6	3 H	W	4			170		9	
7									
8									

Suggested Bidding

WEST	NORTH	EAST	SOUTH
Pass	1♦	Double	2♦
2♥	3♦	3♥	Pass
4♥	Pass	Pass	Pass

East has the right type of hand to make a takeout double of North's 1♦ opening bid. South may raise to 2♦ to try and keep West out of the bidding, but with 8 HCPs and a five-card suit, West should bid 2♥. North has a very good hand and will probably bid on to 3♦, but East also has a medium strength hand — 14 HCPs plus 3 dummy points for the singleton — and should invite partner to game by bidding 3♥. West is on the borderline but should probably accept the invitation.

Suggested Play

In 4♥, West should lose only a heart trick, a diamond trick and a club trick. He can trump his second diamond loser in the dummy. North will do well in a diamond contract, if he is allowed to play there, since he has only three losers: two spades and a club. He can trump his heart losers in the dummy.

Notes

Although bidding 5♦ would get a good result for North-South if East-West reach 4♥, it is unlikely that many pairs will bid that high. North is more likely to double the 4♥ contract, expecting to defeat it. Any East-West pairs that get to 4♠ will probably feel unlucky, since that contract can be defeated if the defense gets one or two heart ruffs.

BOARD #9

Dealer: North
Vulnerable: East-West

NORTH
- ♠ 10
- ♥ J 7 3
- ♦ K J 9 6 5
- ♣ A J 9 2

WEST
- ♠ Q 6 5 2
- ♥ K Q 6
- ♦ A Q 10 8 7
- ♣ 3

EAST
- ♠ J 8 3
- ♥ 9 8 5
- ♦ 4 3
- ♣ K 8 6 5 4

SOUTH
- ♠ A K 9 7 4
- ♥ A 10 4 2
- ♦ 2
- ♣ Q 10 7

ACBL SHORT TRAVELING SCORE
(Mitchell or Howell)

Board No.: **9**

N-S Pair No.	Contract	By	Made	Down	SCORE N-S	SCORE E-W	N-S Match-points	E-W Pair No.	E-W Match-points
1	2 H	S	2		110			9	
2	2 D X	W		3	800			11	
3	3NT	N		1		50		7	
4	2 D X	W		2	500			10	
5	3NT	N	3		400			12	
6	2NT	S	2		120			8	
7									
8									

Suggested Bidding

WEST	NORTH	EAST	SOUTH
	Pass	Pass	1♠
2♦	Double	Pass	Pass
Pass			

After two passes, South opens the bidding 1♠. With 13 HCPs and a good five-card suit, West appears to have a perfectly normal 2♦ overcall. Unfortunately, on this hand he finds North with most of the remaining diamonds and enough strength to make a penalty double. East has no better spot to run to and South should be satisfied with North's decision. North's double is not for takeout since South has already bid a suit. East has nowhere to go and will have to hope that the penalty is not too severe.

Suggested Play

Against the 2♦ doubled contract, North can extract the maximum penalty by leading his singleton spade. South can win, take a second spade trick and lead a third spade for North to ruff. If North-South are familiar with suit preference signals, South should lead back the ♠9, his highest remaining spade, to tell North to lead the higher-ranking of the two obvious suits, hearts. If North leads a heart, South can win the ♥A and lead another spade for North to trump. North will still get the ♣A and two more trump tricks to inflict a three-trick penalty.

Notes

Although it is dangerous to overcall at the two level, especially when partner has passed already and your side is vulnerable, most players would take the risk when playing duplicate bridge. On this hand, however, the risk does not pay off if North-South take the opportunity to collect their penalty. Left to their own devices, North-South will probably end in a partscore contract or overreach to a game contract, which they are unlikely to make.

BOARD #10

Dealer: East
Vulnerable: Both

NORTH
♠ 10 6 3
♥ Q J 8
♦ K 7
♣ A K 8 4 2

WEST
♠ K 9 5 2
♥ 7 4
♦ Q J 9 3 2
♣ J 7

EAST
♠ Q J 8
♥ 6 3
♦ A 10 6 4
♣ Q 10 6 5

SOUTH
♠ A 7 4
♥ A K 10 9 5 2
♦ 8 5
♣ 9 3

| | | | | | | ACBL SHORT TRAVELING SCORE (Mitchell or Howell) | | | | |

Board No. 10

N-S Pair No.	Contract	By	M a d e	D o w n	SCORE		N-S Match-points	E-W Pair No.	E-W Match-points
					N-S	E-W			
1	4 H	S		1		100		9	
2	4 H	S		1		100		11	
3	3NT	N	3		600			7	
4	4 H	S	4		620			10	
5	3 H	S	3		140			12	
6	4 H	S		1		100		8	
7									
8									

Suggested Bidding

WEST	NORTH	EAST	SOUTH
		Pass	1♥
Pass	2♣	Pass	2♥
Pass	4♥	Pass	Pass
Pass			

North is too strong to make a limit raise of South's 1♥ opening bid and starts with a forcing response of 2♣. After South rebids his six-card heart suit, North can put the partnership in the appropriate game.

Suggested Play

West will probably start with the ♦Q and North's ♦K will be trapped. After taking two diamond tricks, the defenders will probably lead a spade, driving out declarer's ♠A and South is in danger of being defeated since he still has two spade losers. South's only hope is to discard one of his losers on an extra winner in the dummy. There is no immediate extra winner, but the length of dummy's club suit offers some potential.

South plans to play the ♣A and ♣K and then lead another club and trump it. If the missing clubs are divided 3–3, dummy's remaining clubs will be winners and South can make an overtrick. When the clubs prove to be divided 4–2, South will have to get back to dummy to lead another club and trump it. Now dummy's remaining club is a winner and declarer can go over to dummy and discard one of his spade losers. Since the only entries to dummy are in the heart suit, South will have to be careful to use his trumps wisely. He can afford to draw only one round before starting on the club suit. He must ruff the third round of clubs with a high trump to avoid being overtrumped and then get back to dummy by leading a second round of trumps. After ruffing another club, dummy's last heart provides the entry he needs.

Notes

Since it is very difficult to make the 4♥ contract, any pair that does will likely be tied for the top result. Any pair that is defeated should carefully go over the hand afterwards to see how the contract can be made. Establishing long suits with the help of the trump suit is an important technique.

LESSON 6

The Team Game

Introducing the Team Game
The IMP Scale
Team Game Tactics
Summary

Workshop Material
Group Activities
Sample Boards

♠ *INTRODUCING THE TEAM GAME* ♠

Team games are a very popular form of duplicate bridge. Four players, made up of two partnerships, can form a team and play against another team of four players. Experienced duplicate players find these team-of-four competitions a challenge. Playing with teammates adds another dimension to the game.

The Basic Team Game

In a *team game*, one team plays a *match*, consisting of a pre-arranged number of boards, against another team of four players. You and your teammates do not play the boards against each other but each partnership (pair) plays all of the boards against one of the partnerships (pairs) on the opposing team. Let's see how this works.

Each team sits one of its pairs North-South at one table and the other pair East-West at a second table. For example, suppose there are two teams, A and B. Team A would sit one pair North-South at Table #1 (Team A's *home table*), and the other pair East-West at Table #2. Team B would fill in the blanks by sitting one of its pairs East-West at Table #1 and the other pair North-South at Table #2 (Team B's *home table*). This arrangement is shown in the diagram below:

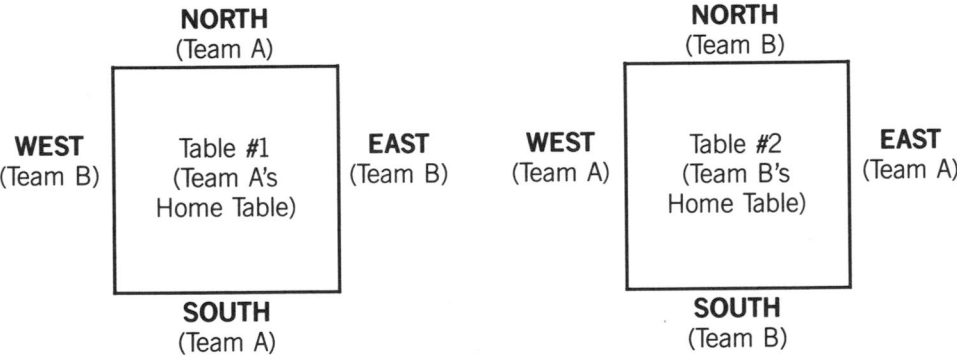

The same boards are played at both tables. If the match is eight boards in length, Table #1 could start by playing Boards 1–4 while Table #2 plays Boards 5–8. When Table #1 is finished playing their four boards, they pass them over to Table #2, and vice-versa. Since the teams are playing the same boards, the tables usually are not located too close to each other. At a tournament, they will be separated in different sections. If you are playing a team game at home, unless the room is very large, you would probably arrange to have the tables in different rooms.

After the eight boards have been played, the East-West pairs return to their home table, where their North-South pair is sitting, and compare results. If you are going to play more than one set of boards, you would now go back and play the same team again, usually playing against the other pair on the opposing team. In this fashion, a match of any length can be played — dividing it into halves, quarters, or even smaller segments if it is a very long match.

Sometimes a team is composed of more than four players, normally up to a maximum of six. Only four can play at one time but, after each break for a comparison of results, you can bring in the player or partnership who sat out.

Swiss Teams

A popular format of team play is *Swiss teams*. Suppose 16 teams enter a Swiss team event. The director arranges eight matches so that each team is playing a match against another team. After the first match is complete, there will be eight winning teams and eight losing teams (ties are possible). In the second round, the director arranges for the winning teams to play against one another and the losing teams to play against one another. At the end of two rounds, there will be only four teams who have won both matches. Again, the director arranges matches so that teams with the same won-lost record play against each other. After the third round there will be only one winning team left. However, the matches continue until the scheduled number of rounds has been completed. The director sets up pairings so that the top two teams play each other, then the next best two, etc. One important provision — teams should not play each other more than once during the event!

One of the reasons for the popularity of Swiss teams is that, if your team loses its first few matches, you find yourself competing against another team with a similar record. As the game progresses, you tend to find yourself playing against teams with whom you are evenly matched. Since masterpoints are awarded for each match you win, everyone has a good chance of winning at least one match and coming away with some masterpoints.

The number of matches and the length of each match will depend on the number of teams entered in the event and the length of the event. In a typical game played in a single session you will find yourself playing four matches of four to seven boards in length.

Other Team Events

There are other formats that can be used to run team games.

Knockout Teams

A *knockout team* event is similar to such an event in tennis. Once you lose a match, your team is out of the event. When you play a knockout match, you usually play the same team for an entire session. The whole event will be run over a number of sessions, perhaps running for several consecutive days, or perhaps one session a week over a number of weeks.

Round-Robin

In a *round-robin team* event, each team plays one match against every other team in the same group. This type of event is often used as a preliminary round for a knockout team contest with, for example, the top four teams going on to play semifinal matches followed by a final match between the winners.

Board-a-Match

The format of *board-a-match* is quite similar to a regular duplicate game. Your North-South pair stays stationary at one table, while your East-West pair moves from table to table, playing a set number of boards against each of the other teams. At the end of the session, the East-West pair goes back to their home table and compares results with their teammates. The movement is coordinated so that the East-West pair plays the same boards as the North-South pair against the same team. It is like having a series of mini-matches of two or three boards each.

This format is quite exciting but it is not used much anymore. It has been replaced with the highly popular Swiss team game.

♠ THE IMP SCALE ♠

Because the team format is somewhat different from a pair event, a different method of score comparison is used.

IMPs

When you finish playing each board, you determine your score in exactly the same way as in a regular duplicate game. If you bid and make a vulnerable 3 NT contract, for example, your score is plus 600 points. When you come back to compare results with your teammates, one of the pairs will have played each board in the North-South direction and the other in the East-West direction. Your team's score on each board is the net total of the two scores. If both pairs have plus scores, your tally will be the sum of the two scores. If both have minus scores, your score will be the sum of the two negative results. If there is a plus and minus score, you will calculate the difference between the two scores. It may end up as zero, or you may have a net plus or a net minus score.

For example, suppose you are sitting North-South and you bid to a vulnerable 4♥ contract, making 10 tricks and scoring 620 points. If the North-South pair at the other table also bids and makes 4♥, your East-West teammates will have lost 620 points. Your net result is zero (620 − 620 = 0). This would be the expected result on every board if both sides bid and played perfectly. Of course, quite often the scores will be different at the two tables. Perhaps the opponents did not bid the game or did not make it. Suppose they bid only 3♥, making 10 tricks and scoring 170 points. Your team would end up with a total of 450 points (620 − 170). Or, perhaps the opposing team made an overtrick in their 4♥ contract and your teammates lost 650 points. When you compare this loss with your 620 point gain, you would end up with a total of −30 points (620 − 650).

Long matches once were scored simply by adding up each side's plus scores. Whichever team scored the most points was the winner. This was called *total point scoring*. The problem with this method is that a large score on one or two boards could affect the outcome of the entire match. For example, because of the large bonuses for small and grand slams, several hundred points could be lost on one board. It takes a lot of partscores and games to recover that amount.

To reduce the effect of a few large scores on the final result, a system was developed whereby the net result of each hand is converted into *International Match Points*, which are referred to as *IMPs*. The scale used for conversion is shown below and there is also a copy inside each Convention Card.

INTERNATIONAL MATCH POINT SCALE

Diff. in Pts.	IMP	Diff. in Pts.	IMP	Diff. in Pts.	IMP
20–40	1	370–420	9	1500–1740	17
50–80	2	430–490	10	1750–1990	18
90–120	3	500–590	11	2000–2240	19
130–160	4	600–740	12	2250–2490	20
170–210	5	750–890	13	2500–2990	21
220–260	6	900–1090	14	3000–3490	22
270–310	7	1100–1290	15	3500–3990	23
320–360	8	1300–1490	16	4000 and up	24

For example, let's see how many IMPs your team would score on a hand where your East-West pair bid and made a non-vulnerable 4♥ game and made an overtrick for a total of 450 points and your North-South defended a 4♥ contract and held it to exactly 10 tricks, losing 420 points. Your team's net result on the board is +30 points (450 − 420). Looking at the IMP Scale, your total result falls between 20 and 40, which would translate into 1 IMP. Your team, then, wins 1 IMP on the board and the other team loses 1 IMP.

If your North-South pair had defeated the contract, collecting 50 points, your side would have a net total of 500 points (450 + 50). This would fall between 500 and 590 on the IMP Scale and would translate into 11 IMPs. If, instead, the opponents had not bid to 4♥ but had stopped in 3♥, making 10 tricks for a total of 170 points, your net result would be 280 points (450 − 170). This falls within the range of 270–310 on the IMP Scale, for a win of 7 IMPs.

The IMP scale still rewards you for bidding and making game contracts, but if you were to miss a game, you might be able to make it up by successfully bidding a couple of part-scores. The strategy of playing in team events, therefore, differs somewhat from the strategy of a pair event. Making an overtrick in a pair event, for example, could mean that you collect all the matchpoints. In a team game, an overtrick is relatively insignificant, being worth only 1 IMP. What is important in a team game is that you bid your game and slam contracts and try to make them. You don't try for overtricks unless your contract is safe.

Winning or Losing

To determine which team won the match, you add up the IMPs you won and lost on each board. If the net total is a plus, you won the match. Otherwise you lost. If you are playing a long knockout match, the difference between winning and losing might come down to a single IMP!

Because the matches in a Swiss team event are quite short, most players feel it is a little much to have the entire match won or lost by a single IMP. Instead, if the margin of victory is only one or two IMPs, the winning team is awarded ¾ of a win and the losing team gets ¼ of a win. As far as the masterpoint awards for the match are concerned, however, they all go to the team who collected more IMPs. For a complete win in a Swiss team event, therefore, a match has to be won by three or more IMPs.

When there are a large number of teams playing in a Swiss team event, it might not be possible to end up with a single winner by the end of the session. For example, if there are four matches played, there may be several teams with four wins. One way of reducing the possibility of a tie is to do a further conversion of the IMP margin in each match into *Victory Points*. A typical Victory Point Scale might look like this:

IMP Diff.	Victory Pts.
0–1	5–5
2–3	6–4
4–6	7–3
7–9	8–2
10–14	9–1
15 or more	10–0

For example, suppose your team wins a match by 5 IMPs. Using the above Victory Point Scale, you would get 7 Victory Points and the losing team would get 3. To get the maximum of 10 Victory Points, you would have to win the match by 15 or more IMPs.

At the end of the session, it is quite likely that one team will have more Victory Points than any of the others, having won all their matches by larger margins than other teams. In fact a team could lose one match by a close margin and win the remaining matches by a large margin and end up with enough Victory Points to win the event.

The Advantage of Team Games

With only two tables, the team game format is a lot more exciting than matchpoints. If you were playing matchpoint pairs, the most you could score on any board would be one matchpoint since the board is played only twice. Even if you do something spectacular, you cannot get more than one matchpoint. On the other hand, if you do a little worse than the pair at the other table, you end up with no matchpoints on the board. The lack of a large number of results to compare means that the game loses some of its excitement.

On any given board in a team event, however, there are lots of potential IMPs to be won or lost. You can battle back and forth for the entire session and it may all come down to a single hand! Team events can be very exciting, and players are usually anxious to get back to their teammates' table to see how they did.

A team event can also provide a fairer competition since your teammates have exactly the same cards as your opponents. Any element of luck is eliminated. Whatever your opponents can do, your teammates will have an equal opportunity at the other table.

♠ *TEAM GAME TACTICS* ♠

Because of the way that team games are scored, you need to approach them in a different fashion from duplicate pair events.

Bidding

In a matchpoint game, you will generally get some of the matchpoints if you make any plus score. Even if you play in a partscore contract when you can make a game, or in a game contract when you could make a slam, some of the other pairs are likely to be in the same contract. In a team game, you play against only one other pair, the pair sitting in the same direction as you at the other table. If they bid and make a game or a slam and you don't, you will lose a large number of IMPs.

In general, then, you want to make sure you bid to your game and slam contracts whenever possible (and make them). Experience has shown that you should generally bid a non-vulnerable game if it has a 50% or better chance of making. For example, you might need a successful finesse to make game. You can bid a vulnerable game with as little as a 40% chance. The idea is that, if you make four out of 10 vulnerable games, you will gain more in the long run than by playing all 10 hands in partscore.

For example, suppose you open the bidding 1♠ with the following hand and your partner makes a limit raise to 3♠, inviting you to game.

♠ A 10 7 6 3
♥ Q J 9 4
♦ 4 3
♣ A Q

With only 13 HCPs plus one point for the five-card spade suit, you should probably reject partner's invitation if you are playing matchpoints. You might make game, but you might even go down in a 3♠ contract if the cards are badly placed. Since other pairs will be faced with a similar situation, some will pass and some will bid game. If game makes, you will get a slightly below average board, but you will get some matchpoints from the other pairs who stopped at partscore. If game does not make, you will be tied for a top result on the board with the other pairs who stopped before game.

On the other hand, if you are vulnerable and playing in a team game, you should probably bid 4♠, even if the contract ends up requiring a finesse or a bit of luck. It is likely to be bid at the other table and the reward outstrips the risk. Suppose there are 10 tricks and you stop in partscore. You will get 170 points. If your opponents bid game, they will get 620 points and you will lose 10 IMPs. If it turns out that only nine tricks can be made and you stop in partscore, you will score 140 points and your teammates will get 100 points for defeating their opponents' 4♠ contract, a total of 240 for 6 IMPs. You can see why the odds favor bidding your close vulnerable games. You have more to gain than to lose.

If you are not vulnerable, it is a little closer decision with the above hand. If you stop in partscore and game happens to make, you will score 170 points and the opponents will score 420 points, a difference of 250 points — 6 IMPs. If it turns out you can make only nine tricks, you will score 140 points and your teammates will score 50, for a total of 190 points — 5 IMPs. It is close to an even proposition.

When considering bidding a small slam, you have to be a little more careful. If you are defeated, you not only lose the slam bonus but also the game bonus. Therefore, you would like your chances for slam contracts to be better than those required for game contracts. If you never bid a slam that requires more than a finesse, you are probably in the right ball park.

You need to be very sure before you bid a grand slam, because if you are defeated, you lose not only the game bonus but also the small slam bonus. Your teammates would be disappointed if you went down one in a grand slam when your opponents did not even reach the small slam contract.

All this is not to say that partscores are not important. If you can make a partscore while the opponents are being defeated in a similar contract, that is worth about 6 IMPs. You should be reasonably aggressive even when competing for partscores.

On the other hand, you should be careful about doubling your opponents in a partscore unless you are very sure of defeating them. In a matchpoint game you are risking a top or a bottom on a single board, which you might recover by making an overtrick on the next board. In a team game, your are risking the whole match, since it can be won or lost by a single IMP.

Play

When you are playing for matchpoints, you are trying, whenever possible, to beat all the other pairs in your direction. Risking your contract to make an overtrick can benefit you if, in the long run, you get more tops than bottoms. In a team game, the odds are much different. Making an overtrick is worth only 1 IMP, whereas going down in a game can cost 10 or more IMPs. The odds would have to be heavily in your favor before you would risk the contract for the chance of an overtrick.

In fact, you should always look for the safest line of play to take the number of tricks you need. Consider the following hand where you are declarer in a contract of 3 NT:

DUMMY
♠ 9 7 3
♥ 6 4
♦ A K Q 9 7 6
♣ J 5

DECLARER (**YOU**)
♠ A K 2
♥ A K 7 2
♦ 5 3
♣ Q 10 8 4

In your contract of 3 NT, you need to take nine tricks. Playing matchpoints, your approach would be very straightforward. You have two spade tricks, two heart tricks and likely six diamond tricks if the missing diamonds are divided 3–2. Since overtricks are important, you would try for your 10 tricks by playing the ♦A, ♦K and ♦Q, hoping the remaining diamond tricks are established. If you are unlucky and the missing diamonds are divided 4–1, you will go down, but so will the other declarers who take the same reasonable view.

In a team game, you want to give yourself the best chance of taking **nine** tricks. The overtrick is unimportant relative to the importance of making your contract. You can protect yourself against the missing diamonds being divided 4–1 by giving up the first diamond trick to the opponents. If the missing diamonds were originally divided 3–2, you have given up an overtrick — 1 IMP. On the other hand, if they were divided 4–1, you will still make your contract because you have a little diamond left to get to your diamonds in the dummy. You will have saved 10 or more IMPs. This type of play is called a *safety play* because you do something that helps guarantee your contract, even if it ends up costing you an overtrick. It is not a good idea to use the safety play at matchpoints unless you are in a contract that you do not think the other players will have reached. On the other hand, the safety play is an excellent team tactic.

Defense

Just as making your contract when you are declarer is very important in a team game, so is defeating the opponents' contract whenever possible. When you are playing matchpoints, merely defeating the opponents' contract might not be enough. You are trying to defeat it by more tricks than other pairs in your direction. In a team game, however, you are playing against only one other pair and therefore should not take any risks. The general idea is to take the setting trick.

Consider the following hand:

```
              NORTH (DUMMY)
              ♠ Q J 9 4
              ♥ K J 3
              ♦ Q 8 2
              ♣ A 8 2

WEST (YOU)
♠ K 3
♥ A 9 7 5
♦ J 10 9 5
♣ 7 6 3
```

The opponents reach 4♠ after South has opened the bidding 1♠, and your opening lead is the ♦J. Declarer plays low from dummy, your partner encourages with the ♦7 and your jack wins the first trick. You lead another diamond and your partner wins the trick with the ♦K and plays the ♦A, which declarer trumps. Declarer now leads a low heart toward the dummy. What should you do?

Playing matchpoints, you might have some reason to play second hand low. If declarer has two hearts, perhaps he will guess incorrectly and you will defeat the contract an extra trick. In a team game, however, you should not even think twice. By taking the ♥A you

can be sure that the contract will be defeated since you will also get a trick with your ♠ K. Don't give declarer the chance to slip a trick by you. The complete hand might look like this:

```
              NORTH
              ♠ Q J 9 4
              ♥ K J 3
              ♦ Q 8 2
              ♣ A 8 2

WEST                        EAST
♠ K 3                       ♠ 6
♥ A 9 7 5                   ♥ Q 10 8 6 2
♦ J 10 9 5                  ♦ A K 6 4
♣ 7 6 3                     ♣ 10 9 4

              SOUTH
              ♠ A 10 8 7 5 2
              ♥ 4
              ♦ 7 3
              ♣ K Q J 5
```

If you play low on the heart and declarer plays dummy's ♥ K, you will never get a heart trick. Playing a small card could cost 10 or more IMPs.

♠ *SUMMARY* ♠

Teams are a form of competition whereby you and your partner play with another pair to form a team to play against four other players. Both teams play the same boards. You play in the opposite direction to your teammates so that, as a team, you play each board once in the North-South direction and once in the East-West direction.

At the end of the match you compare scores with your teammates. You add together your results and the net total is converted into IMPs. You total up the IMPs won and lost on each board to determine which team won the match.

♠ *GROUP ACTIVITIES* ♠

Exercise One — The Team Game

You and your partner are playing in a team game.

- If your teammates sit North-South, which direction will you sit?

- What do you do when you are finished playing the boards that were originally put on your table?

- Where do you go at the end of the match?

- Do you need to keep track of your scores?

Exercise Two — IMPs

You and your teammates are comparing scores from the first four boards of your match. These are the results from each table:

Table #1 (N-S)				Table #2 (E-W)				Net Score	IMPs
Board	Contract	Result	Score	Board	Contract	Result	Score		
1	3NT N	3	+400	1	3NT N	3	−400		
2	2♠ E	3	−140	2	4♠ E	−2	−100		
3	4♥ S	4	+420	3	3NT N	3	−400		
4	5♣ X W	−1	+200	4	3NT E	3	+600		

Using the IMP scale in your Convention Card, calculate the IMPs won or lost on each board. Did your team win the match?

Exercise Three — Team Game Tactics

You are in a contract of 4♥ and the opening lead is the ♦9. How would you play the following deal in a team game? What might you do differently if you were playing matchpoints?

DUMMY
♠ Q 8 2
♥ 10 9 5
♦ A Q J 8 5
♣ J 5

Lead: ♦ 9

DECLARER (**YOU**)
♠ J 3
♥ A Q J 8 4 2
♦ K 10 2
♣ A 7

1. How many losers can you afford in your 4♥ contract?

2. How many losers do you have?

3. What might you be able to do with your spade losers?

4. How might you avoid the heart loser?

5. What about the club loser?

6. Do you plan to start by playing the diamond suit to discard your losers or by drawing trumps?

7. Is there any danger in taking the heart finesse? After all, if it loses, the opponents can take only two spade winners and you will later be able to draw the remaining trumps and discard your club loser.

8. How, then, should you plan to play the trump suit in a team game?

9. How might you play the hand at matchpoints?

♠ *SAMPLE BOARDS* ♠

The sample hands are discussed as though they were played in a match between two teams. Team #1 is sitting North-South at Table #1 and East-West at Table #2. Team #2 is North-South at Table #2 and East-West at Table #1. The score recorded at each table is shown.

BOARD #1

Dealer: North
Vulnerable: None

NORTH
♠ Q 6
♥ A Q 8 3
♦ K 10 7
♣ K Q 6 3

WEST
♠ A 9 4
♥ J 10 5
♦ 8 5 3 2
♣ 10 8 5

EAST
♠ K J 7 5 2
♥ 7 2
♦ A 6
♣ J 9 7 2

SOUTH
♠ 10 8 3
♥ K 9 6 4
♦ Q J 9 4
♣ A 4

Results:

Table #1: 4 ♥ by North, making 10 tricks (+420 for N-S, −420 for E-W).

Table #2: 3NT by North, down two (−100 for N-S, +100 for E-W).

Suggested Bidding

WEST	NORTH	EAST	SOUTH
	1 NT	Pass	2♣
Pass	2♥	Pass	4♥
Pass	Pass	Pass	

When North opens the bidding 1 NT, South knows there should be enough combined strength for game. The only question is whether the partnership belongs in a major suit or in 3 NT. Holding a four-card heart suit, South can find out whether North holds four hearts by making use of the Stayman convention. In response to South's 2♣ bid, North bids his four-card heart suit. This is all the information South needs to jump to the best game contract.

Suggested Play

Since the missing hearts are divided 3–2, North has only two spade losers, a diamond loser and a club loser to worry about in a 4♥ contract. There is nothing he can do about the spade and diamond losers if the opponents take their tricks, but the club loser can be trumped in the dummy or discarded on the extra diamond winner in the dummy once the ♦A has been driven out. If the opponents do not find their spade tricks soon enough, declarer may be able to discard one of his spade losers on dummy's extra diamond and make an overtrick.

If North plays in 3 NT, East will probably lead a small spade and East-West will end up taking the first five spade tricks and the ♦A to defeat the contract two tricks.

Notes

North-South at Table #1 got to 4♥, making, while 3 NT at the other table was defeated two tricks. Perhaps the North-South pair at Table #2 were not familiar with the Stayman convention, or South decided not to use it on this hand. Team #1 was +420 at Table 1 and +100 at Table 2, a net gain of 520, worth 11 IMPs.

BOARD #2

Dealer: East
Vulnerable: North-South

NORTH
♠ J 10 8 6
♥ K 8 5
♦ Q 2
♣ K Q 9 7

WEST
♠ A Q 7 5 2
♥ 10 4 3
♦ K 4 3
♣ 6 4

EAST
♠ 9 3
♥ 7
♦ A J 10 8 7 6 5
♣ 10 8 3

SOUTH
♠ K 4
♥ A Q J 9 6 2
♦ 9
♣ A J 5 2

Results:

Table #1: 5 ♦ doubled by East, down one (+100 for N-S, −100 for E-W).

Table #2: 4 ♥ by South, making 10 tricks (+620 for N-S, −620 for E-W).

Suggested Bidding

WEST	NORTH	EAST	SOUTH
		3♦	3♥
5♦	Double	Pass	Pass
Pass			

If East opens with a preemptive 3♦ bid, South has enough to overcall 3♥. West now has an interesting choice of calls. If West passes, North will raise to 4♥, knowing South must have better than a minimum hand to overcall at the three level. Anticipating this, West should consider raising East's suit to try to prevent the opponents from finding their best contract. Looking at his own hand, and knowing that his partner has a weak hand, it is unlikely that his side will have enough tricks to defeat 4♥. Since North-South are vulnerable and East-West are not, it is unlikely that the penalty will compensate them for their game even if the opponents double.

In such situations, West should bid as high as he can as soon as he can. By jumping to 5♦, he makes the auction very difficult for North. North will have to decide whether to double or to bid on to 5♥. When in doubt, North should usually settle for the "sure" plus score.

Suggested Play

If East plays 5♦, he has to lose only a heart trick and two club tricks. He can take the spade finesse to avoid a spade loser and he can trump his third club loser in the dummy after the missing trumps are drawn.

If North-South are allowed to play 4♥, they will lose only two spade tricks and a diamond trick. Of course, if they push on to 5♥ over the opponent's 5♦ bid, they will still lose the same three tricks and end up going one down.

Notes

North-South at Table #2 were allowed to play in 4♥ and made it. At Table #1, East-West found the 5♦ "sacrifice" and the best North-South could do was collect 100 points for defeating 5♦ doubled. Team 2 was +620 at Table 2 and –100 at Table 1, a net plus of 520, worth 11 IMPs.

BOARD #3

Dealer: South
Vulnerable: East-West

NORTH
♠ K
♥ J 10 9 7 5
♦ J 9 5
♣ J 8 6 4

WEST
♠ A Q 7 5 2
♥ Q 4
♦ K Q 6 3
♣ 9 2

EAST
♠ J 10 6 3
♥ A 8 3 2
♦ A 8
♣ Q 10 3

SOUTH
♠ 9 8 4
♥ K 6
♦ 10 7 4 2
♣ A K 7 5

Results:

Table #1: 4♠ by West, down one (+100 for N-S, −100 for E-W).

Table #2: 3♠ by West, making nine tricks (−140 for N-S, +140 for E-W).

Suggested Bidding

WEST	NORTH	EAST	SOUTH
			Pass
1♠	Pass	3♠	Pass
Pass	Pass		

South does not have enough to open the bidding, but West has enough to open with 1♠. After North's pass, East can make a limit raise to 3♠, showing about 11–12 points, if that is the partnership style. West has a difficult decision to make. He has 13 HCPs plus 1 point for the five-card suit. This puts him on the borderline. The more aggressive players will accept the invitation, while others will settle for the safer partscore.

Suggested Play

Against 3♠, North will probably lead the ♥J, and if declarer plays a small heart from dummy, South will win the ♥K. South may also take the ♣A and ♣K, leaving declarer only the spade suit to worry about since he can trump his diamond loser or discard it on one of dummy's extra winners. West may try the spade finesse which will lose to North's singleton ♠K.

When the hand is over, West may feel unlucky to have lost to North's singleton king, since playing the ♠A is not usually the best way to avoid a spade loser. On this hand, however, there is a strong indication that North has the ♠K and the finesse is doomed to fail. If the defense goes as outlined above, South will already have shown up with the ♥K, ♣A and ♣K. If he held the ♠K as well, he would have had enough to open the bidding. Since he passed originally, there is a strong inference that North has the ♠K. Therefore, West should play the ♠A since his only hope is that the ♠K is singleton. West will be well rewarded for his effort, especially if he bid aggressively to 4♠.

Notes

The East-West pair at Table #1 pushed to game while the East-West pair at Table #2 stopped in partscore. Neither declarer worked out to play the ♠A and drop North's singleton ♠K, so the East-West pair at Table #1 had a net loss of 240 points worth 6 IMPs. They missed a chance to win 10 IMPs by failing to work out the spade position.

BOARD #4

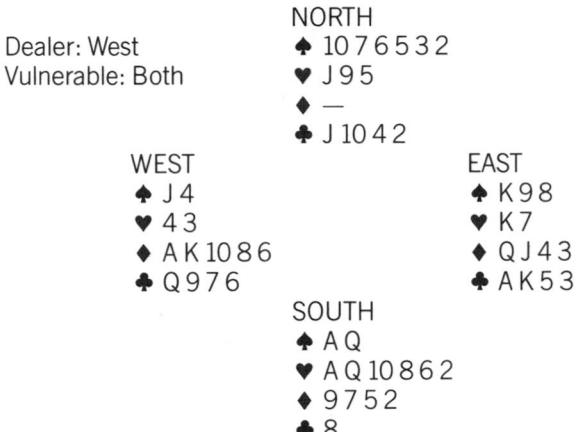

Dealer: West
Vulnerable: Both

NORTH
♠ 10 7 6 5 3 2
♥ J 9 5
♦ —
♣ J 10 4 2

WEST
♠ J 4
♥ 4 3
♦ A K 10 8 6
♣ Q 9 7 6

EAST
♠ K 9 8
♥ K 7
♦ Q J 4 3
♣ A K 5 3

SOUTH
♠ A Q
♥ A Q 10 8 6 2
♦ 9 7 5 2
♣ 8

Results:

Table #1: 4♥ doubled by South, making 10 tricks (+790 for N-S, −790 for E-W).

Table #2: 3NT by East, making nine tricks (−600 for N-S, +600 for E-W).

Suggested Bidding

WEST	NORTH	EAST	SOUTH
Pass	Pass	1 NT	2♥
3 NT	4♥	Pass	Pass
Double	Pass	Pass	Pass

With the majority of the strength in the East-West hands but some unusual distribution in the North-South hands, this could prove to be one of the most exciting hands in the match. East has a normal 1 NT opening bid and South has a good enough suit to overcall at the two level. With 10 HCPs, West should raise partner to 3 NT, as he would have done had South passed. Now, it is up to North. If North passes, that will be the end of the auction (East and South will pass). With a void in diamonds and three-card support for partner's suit, however, North may decide to push on to 4♥. North is not expecting that this contract will make. However, since partner has made a vulnerable overcall, he does not expect to be in too much trouble — any penalty may be less than the value of the opponents' game. If he does bid 4♥, one of the opponents should double and that will end the auction.

Suggested Play

East-West may be quite disappointed if they end up defending 4♥ since they cannot defeat that contract despite their high-card strength. If West leads the ♦A, for example, declarer can trump in the dummy, lead a spade to his ♠Q and trump a second diamond in the dummy. He can come back to the ♠A and trump another diamond in the dummy. Eventually, he loses a heart trick, a diamond trick and a club trick.

If East is allowed to play 3 NT, he will make it after South leads a heart. Declarer can win the first trick with the ♥K and take five diamond tricks and three club tricks.

Notes

At Table #2, North did not risk the 4♥ bid and ended up defending 3 NT, which made. This proved an unlucky decision since the North-South pair at Table #1 made their 4♥ doubled contract. This was a big win for Team #1 — a *double game swing* (a game made in both directions).

BOARD #5

Dealer: North
Vulnerable: North-South

NORTH
♠ 9 3
♥ A Q 10 7 5 3
♦ 9
♣ K Q 8 4

WEST
♠ Q J 6 4 2
♥ J 6
♦ A K J 3
♣ 7 3

EAST
♠ A 10 7 5
♥ 9
♦ Q 6 4 2
♣ A J 10 5

SOUTH
♠ K 8
♥ K 8 4 2
♦ 10 8 7 5
♣ 9 6 2

Results:

Table #1: 4♠ by West, making 10 tricks (−420 for N-S, +420 for E-W).

Table #2: 4♠ by West, down one (+50 for N-S, −50 for E-W).

Suggested Bidding

WEST	NORTH	EAST	SOUTH
	1♥	Double	2♥
4♠	Pass	Pass	Pass

East has 11 HCPs and can add 3 dummy points for the singleton heart to give him enough to make a takeout double over the 1♥ opening. South has enough to raise to 2♥, but West has more than enough to jump to a game in spades.

Suggested Play

North might lead his singleton diamond, hoping to get a ruff, or might lead the ♥A and then switch to the singleton diamond. Playing matchpoints, West would probably try the spade finesse, hoping to make an overtrick if North started with the ♠K. Playing in a team game, West should be looking for the safest way to make the contract. There appears to be only one spade loser, one heart loser and one club loser since declarer's second heart loser can be trumped in the dummy. The only danger is that the opponents can get a ruff. Instead of taking the spade finesse, West should play the ♠A first and then lead another spade, eliminating the opponents' trumps as quickly as possible. Declarer can afford one trump loser but not two.

Notes

Game was reached at both tables, but at Table #2 West tried the spade finesse after North had led his singleton diamond. South won the ♠K and, figuring out why North had led a diamond rather than a heart, led another diamond so that North could trump with his remaining spade. North took the ♥A and later got a club trick to defeat the contract. The West player at Table #1 made the safety play of taking the ♠A right away and leading another spade, and was well rewarded for his careful play, winning 10 IMPs.

BOARD #6

NORTH
Dealer: East
Vulnerable: East-West
- ♠ 6 3
- ♥ 7 4 2
- ♦ 9 6 3
- ♣ A K Q 8 3

WEST
- ♠ 9 5
- ♥ 1 0 9 6 5 3
- ♦ 1 0 7
- ♣ 1 0 9 6 5

EAST
- ♠ K J 1 0 8 4
- ♥ Q J
- ♦ K Q J 8
- ♣ J 4

SOUTH
- ♠ A Q 7 2
- ♥ A K 8
- ♦ A 5 4 2
- ♣ 7 2

Results:

Table #1: 3 NT by South, down one (−50 for N-S, +50 for E-W).

Table #2: 3 NT by South, making nine tricks (+400 for N-S, −400 for E-W).

Suggested Bidding

WEST	NORTH	EAST	SOUTH
		1♠	1NT
Pass	3NT	Pass	Pass
Pass			

South has a stopper in spades and so, with a balanced hand and 17 HCPs, overcalls 1NT over the 1♠ opening bid. With 9 HCPs plus 1 for the five-card club suit, North has enough to raise to game.

Suggested Play

East should lead the ♠9, top of a doubleton in partner's suit. Declarer has two spade tricks, two heart tricks, one diamond and three sure club tricks for a total of eight tricks. Two extra tricks can be developed in clubs if the missing clubs are divided 3–3. However, the missing clubs are more likely to be divided 4–2, so South should take the precaution of playing a low club from both hands after winning the first spade trick. When the opponents lead another spade, South can win and play his remaining club over to dummy's ♣A, ♣K and ♣Q. Even though the suit breaks 4–2, dummy's remaining ♣8 is a winner since one round of clubs has already been played.

Notes

The South player at Table #1 did not foresee the need to give up a club trick. He won the first spade trick and then took the next three club tricks. When the suit did not divide 3–3, he could establish another club winner by giving up a club trick, but there was no way to get back to the dummy to take the club winner. Declarer went down a trick. The South player at Table #2 found the safe line of play for the contract and his team won 10 IMPs for their net score of +450.

♠ *RESULT OF THE MATCH* ♠

TEAM #1

Table #1 (N-S)				Table #2 (E-W)				Net Score	IMPs
Board	Contract	Result	Score	Board	Contract	Result	Score		
1	4♥ N	4	420	1	3NT N	−2	100	+520	11
2	5♦ E X	−1	100	2	4♠ S	4	−620	−520	−11
3	4♠ W	−1	100	3	3♠ W	3	140	+240	6
4	4♥ S X	4	790	4	3NT E	3	600	+1390	16
5	4♠ W	4	−420	5	4♠ W	−1	−50	−470	−10
6	3NT	−1	−50	6	3NT S	3	−400	−450	−10
									+2

TEAM #2

Table #1 (E-W)				Table #2 (N-S)				Net Score	IMPs
Board	Contract	Result	Score	Board	Contract	Result	Score		
1	4♥ N	4	−420	1	3NT N	−2	−100	−520	−11
2	5♦ E X	−1	−100	2	4♠ S	4	620	+520	11
3	4♠ W	−1	−100	3	3♠ W	3	−140	−240	−6
4	4♥ S X	4	−790	4	3NT E	3	−600	−1390	−16
5	4♠ W	4	420	5	4♠ W	−1	50	+470	10
6	3NT	−1	50	6	3NT S	3	400	+450	10
									−2

After an exciting match, Team #1 won by 2 IMPs. With all the big exchanges of IMPs, there will be plenty of hands to discuss following the game.

LESSON 7

The Individual

Introducing the Individual
New Partnerships
Tactics—Sacrificing
Summary

Workshop Material
Group Activities
Sample Boards

So far, we have seen how duplicate can be played as either a pair event or a team event. In both types of game, you play with the same partner or teammates throughout the event. In this lesson, we will look at another exciting form of duplicate bridge, one which lets you play with a number of different partners throughout the game.

♠ *INTRODUCING THE INDIVIDUAL* ♠

The format which allows you to play with different partners throughout the game is called an *Individual*. For those who have a spirit of adventure and like to meet new people, the Individual can be one of the most fascinating types of game.

How It Works

In an Individual, you play from one to three hands with as many different partners as time permits. You have only a few moments to discuss conventions with each of your new partners, so your overall result will depend on both your playing skill and your ability to get along with unfamiliar partners.

In a typical movement, you are assigned a player number and given a starting table and direction. For example, suppose you start off as the East player at Table #3. The director puts three boards on the table and tells you to shuffle them and play only the first board with your current partner, the player sitting West. After the first board is completed, the director instructs the East and South players to exchange places. You will now be North's partner for the second board. For the third board, the director instructs the current South and West players to exchange places so that you will be partnered by the original South player who is now sitting in the East chair. Your movement would look something like this:

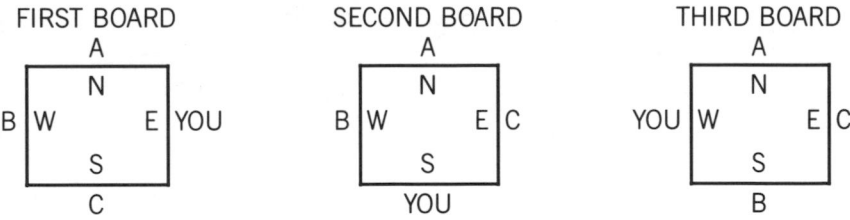

At the end of three boards, the director will announce the move for the next round. The North players usually remain stationary while the East, South and West players each move to different tables. There are various types of movement, but this is a common one. All of this may sound a bit confusing, but the idea is to allow you to partner as many of the other players as possible while making sure that you do not play the same board more than once. The director will take care of organizing the movement. All you need to do is follow the instructions and have a good time.

Scoring an Individual

Since North usually remains stationary, he is responsible for scoring. Because the other players play in different directions, you have to keep track of each of them using the player number which they were originally assigned. A typical Individual scoreslip looks like this:

N-S Players' Nos.	Contract	By	M a d e	D o w n	SCORE		N-S Match-points	E-W Players' Nos.	E-W Match-points
					N-S	E-W			
/								/	
/								/	
/								/	
/								/	
/								/	
/								/	
/								/	
/								/	

OFFICIAL TRAVELING SCORE
(Individual)

Board No. [ ]

North must be careful to put the appropriate pair numbers in the column marked "N-S Players" and the appropriate East-West pair numbers in the column for "E-W Players." The rest of the scoreslip is very similar to that for a regular duplicate game.

At the end of the game, the director will matchpoint the boards and give each individual the appropriate number of matchpoints for each board on the recap sheet. The winner will be the player with the largest total of matchpoints. The reason the game is a little more difficult for the director is that he has twice as much work to do in entering the results since they are entered for each player rather than each pair.

♠ *NEW PARTNERSHIPS* ♠

Since you do not have much time to discuss your conventions with each new partner in an Individual event, it is best to keep things very simple. In fact, this is the same type of approach you should take with any unfamiliar partner, even if you are playing together for an entire game. You need discuss only the most fundamental methods that you will use. Players who come from the same area will usually be using the same general approach.

At an Individual Event

When playing in an Individual — where you have a minute or less to discuss your "system" — it is important to focus on only a few key questions. Here are some suggestions:

- Do you play the Stayman convention?
- Do you play limit or jump raises?

The assumption is that anything you do not have time to discuss is treated as natural. You will notice, for example, that you did not bother to ask about the notrump range. Usually people who play regularly in the same game will know whether the standard range is 15–17 or 16–18. It may be that you are playing a 15–17 range and your partner will assume that you are playing 16–18. The one point difference is unlikely to be significant. First, the particular board you play with that partner may not involve a notrump opening bid and, even if it does, the responses are similar whichever the range. It is likely you will get to the same contract as everyone else. Of course, if some players in your area play the weak notrump, 12–14, then you might want to clarify the range.

At any rate, assume that partner's opening bid shows his longest suit and about 13–21 points and that new suits by responder are forcing. The other players will make the same assumptions about your bids. Notice that you do not bother asking about any exotic conventions. It is unlikely that the need for such conventions will come up while you are playing a board or two with any particular partner and it is best to avoid using anything that you have not fully discussed. Not all players agree on how the same convention should be used.

There will always be times when you are destined to have a bidding misunderstanding. This is what makes an Individual a lot of fun. Although you might end up in a ridiculous contract, it is just one board and, presumably, you are competing against pairs who will also have bidding misunderstandings. It tends to even out in the end; you will get both bottom and top boards through such bidding adventures.

Playing with a New Partner

It is not only in an Individual event that you encounter the experience of playing with an unfamiliar partner. You might arrive at a game with no partner and the director will pair you with someone with whom you have never played. Or, halfway through a team game, you might rearrange your partnerships. In these situations, you will have a little longer to fill out your Convention Card, so let's look at the approach you should take.

Completing the Convention Card

Filling out the Convention Card is a useful way of finding out your partner's approach to the game, even though the Convention Card is primarily for the opponents' use during the game. Normally, you fill it out by starting at the top and going through the sections step by step.

If you have never met your partner before, getting his name is the first step. The next is to take a look at the big picture. What is your general approach? Hopefully you have both agreed to play "standard." We won't go through the entire card in detail, but let's look at how you might organize your discussion of a particular section. If we look at the section on notrump opening bids, here are the types of points you might want to cover:

- What is the range of the 1 NT opening bid? For example, it might be either 15–17 or 16–18. It is assumed that responses are standard. For example, with 0–7 points, you either pass or bid a five-card or longer suit (except clubs) at the two level.
- Do you play the Stayman convention? If the answer is yes, the next question is what type of Stayman? Is a 2♣ response forcing all the way to game or only for one round (the standard approach, referred to as *Non-forcing Stayman*).
- What do jumps in a minor suit show? What do jumps in a major suit show? You may want to discuss other variations such as how you handle interference by the opponents. The amount of detail you go into will depend on how experienced the two of you are. In general, try not to go above your heads. Keep things to the level of the least experienced member of the partnership.
- What is the range of an opening 2 NT bid? What does an opening 3 NT bid show?

In general, discuss each section as much as time permits until you are fairly sure you are both on the same wavelength. Do not be upset if your partner does not want to play the same conventions as you do. The number of conventions a player has at his disposal is not indicative of his skill level. Many players assume that someone who does not play as many conventions as they do is an inferior player. They might even go back to the director to get another partner — only to find, at the end of the game, that they gave up a winner.

Handling the Partnership

The game of bridge involves a combination of skill, luck and the ability to get on with your partner. Having a good relationship with your partner is important in both regular and new partnerships. It goes beyond being polite. Remember, you and your partner are on the same team. If you are so much better than your partner that you cannot help being irritated by the way he bids or plays throughout the game, or you are so much less experienced than your partner that you continually feel intimidated and ill at ease, it is time to find another partner. On the other hand, many very fine players enjoy playing with someone less experienced than they are. It gives them an opportunity to get back to the basics and presents the challenge of trying to make every bid and signal as clear as possible to their partner.

Any detailed discussion of the way a board was bid or played should be left until you are away from the table. It may help to immediately clarify a misunderstanding over a convention you are using which is likely to come up again during the game, but any further discussion should be left until after the heat of the battle. Most players are not able to correctly analyze a board very quickly at the table. What may appear obvious on the surface may involve a number of factors not so apparent to one or both partners.

You want to avoid making a remark or comment that you may later regret. Making polite and encouraging remarks is a very effective way to get the best performance from the partnership. When partner puts down the dummy, you should say, "Thank you, partner," even if it is not the dummy you were expecting. There is no point in encouraging the opponents by letting them know that you are dissatisfied with the contract. An occasional "Well played, partner" at the end of board will help the partnership harmony. Never point out an apparent mistake by partner — or by an opponent — at the end of a board. A simple "Bad luck" or "I would have played it the same way" will suffice. Partner will already be feeling bad enough if he realizes that he has made a mistake. If he has not seen the mistake, so much the better — especially if further analysis shows it was not a mistake at all.

♠ TACTICS—SACRIFICING ♠

The general approach to duplicate bridge is to try to bid the contracts your side can make and to try to defeat the opponents in the contracts that they bid. However, since you get matchpoints for every pair you beat in your direction, you can also do well if you lose fewer points than other pairs holding your cards.

The Sacrifice

Suppose your opponents, who are vulnerable, bid 4♥ and can take 10 tricks. They will get 620 points for bidding and making their game. If this is the normal result on the board, then the only way to do better than the other pairs is by losing fewer than 620 points. You might be able to do this by bidding a contract of your own, such as 4♠, which, even though it will not make, will cost fewer than 620 points. If you are not vulnerable you can afford to be beaten as many as three tricks and still show a profit because, even if doubled, you will lose only 500 points. This is called taking a *sacrifice*.

Of course, you may be risking a bad result by bidding if you are defeated four tricks. Now if the contract is doubled and you are not vulnerable, your opponents will get 800 points and likely a top board. It is a delicate decision whether or not a sacrifice will be worthwhile. The opponents may not be able to make their game contract and you would lose several hundred points instead of collecting the penalty for defeating them.

How can you be sure that the opponents will make their contract and the penalty you will suffer will be less than the value of their game? There is no way to be sure. You have to use your judgment. For example, suppose partner opens the biding 3♠, the opponent on your right overcalls 4♥, and this is your hand:

♠ Q 10 7 5
♥ 7 3
♦ A 8 6 4 2
♣ 6 4

If you are not vulnerable and your opponents are vulnerable, bidding 4♠ is likely to be the right decision. Your partner has shown a weak hand with about seven spades. Even if partner holds both the ace and king of his suit, you will not be able to take more than one spade trick since you hold at least 11 spades between you. Combined with your ♦A, it looks as if the opponents have at most two losers. They should make their 4♠ contract, likely with one or more overtricks. If partner has a singleton diamond, he may be able to get a ruff, but you still do not expect to defeat the contract. Since partner has a weak hand, you do not expect to make your 4♠ contract. On the other hand, you do not expect to be defeated more than three tricks. Partner should get at least six spade tricks and the ♦A. If the opponents double you, it will cost, at most, 500 points rather than 620 points.

Another advantage of bidding 4♠ is that the opponents may not want to double you but prefer to bid on to 5♥. Your chance of defeating this contract is better than that of defeating 4♥. If they do bid 5♥, you can still decide whether or not it would be reasonable to sacrifice in 5♠. Note that your partner will not be able to make this decision. He has described his hand and does not know whether your 4♠ bid was made as a sacrifice or with the intention of making the contract.

Usually, pushing the opponents one level beyond game is enough since you have probably placed them at a disadvantage with respect to the other players in the field. You must also be careful not to push the opponents into a contract they would not otherwise reach but which is likely to succeed. If you bid 5♠ with the above hand, it may turn out to be a profitable sacrifice but the opponents might decide to bid 6♥. Can you be sure of defeating that contract? If you do not think so, you may find yourself bidding 6♠ and the penalty may become greater than the value of their game. You will get a poor result relative to the rest of the field if no other pair bids up to the six level.

Good playing strength combined with not much defensive strength tends to make a sacrifice worthwhile. Let's look at a typical situation where it is not best to bid on. Your partner opens 1♠, your right-hand opponent overcalls 2♥, and this is your hand:

♠ 9 7 6 5
♥ A J
♦ J 10 9 3
♣ 8 4 2

You raise to 2♠ and your left-hand opponent bids 4♥. Partner passes as does the opponent on your right, and it is back to you. Do you sacrifice? If you look only at your hand, you might expect the opponents to make their contract since you have only the ♥A as a sure defensive trick. However, it would be poor tactics to make a sacrifice bid of 4♠ with this hand since you do not have any real idea of the offensive or defensive potential of the combined partnership hands. You have accurately described your hand to partner with your raise to 2♠. It is now up to him. He may have enough defensive strength to give you a good chance of defeating the contract. He may also have inadequate offensive strength to prevent your side being defeated too many tricks in a contract of 4♠. For example, suppose this is your partner's hand:

> ♠ A Q 8 4 3
> ♥ 10 9 8
> ♦ K 4
> ♣ K J 3

Looking at the combined hands, you might expect to defeat 4♥. On the other hand, if you were in 4♠, it is unlikely you would make it and the penalty could be very large. Let's change opener's hand to the following:

> ♠ K Q J 4 3 2
> ♥ 7 3
> ♦ A Q 4 2
> ♣ 7

With this type of hand, partner would be quick to bid 4♠ over the opponents' 4♥ bid. He may not be able to make 4♠, but it is unlikely that this type of hand will provide enough defensive tricks to defeat the opponents' 4♥ contract. Any penalty suffered is likely to be less than the value of the opponents' game. Sacrificing in 4♠ might also push them to 5♥, where you stand a better chance of defeating them.

If you are planning to save (sacrifice), it is generally a good tactic to bid as high as you can as soon as you can. The more room you take away from the opponents — and the sooner you take it from them — the more pressure you put on them and the more likely they are to make a mistake. For example, suppose partner opens with a preemptive 3♥ bid, the opponent on your right passes, and you have this hand:

> ♠ 5
> ♥ K 5 4 3
> ♦ J 9 8 5 2
> ♣ 9 4 2

Opposite partner's weak three-bid, you certainly do not expect to make a game. Since your right-hand opponent has passed, you might think your side could end up playing the contract in 3♥. However, this is unrealistic. It is more than likely that the missing strength is held by your left-hand opponent. Looking at all your hearts and the singleton spade, it is quite likely that the opponents will make any contract they bid if they do come into the auction. They should be able to make at least 4♠ and maybe a small or grand slam. With this type of hand, you should take action immediately to try and put the maximum pressure on your opponents.

You might try bidding 4♥. Perhaps this will persuade your left-hand opponent you have a strong hand and he will not enter the auction. This might be a good tactic against inexperienced opponents. However, it is unlikely to work against experienced opponents. You want to bid as high as you are willing to go right away. A bid such as 5♥ would leave the opponents with very little room to explore their best contract. Such a tactic is called taking an *advance sacrifice* since you are sacrificing in advance of their decision.

♠ *SUMMARY* ♠

In an Individual event you play with a number of different partners and the overall winner is the player who accumulates the most matchpoints. Since you do not play many boards with each partner, there is no time to discuss your bidding methods in any detail. You should try keep your bidding as simple as possible, using only the "standard" conventions that you are sure your partner is familiar with.

When playing with a new partner, use the process of filling out the Convention Card as a basis for discussion of the methods you are playing. Make sure that you limit your conventions to only those that are familiar to the least experienced member of the partnership. Avoid any detailed discussions during the game. There will be plenty of time after the game to deal with any problems the partnership might have encountered.

If the opponents bid to a contract that is likely to make, one way to try to improve your score is by taking a sacrifice — bidding a contract that is unlikely to make but where the penalty, even if doubled, is likely to be less than the value of the opponents' contract. The best boards for a sacrifice are those with good offensive potential but little defensive potential.

♠ *GROUP ACTIVITIES* ♠

Exercise One — The Individual

You are playing in an individual event and the director assigns you a starting position as South at Table #2. Sitting North at your table is Player A. Sitting West is player B and sitting East is player C. You are to play one board with each player as a partner. The director instructs the players sitting South and East to exchange places after the first board and the players then sitting South and West to exchange places after the second board.

    1. Who will be your partner on the first board?
    2. Who will be your partner on the second board?
    3. Who will be your partner on the third board?
    4. Which player will enter the results on the scoreslip for each board?

Exercise Two — New Partnerships

You are playing in an individual and you have time to ask your new partner only two quick questions about his bidding style before you start to play. What might you ask?

Exercise Three — Tactics—The Sacrifice

Your side is not vulnerable and the opponents are vulnerable. Partner opens the bidding with a preemptive bid, 3♠, the opponent on your right doubles and you hold the following hand:

♠ K J 5
♥ 8 6 3
♦ K Q 7 6 5
♣ 7 2

If you assume that your partner's hand looks something like this:

♠ A Q 7 6 4 3 2
♥ 9
♦ 8 4 2
♣ 8 5

    1. What do you think will happen if you say pass?
    2. How many tricks might your side take in a spade contract?
    3. How many tricks might your side take defending a heart contract?
    4. What should you bid? Why?

♠ *SAMPLE BOARDS* ♠

BOARD #1

Dealer: North
Vulnerable: None

NORTH
♠ A J 8
♥ A 5
♦ A K 8 5 2
♣ A J 10

WEST
♠ 10 6 4 2
♥ Q 6
♦ Q J 9 6 4
♣ 7 4

EAST
♠ K 9 5
♥ J 8 4 2
♦ 10 3
♣ K Q 9 2

SOUTH
♠ Q 7 3
♥ K 10 9 7 3
♦ 7
♣ 8 6 5 3

OFFICIAL TRAVELING SCORE
(Individual)

Board No. 1

N-S Players' Nos.	Contract	By	Made	Down	SCORE N-S	SCORE E-W	N-S Match-points	E-W Players' Nos.	E-W Match-points
1/13	4 H	S		1		50		7/19	
6/18	3 NT	N	3		400			12/24	
5/17	4 H	S		2		100		11/23	
4/16	3 NT	N		1		50		10/22	
3/15	3 NT	N	3		400			9/21	
2/14	3 NT	N		1		50		8/20	

Suggested Bidding

WEST	NORTH	EAST	SOUTH
	2 NT	Pass	3♥
Pass	3 NT	Pass	Pass
Pass			

With a balanced hand and 21 HCPs plus 1 point for the five-card diamond suit, North has enough to open the bidding 2 NT. South, holding 5 HCPs plus 1 for the five-card heart suit, knows there is enough combined strength for game. The only decision is whether the partnership belongs in hearts or notrump. South can find out by bidding 3♥, which is forcing and asks North to choose between 3 NT and 4♥. With only a doubleton heart, North chooses 3 NT.

Suggested Play

With only two touching high cards, East will probably lead a low club against 3 NT and North will win the first trick with the ♣10, giving him two sure tricks in the suit. Even if East led the ♣K, North can get two tricks in the suit. In addition to the two club tricks, North has one sure trick in spades, two in hearts and two in diamonds. Two more tricks are needed to make the contract. One trick could be developed in spades by driving out the opponents' ♠K or a trick might be developed in diamonds if the missing diamonds are divided 4–3. The heart suit, however, offers the best potential for extra tricks. By playing the ♥A and ♥K and leading the suit again, two extra tricks will be developed if the missing hearts divide 3–3 or, as on the actual hand, one of the opponents' high hearts appears on the second round. In this case the other heart honor can be driven out by leading dummy's ♥10 (or ♥9).

When East wins the ♥J, he will probably lead another club to drive out North's remaining high card. North still needs an entry to dummy to get to the established hearts. He can do this by leading a spade toward dummy's ♠Q, hoping that East has the ♠K. East can win the ♠K and take his two club tricks, but declarer has the rest.

Notes

Since there are many pitfalls in getting to the best contract and making it, any North-South pair that bids and makes 3 NT should get an excellent result.

BOARD #2

Dealer: East
Vulnerable: North-South

NORTH
♠ A 10 8 3
♥ K J 7 4
♦ 8 4
♣ A J 5

WEST
♠ J 7 6
♥ A 10 5
♦ A Q 7 2
♣ Q 8 6

EAST
♠ K Q 5
♥ 9 8 3
♦ J 10 6 5 3
♣ 9 3

SOUTH
♠ 9 4 2
♥ Q 6 2
♦ K 9
♣ K 10 7 4 2

OFFICIAL TRAVELING SCORE
(Individual)

Board No. | 2

N-S Players' Nos.	Contract	By	Made	Down	SCORE		N-S Match-points	E-W Players' Nos.	E-W Match-points
					N-S	E-W			
1/19	2 D	W	3			110		7/13	
6/24	4 C	S		2		200		12/18	
5/23	3 D	W	3			110		11/17	
4/22	3 D	W	3	50				10/16	
3/21	3 C	S		1		100		9/15	
2/20	3 C	S	3		110			8/14	

Suggested Bidding

WEST	NORTH	EAST	SOUTH
		Pass	Pass
1♦	Double	2♦	3♣
Pass	Pass	3♦	Pass
Pass	Pass		

This may prove to be a lively partscore battle. With 13 HCPs and support for the unbid suits, North should make a takeout double of West's 1♦ opening bid. If East raises to 2♦, this should not stop South from competing with 3♣. He has 8 HCPs and a five-card suit. North will not expect too much from South since South could jump a level if he were interested in inviting to game. When the bidding gets back to East, he will have to decide whether to defend 3♣ or bid on to 3♦. With five-card support for partner's suit and only a doubleton club, East will probably elect to bid again.

Suggested Play

North-South can defeat 3♦ if they lead hearts soon enough. They will get two heart tricks, two club tricks and the ♠A. However, most North players will start by leading the ♣A and, if South makes an encouraging signal, continue by leading a club to South's ♣K. This establishes West's ♣Q as a trick and he can use it to discard one of dummy's hearts. Now West can give up a heart and trump his remaining loser in the dummy. When the diamond finesse proves successful, West ends up making the contract.

If South plays in clubs, there is a variety of possible results. In theory, East-West should get two spade tricks, a heart trick and two diamond tricks by trapping South's ♦K. They might also get a club trick if South does not guess who has the missing ♣Q. In practice, West may lead the ♦A, establishing South's ♦K as a trick, or the defenders may not lead spades soon enough, allowing South to establish his heart suit and discard a spade loser on an extra heart winner in dummy. If South also guesses to play a club to the ♣J, finessing against West's ♣Q, he might even make the contract.

Notes

The vulnerability can play an important part in the scoring when both sides are competing. Since North-South are vulnerable, they cannot afford to be defeated two tricks — or even one if they are doubled — since they will get a bottom board.

BOARD #3

Dealer: South
Vulnerable: East-West

NORTH
♠ 6
♥ 7 6 5 4
♦ K 9 3 2
♣ A 9 6 3

WEST
♠ A Q 9 4
♥ K Q 8 3
♦ A 8 7 5
♣ 10

EAST
♠ K J 7 5 2
♥ A 10 9 2
♦ Q 10 6
♣ 8

SOUTH
♠ 10 8 3
♥ J
♦ J 4
♣ K Q J 7 5 4 2

OFFICIAL TRAVELING SCORE
(Individual)

Board No. 3

N-S Players' Nos.	Contract	By	M a d e	D o w n	SCORE		N-S Match-points	E-W Players' Nos.	E-W Match-points
					N-S	E-W			
1/7	3 C	S		1		50		19/13	
6/12	4 S	E	5			650		24/18	
5/11	5 C X	S		3		500		23/17	
4/10	5 C	S		3		150		22/16	
3/9	5 S	E		1	100			21/15	
2/8	5 S	E	5			650		20/14	

Suggested Bidding

WEST	NORTH	EAST	SOUTH
		3♣	Double
Double	5♣	Double (?)	Pass
Pass	Pass		

South should open with a preemptive bid of 3♣, showing a weak hand with a long suit. West has the right type of hand to make a takeout double to compete for the contract. Since his side is not vulnerable, North may decide to take a sacrifice in 5♣. By jumping to 5♣ right away, he puts the maximum pressure on the opponents. In view of his partner's takeout double, East knows that his side has the majority of strength. However, he must make his first bid at the five level. A penalty double is a reasonable choice, but a bid of 5♠ may result in a better score. If East bids 5♠, however, West may be tempted to carry on to 6♠, getting the partnership too high. Such auctions make the game exciting for both sides.

Suggested Play

If North-South reach 5♣, they will probably lose only one spade trick, one heart trick and one diamond trick. South can trump his remaining spade losers in the dummy and can avoid two diamond losers by leading toward dummy's ♦K.

If West ends up playing 5♠, he will have to be careful to avoid losing two diamond tricks along with a club trick. After drawing trumps, West can take the ♦A and lead a diamond toward the ♦Q and ♦10 in his hand. If North plays a low diamond, West will have to guess whether to play the ♦Q, hoping North has the ♦K, or the ♦10, hoping North has the ♦J.

Notes

Since East-West can make 4♥ or 4♠, probably with an overtrick, a North-South sacrifice in 5♣ will work out well, even if the contract is doubled. Most pairs will find the sacrifice, so any North-South pair that lets East-West play the hand at 4♥ or 4♠ will get a poor result. If East-West choose to bid on to 5♥ or 5♠, rather than defend 5♣, they will do well — provided they make the contract!

BOARD #4

Dealer: West
Vulnerable: Both

NORTH
♠ Q95
♥ J52
♦ QJ
♣ A10874

WEST
♠ AK73
♥ 86
♦ A875
♣ KQ2

EAST
♠ J6
♥ AK74
♦ 6432
♣ J65

SOUTH
♠ 10842
♥ Q1093
♦ K109
♣ 93

OFFICIAL TRAVELING SCORE (Individual)									
Board No.								4	

N-S Players' Nos.	Contract	By	Made	Down	SCORE		N-S Match-points	E-W Players' Nos.	E-W Match-points
					N-S	E-W			
2/14	2 NT	W	2			120		8/20	
1/18	3 NT	W		2	200			11/21	
6/16	3 D	W	3			110		9/22	
5/13	2 NT	W		1	100			12/23	
4/17	3 NT	W		1	100			10/24	
3/15	1 NT	W	3			150		7/19	

Suggested Bidding

WEST	NORTH	EAST	SOUTH
1 NT	Pass	2♣	Pass
2♠	Pass	2 NT	Pass
Pass	Pass		

With 9 HCPs, East has enough strength to invite partner to game after the 1 NT opening bid. Holding a four-card heart suit, East should start off by using the Stayman convention to find out if West also has four hearts. When West shows his four-card spade suit, East can go back to 2 NT, showing the invitational strength of his hand. If he held 10 or more points, he would jump to game. With only 16 HCPs, West should decline the invitation.

Suggested Play

Against a notrump contract, North should start off by leading a low club, hoping to develop tricks in the suit. West has two sure spade tricks, two heart tricks and a diamond trick. With the opponents leading clubs, he will get two tricks in that suit and needs one more trick to make 2 NT. There are two ways West can try to develop the extra trick he needs. He can win the first club trick in his hand and lead a small spade toward dummy's ♠ J, hoping North has the ♠ Q. Whether or not North takes the ♠ Q, West will end up with three spade tricks, rather than two. The other choice is to play diamonds, giving up two tricks to the opponents and hoping the missing diamonds are divided 3–2. On the actual hand, either method will work.

If West gets to 3 NT, he will need both the extra spade trick and the extra diamond trick. Unfortunately, this means giving up the lead three times. In the meantime, North can develop enough club tricks to defeat the contract.

Notes

With the temptation to bid game whenever the opportunity arises, some East-West pairs will get overboard on this deal and, unless they are very lucky, will suffer defeat. The more conservative East-West pairs will be rewarded on this deal.

BOARD #5

NORTH
Dealer: North
Vulnerable: North-South
♠ 762
♥ A 10 7 3
♦ 9 4 2
♣ K 9 3

WEST
♠ 10 9 4
♥ Q 6 5
♦ A 10 8 7 3
♣ 7 6

EAST
♠ Q J 8 3
♥ J 9 4 2
♦ Q 6
♣ Q 10 5

SOUTH
♠ A K 5
♥ K 8
♦ K J 5
♣ A J 8 4 2

OFFICIAL TRAVELING SCORE (Individual)									
Board No.							5		

N-S Players' Nos.	Contract	By	Made	Down	SCORE		N-S Match-points	E-W Players' Nos.	E-W Match-points
					N-S	E-W			
2/20	3 NT	S		1		100		8/14	
1/21	3 NT	S	4		630			11/18	
6/22	3 NT	N	5		660			9/16	
5/23	3 C	S	4		130			12/13	
4/24	3 NT	S	4		630			10/17	
3/19	3 NT	S		1		100		7/15	

Suggested Bidding

WEST	NORTH	EAST	SOUTH
	Pass	Pass	1♣
Pass	1♥	Pass	2 NT
Pass	3 NT	Pass	Pass
Pass			

With 19 HCPs and a five-card suit, South is too strong to open 1 NT. Instead, he should start with 1♣ and jump to 2 NT over North's response to show his strength. With 7 HCPs and knowing South has 19–21 points, North can raise to game.

Suggested Play

West should start off by leading a low diamond from his long suit and East should play the ♦Q, third hand high. After South wins the ♦K, he wants to avoid letting East get the lead because East can lead his remaining diamond, trapping South's ♦J and letting West take four diamond tricks to defeat the contract. East has become the *dangerous opponent*. There is no danger if a trick is lost to West since West cannot trap South's ♦J. Whether West plays the ♦A or a low diamond, South will get a trick with the ♦J.

Since it is safe to lose a trick to West, declarer should play a low club to dummy's ♣K and a low club back toward his hand. When West's ♣10 appears, South should finesse the ♣J. On the actual hand, the ♣J wins the trick and declarer ends up with two spade tricks, two heart tricks, a diamond trick and five club tricks — making an overtrick. If the finesse had lost, South would still end up with at least nine tricks.

Notes

Most pairs should get to 3 NT and make an overtrick. If, however, declarer plays the ♣A and ♣K, rather than taking the finesse, he is likely to go down in his contract if the opponents take their diamond tricks.

BOARD #6

Dealer: East
Vulnerable: East-West

NORTH
♠ A K J 6
♥ 10 8 7 3
♦ 8
♣ A 10 7 3

WEST
♠ Q 7 3
♥ A J 5 2
♦ 10 6 2
♣ J 8 4

EAST
♠ 8 4
♥ K 4
♦ A K Q J 7 4
♣ Q 6 2

SOUTH
♠ 10 9 5 2
♥ Q 9 6
♦ 9 5 3
♣ K 9 5

OFFICIAL TRAVELING SCORE
(Individual)

Board No. 6

N-S Players' Nos.	Contract	By	Made	Down	SCORE		N-S Match-points	E-W Players' Nos.	E-W Match-points
					N-S	E-W			
2/8	3 NT	W	3			600		20/14	
1/11	3 NT	W	4			630		21/18	
6/9	3 NT	W		2	200			22/16	
5/12	3 D	W	3			110		23/13	
4/10	3 S	S		2		100		24/17	
3/7	3 D	W		1	100			19/15	

Suggested Bidding

WEST	NORTH	EAST	SOUTH
		1♦	Pass
1♥	Double	3♦	Pass
3NT	Pass	Pass	Pass

After East's opening bid of 1♦ and West's response of 1♥, North has the right type of hand to make a takeout double. He has 12 HCPs plus 3 dummy points for the singleton diamond and he has support for the unbid suits, spades and clubs. North's double should not affect East's rebid. With 15 HCPs plus 2 points for the six-card suit, East has a medium strength hand and can show this by jumping to 3♦. With 8 HCPs, West has a close decision as to what to do over his partner's invitational bid. An aggressive West will elect to try for the 3NT game rather than stop in the partscore of 3♦.

Suggested Play

If West plays 3NT, North's defense will determine whether or not the contract is made. If he leads a low spade, West will win the trick with the ♠Q and take two heart tricks — three, if he takes the finesse — and six diamond tricks. A better lead for North is the ♠A, keeping the lead and waiting to see what his partner does. Without the ♠Q, South should play a low spade as a discouraging signal. If North interprets this correctly, he will realize that West has the ♠Q and he will want to get over to partner's hand so that he can lead a spade through and trap West's queen. Should he switch to a heart, hoping South has the ♥A, or to a club, hoping South has the ♣K? North's best play is to take the ♣A to see what South does. When South makes an encouraging signal by playing the ♣9, North will lead a club over to South's ♣K and South will lead a spade back to defeat the contract two tricks. If South had played a discouraging low club, North would lead a heart rather than another club.

Notes

The defense to 3NT is not easy, so any aggressive East-West pair that bids the game is likely to make it. Some East-West pairs will remain in partscore, however, and will consider themselves fortunate if North is the type of player who would find the winning defense against 3NT.

BOARD #7

Dealer: South
Vulnerable: Both

NORTH
♠ A K 8
♥ A 9 6
♦ A J 10
♣ 8 5 4 2

WEST
♠ 9 5 4
♥ Q 10
♦ K Q 8 5 3
♣ A K 3

EAST
♠ Q 10 6 3
♥ K 7 4 3
♦ 7 6
♣ J 7 6

SOUTH
♠ J 7 2
♥ J 8 5 2
♦ 9 4 2
♣ Q 10 9

OFFICIAL TRAVELING SCORE
(Individual)

Board No. 7

N-S Players' Nos.	Contract	By	Made	Down	SCORE N-S	SCORE E-W	N-S Match-points	E-W Players' Nos.	E-W Match-points
3/18	1 NT	N		1		100		11/20	
2/17	2 H	S		2		200		12/19	
1/15	1 NT	N	1		90			8/22	
6/14	2 D	W	2			90		10/21	
5/16	1 NT	E		1	100			7/24	
4/13	2 D	W		1	100			9/23	

Suggested Bidding

WEST	NORTH	EAST	SOUTH
			Pass
1♦	1 NT	Pass	Pass
Pass			

West will probably open 1♦ and North has a natural overcall of 1 NT. That should end the auction since East does not have enough to bid or double, South has nothing to say and West should not bid again. Other auctions are possible, however. North might choose to make a takeout double of the 1♦ opening bid. Alternatively, with 14 HCPs and a five-card suit, West might elect to open 1 NT if the partnership is playing 15–17 1 NT opening bids. In either case, the auction would take a different turn. With the points evenly divided, one side or the other should end up playing in a partscore contract.

Suggested Play

If North plays 1 NT, East will probably lead a diamond, partner's suit. North will end up with two diamond tricks to go with his two spade tricks and one heart trick. To develop the additional tricks he needs, North will have to play the club suit carefully. He should lead a small club toward dummy and finesse the ♣9 (or ♣10), hoping that East has the ♣J. When this finesse is successful, North can repeat it when he regains the lead. Eventually, North will get a trick with dummy's ♣Q and another trick from the fourth club in his hand, enough to make the contract. Of course, North may not spot this line of play and could end up being defeated.

Notes

As the scoreslip reflects, either side might end up declaring the contract. The number of matchpoints they get will depend on the number of tricks they make. If declarer makes his contract, he should get a good result. If he goes down, it will be the opponents who get a good result. This is normal on partscore hands where the points are evenly divided. Whichever side gets a plus score will tend to get the majority of the matchpoints.

BOARD #8

NORTH
Dealer: West
Vulnerable: None
♠ 8 7 3
♥ K Q J 9 7 2
♦ A J
♣ 9 2

WEST
♠ A Q J 10 6 4
♥ 6
♦ K Q 9
♣ Q 6 3

EAST
♠ K 9 5 2
♥ 4 3
♦ 8 7 4
♣ A 8 5 4

SOUTH
♠ —
♥ A 10 8 5
♦ 10 6 5 3 2
♣ K J 10 7

| | | | | | OFFICIAL TRAVELING SCORE (Individual) | | | | |

| | | | | | | | Board No. | 8 | |

N-S Players' Nos.	Contract	By	M a d e	D o w n	SCORE		N-S Match- points	E-W Players' Nos.	E-W Match- points
					N-S	E-W			
3/20	4 H	N	4		420			11/18	
2/19	5 H X	N		1		100		12/17	
1/22	4 S	W		1	50			8/15	
6/21	4 S	W	4			420		10/14	
5/24	5 H X	N	5		650			7/16	
4/23	4 H	N	5		450			9/13	

Suggested Bidding

WEST	NORTH	EAST	SOUTH
1♠	2♥	2♠	4♥
4♠	Pass	Pass	Pass

After West's 1♠ opening bid, North has a good hand to compete and overcalls 2♥. East has a natural raise to 2♠ and then it is up to South. With 8 HCPs plus 5 points for the spade void, South has enough to take partner to the game level, 4♥. Now, it is up to West. With only 14 HCPs and a six-card suit, he does not have enough to expect to make 4♠ after partner's raise to only 2♠. Nonetheless, defending 4♥ does not look like a good prospect either and West should probably "sacrifice" by bidding 4♠. This could make on a lucky day or drive the opponents up to 5♥. Even if West is defeated, the penalty will likely be less than the value of the opponents' game, assuming they can make it. The 4♠ bid may well end the auction since neither North nor South have enough to double. North or South might consider bidding 5♥, either hoping to make the contract or as a "sacrifice" if 4♠ is making.

Suggested Play

If West is left in 4♠, he will probably lose a heart trick, two diamond tricks and a club trick unless the defense gets careless. If North leads the ♦A, for example, West will lose only one diamond trick and end up making the contract.

If North plays in hearts, a lot will depend on how he guesses to play the club suit. If he finesses dummy's ♣J, he will likely end up losing two club tricks and one diamond trick. If he guesses to play a club toward dummy's ♣K, he will only lose one club trick and one diamond trick.

Notes

The scoreslip shows a number of different results, with large swings in both directions. Both sides have to decide whether to defend against the opponents' contract or bid on to try to buy the contract. Even when the contract is decided, a lot may hinge on the play. Game might be made in either direction.

BOARD #9

Dealer: North
Vulnerable: East-West

NORTH
♠ 9 5
♥ Q J 10 5 2
♦ A 6 2
♣ K 9 8

WEST
♠ 6 4 3 2
♥ 9 6 3
♦ J 8
♣ Q 10 6 3

EAST
♠ A K 7
♥ K 8
♦ K Q 10 7 5
♣ J 4 2

SOUTH
♠ Q J 10 8
♥ A 7 4
♦ 9 4 3
♣ A 7 5

OFFICIAL TRAVELING SCORE
(Individual)

	Board No.	9

N-S Players' Nos.	Contract	By	Made	Down	SCORE		N-S Match-points	E-W Players' Nos.	E-W Match-points
					N-S	E-W			
3/11	1 NT	E	1			90		20/18	
2/12	2 H	N	3		140			19/17	
1/8	1 NT	E		1	100			22/15	
6/10	4 H	N		1		50		21/14	
5/7	1 NT	E		2	200			24/16	
4/9	3 H	N	3		140			23/13	

Suggested Bidding

WEST	NORTH	EAST	SOUTH
	Pass	1 NT	Pass
Pass	Pass (?)		

North does not have quite enough to open the bidding in first position. East has a balanced hand with 16 HCPs and should open 1 NT. South does not have the right type of hand to enter the auction and West has nowhere to go. The spotlight now falls on North. He has already passed and is now in the balancing position. If he passes, that will end the auction. An aggressive North player might overcall 2♥, hoping partner will remember that he passed originally and therefore will not get too excited.

Suggested Play

If East is left to play in 1 NT, South will probably lead the ♠Q, top of a sequence. After winning the ♠K, East should try to establish his diamond suit by driving out North's ♦A. If North leads back a spade, partner's suit, East can take the trick with his ♠A and take his four diamond tricks. North-South will end up taking the rest of the tricks, but down one is not a bad result given the rather meager-looking dummy. North, however, has a chance to shine when he wins the ♦A. If he plays the ♥Q, East's ♥K will be trapped and the defenders can take five heart tricks to go with the ♦A, the ♠A and the ♣K, to defeat the contract two tricks. There is nothing East can do.

If North plays in a heart contract, he should lose only two spade tricks and two diamond tricks. He can avoid losing a heart trick by leading his ♥Q and trapping East's ♥K. If East leads the ♠A and ♠K before establishing his diamond tricks, North will be able to discard his diamond losers on dummy's remaining spades once trumps are drawn.

Notes

The vulnerability plays an important role on this board. Since North-South can make a partscore in hearts, East does not fare badly if he is defeated only one trick in 1 NT. If North-South find the defense to defeat East two tricks, however, they will collect 200 points and an excellent score. This may make some North players regret that they decided to balance with 2♥ and miss the chance to score 200 points.

BOARD #10

Dealer: East
Vulnerable: Both

NORTH
♠ J 4
♥ K 10 8 4 2
♦ J 9 7 2
♣ K 6

WEST
♠ K 8 2
♥ Q 3
♦ A 10 6 3
♣ J 7 4 2

EAST
♠ A Q 10 9 7 6 3
♥ 7 5
♦ 5
♣ 10 9 3

SOUTH
♠ 5
♥ A J 9 6
♦ K Q 8 4
♣ A Q 8 5

OFFICIAL TRAVELING SCORE
(Individual)

Board No. | 10

N-S Players' Nos.	Contract	By	M a d e	D o w n	SCORE		N-S Match-points	E-W Players' Nos.	E-W Match-points
					N-S	E-W			
4/15	4 H	N	4		620			12/21	
3/16	5 H	N		1		100		8/23	
2/13	4 H	N	5		650			11/22	
1/14	4 S X	E		2	500			10/24	
6/17	4 H	N		1		100		7/20	
5/18	4 S X	E		1	200			9/19	

Suggested Bidding

WEST	NORTH	EAST	SOUTH
		3♠	Double
Pass (?)	4♥	Pass	Pass
Pass (?)			

East has the perfect hand for a preemptive opening bid of 3♠ — a good seven-card suit and no defensive strength in the other suits. This does not present South with much of a problem since he has the right distribution for a takeout double. This will probably result in North-South playing at least at the four level, but South has some extra strength and does not want to be pushed around by East's preempt. West has a difficult decision as to whether or not to sacrifice in 4♠. He has some support for partner but also some defense against the opponents' contract. If he passes, North will have an easy choice of bidding 4♥ and, when this comes back to West, he will again have to decide what to do. In general, West should bid 4♠ right away if he wants to sacrifice. North may misjudge the hand and bid 5♥ rather than defend 4♠.

Suggested Play

In a 4♥ contract, North has to lose a spade and a diamond but is unlikely to lose a trick to West's ♥Q (eight ever, nine never). East, however, has a chance to defeat the contract if he leads his singleton diamond. West can win the ♦A and lead back a diamond for East to trump. West should lead back a high diamond, a suit preference signal for the higher-ranking suit, spades. If East interprets this correctly, he will lead a small spade over to West's ♠K and West will lead another diamond for East to trump. It is unlikely that many pairs will find this brilliant defense, however.

If East plays in a spade contract, he will have to lose two heart tricks and three club tricks, unless the defense gets careless and fails to untangle all its tricks.

Notes

Since the defense to defeat 4♥ is very difficult to find, East-West will probably get a good result for sacrificing in 4♠. If North bids on to 5♥, however, he will get a poor result if the defenders find their diamond ruff.

LESSON 8

Putting It Together

ACBL
Where Next?
Tactics — Defense
Summary

Workshop Material
Group Activities
Sample Boards

♠ *ACBL* ♠

In 1937, the American Bridge League and the United States Bridge Association merged to become the American Contract Bridge League. Since that time, this organization has grown into a full-time operation with headquarters in Memphis, Tennessee, and a membership approaching a quarter of a million. Once you become involved in duplicate bridge, you will become familiar with a variety of services that ACBL offers.

The Role of ACBL

The American Contract Bridge League, commonly known as *ACBL*, organizes duplicate bridge games at all levels across North America. It promotes the establishment of bridge as a competitive sport as well as a social pastime. ACBL does a large amount of charitable work. Over the years, it has helped raise millions of dollars for the benefit of a variety of charitable organizations.

Since the mid 1980's, ACBL has focused much of its energy on developing bridge teaching programs to bring the game to newcomers so that they can learn it in a way that is both comfortable and rewarding. The ACBL *Club, Diamond, Heart* and *Spade Series* are part of this program. ACBL is also busy finding new ways to promote the game to all parts of the community — schools, colleges, departments of recreation, etc.

Structure of ACBL

ACBL is primarily a membership organization. You can become a member of ACBL by sending in an application form along with an annual membership fee. When you join ACBL, you automatically become a member of your local *Unit*. Each Unit has its own board of directors, consisting of volunteers from the area who have been elected by the membership. The Unit is responsible for the promotion and advancement of bridge in the local community. There are more than 300 Units in North America, including Units in Canada, Mexico and Bermuda.

One of the major roles of the Unit is to schedule and organize local tournaments. These can be special events, such as a Unit-wide charity game or *sectional* tournaments. Each sectional tournament lasts for two or three days and consists of a variety of games for players of all levels. The Unit often organizes special social events to go alongside the bridge games — dinners, dances, panel shows, and so forth. In most areas, the Units work closely with the local bridge clubs and the clubs might have representatives on the Unit board of directors. Most Units put out a local publication informing members of the bridge activities in the area. These publications help you find out where the bridge clubs are located and where local tournaments are taking place. The publications often highlight the local winners of tournaments and often include articles about local bridge players.

Each Unit is part of a larger organization called a *District*. There are 25 Districts in North America. Each one elects a representative to the ACBL Board of Directors and three representatives to the Board of Governors of the ACBL. The District coordinates the efforts of the various Units and is responsible for scheduling and organizing *regional* tournaments, which are held in major population centers and last for about five days.

Each Member of the ACBL Board of Directors is elected for a three-year term. The directors determine the policies and make the major decisions concerning ACBL and its operation. They receive input from the Board of Governors and various committees that have been set up to deal with specific issues within the organization. Another function of the Board of Directors is the allocation and scheduling of the three *North American tournaments* that are run each year — the Spring, Summer and Fall North American Bridge Championships. These tournaments run for 10 days and comprise the major North American championship events.

The ACBL Management team, located at ACBL's headquarters, is responsible for carrying out the directives of the Board and performing the day-to-day administrative tasks necessary to keep the organization running effectively.

The Functions of ACBL

ACBL provides many benefits to its members. One of its major functions is to record the masterpoints won by each member in local clubs and at tournaments. In addition, each member receives the *ACBL BULLETIN* each month, a magazine filled with articles on bridge, schedules of upcoming events, winners of tournaments, book reviews and anything else of interest to the membership. ACBL also publishes newsletters for special interest groups, such as students, teachers and volunteer workers.

ACBL sanctions bridge clubs to run games for which masterpoints can be awarded. There are more than 4000 bridge clubs affiliated with ACBL. ACBL provides training for club directors and administers a test for certification. The affiliated clubs hold many special events organized by ACBL, such as charity games to support local and national charities, and International Fund Games to support players representing ACBL in international events. In these events, the deals are usually *pre-dealt* so that the same deals can be played at a number of different locations. The director passes out *hand records* to each table and asks the players to construct the hand shown on each record and put it in the appropriate duplicate board. The players then pass the boards they have made to another table so that they do not play the boards they have constructed. Analyses of the boards are written beforehand and then distributed to all the participants following the game. One of the most popular events of this type is the annual Epson Pairs in which ACBL members play the same hands as players from many other countries around the world.

ACBL sanctions the sectional, regional and NABC tournaments, and automatically records the masterpoints won by the participants at these events. In most tournaments, the boards are also pre-dealt and duplicated so that the players in different sections of each event can play the same boards.

Working with similar organizations around the world, ACBL arranges international bridge events and sends representatives to the World Bridge Federation meetings. Qualifying events are scheduled to help select the competitors who will represent ACBL in the world championships. ACBL also works with other countries in the development of the laws and regulations of the game.

ACBL provides an accreditation course for teachers, along with the supporting teacher manuals and student texts. It assists Unit Education Liaisons, many of whom coordinate in their areas the teachers and classes and arrange special student games (Bridge Plus+) for the graduates from the various bridge courses.

♠ WHERE NEXT? ♠

Finding a Game

When you are ready to play duplicate bridge, the next challenge is to locate your local duplicate bridge game. There are different levels of duplicate games organized in each area. There are more than 4000 ACBL bridge clubs. Clubs differ from one part of the country to another. Some run a game only one night a week which may be held in a church hall, a school, a golf club, a hotel, the cafeteria of a business, a local company — wherever the organizer can put enough tables and chairs. Other clubs have full-time premises and run games every day of the week. Many of the clubs run games for different levels of players and some have lesson programs where you can continue to improve your skill. When you play in a duplicate club that is affiliated with ACBL, you can earn the masterpoint awards given out for various levels of achievement.

You can usually locate a game by talking to friends who play or by looking in the phone book. If you have been taking lessons, your bridge teacher will know the location of local clubs and there might be a special *student game* (Bridge Plus+) in your area for the graduates from other bridge classes. If you have any difficulty, you can contact ACBL (2990 Airways Boulevard, Memphis, TN 38116–3847, 901–332–5586) and request a club directory.

When contacting a club, find out whether or not the club has special games for beginning players. Some areas hold student games (Bridge Plus+) and most clubs hold a *novice game* on at least one night during the week. Regular duplicate games are called *open games* — you are unlikely to be ready for such a game on your first time out. They play about 24 to 27 boards in a session, which usually lasts about three and a half hours. This can be quite a step up from a lesson environment. It is probably wise to start with a Bridge Plus+ or novice game. Most areas hold novice games during their local tournaments and this might be a place to start if none of the local clubs has an introductory game.

The First Time Out

Once you have found a game and decided to go, you may go with a partner or go on your own. Although some clubs arrange partnerships, you are likely to be more comfortable with someone you know. Do not feel that you have to find a whole table of four people; the organizers do that for you.

For your first game, make sure you arrive early. The person running the game will get very busy as game time approaches — selling entries, finding partners, setting up the movement. You want your introduction to be as relaxed as possible. When you arrive at the game, you will usually find people milling about, discussing hands from previous games or filling out Convention Cards. Your first step should be to talk to the organizer or director. When you explain that you are new to the game, the director will usually show you around or, if he is busy, introduce you to someone who can help you feel at ease. If you need a partner, let the director know early so that he can find someone suitable.

The size of the game will vary from club to club. Some will have 12 people, 3 tables, and others may have as many as 80 people, 20 tables. The director will organize the game and give you an entry form which will tell you your starting table. Once the game gets under way, you will soon find yourself getting involved in the familiar aspects of bidding and play and your surroundings will fade into the background. After a couple of sessions at the same club, you will feel like a regular and it won't be long before you know the names of many of the players you meet during the game.

Continuing On

Once you are comfortable playing in one or more of your local clubs, it is time to decide where you want to go from there. Many players are quite content to play in the same game every week. You will find your skill improves with experience, as you pick up pointers from the other players. If you are more ambitious, you will probably want to improve further by playing against better competition. You can move up from the Novice Game to the Open Game and then start playing in the local tournaments.

There are other ways to improve your game as well. You can take lessons on the more advanced aspects of the game. ACBL offers the Tournament Players' Lecture Series at its NABCs and there will be similar opportunities in your local area. There are many excellent books written about the game, although you should be careful to choose something that is not too far above your current level of play. Usually your teacher, club director or bridge-playing friends can recommend something at the appropriate level. When it comes to bidding, try to read the same books as your partner so that you are both on the same wavelength. It will not do you much good to play a fancy new convention if your partner is not familiar with it. After a game, you will see groups of players standing around discussing the boards. There is always room to learn something new.

♠ *TACTICS — DEFENSE* ♠

When you are in a rubber bridge game or a team game, your defensive objective is quite clear: to try to defeat the contract whenever possible. If you end up giving declarer an extra trick through your efforts to defeat him, the cost is small compared to the potential gain if you set the contract. In a matchpoint duplicate game, however, the situation is different. While the defenders are still trying to defeat the contract whenever possible, they must keep in mind that their real objective is to try to get a better result than the other pairs who hold the same cards that they hold. This often affects the defenders' tactics.

Take Your Tricks

A single extra trick made by declarer can give you a bottom result on a board if none of the other defenders in your direction allowed declarer to make the same extra trick. You must be careful to give nothing away. For example, suppose the auction has gone as follows:

WEST (YOU)	NORTH	EAST (PARTNER)	SOUTH
	1 NT	Pass	3♠
Pass	4♠	Pass	Pass
Pass			

You lead the ♥J against a contract of 4♠ and you see the following cards:

NORTH (DUMMY)
♠ Q J 9
♥ 7 3
♦ A K J 10 2
♣ K Q 2

WEST (YOU)
♠ K 3
♥ J 10 9 6 5
♦ Q 5
♣ A 7 6 3

Declarer wins the first trick in his hand with the ♥A, plays a low diamond to dummy's ♦K and then leads dummy's ♠Q, taking a finesse which loses to your ♠K. What now? You have one spade trick and you can see that your side is not going to take any diamond tricks. The only possible tricks for the defense are in hearts and clubs. Declarer won the first trick with the ♥A, so it is possible that partner holds the ♥K and ♥Q and your side can take a heart trick if you lead another heart. It is also possible, however, that declarer holds the ♥K. There is nothing to prevent him from winning the first trick with the ♥A and keeping the ♥K concealed to try to make things more difficult for the defense. What about the club suit? It looks as though you are entitled to only one trick. Declarer will be able to lead toward dummy's ♣K and ♣Q or may be able to discard any club losers on dummy's extra diamond winners.

After taking all this into consideration, you should *play the* ♣A. This is highly unlikely to help declarer make the contract since it appears that you are not going to be able to defeat it anyway. It does not give up your opportunity to take a heart trick since you can still lead a heart after you win a trick with the ♣A. Most importantly, it ensures that you get all the tricks to which you are entitled on the hand. Suppose this is the complete hand:

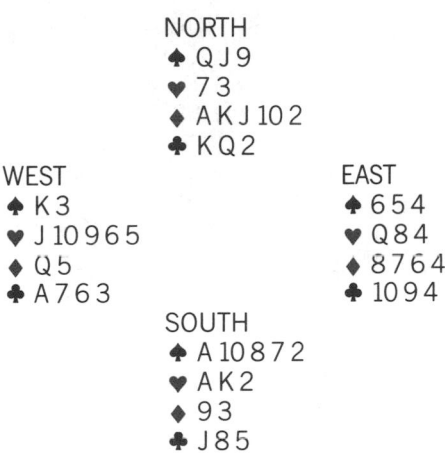

NORTH
♠ Q J 9
♥ 7 3
♦ A K J 10 2
♣ K Q 2

WEST
♠ K 3
♥ J 10 9 6 5
♦ Q 5
♣ A 7 6 3

EAST
♠ 6 5 4
♥ Q 8 4
♦ 8 7 6 4
♣ 10 9 4

SOUTH
♠ A 10 8 7 2
♥ A K 2
♦ 9 3
♣ J 8 5

If you were to lead another heart, declarer would win the trick, trump his losing heart in dummy, draw the remaining trumps and then lead a diamond. When your ♦Q appears, declarer would be able to discard all three of his clubs on the diamonds and end up making two overtricks. By taking your ♣A, you hold declarer to eleven tricks, ensuring that you get your fair share of the matchpoints on the board. If you let declarer make that extra overtrick, you might find yourself with a bottom result on the board if the other defenders all took their opportunity to take the ♣A.

Here is another example. Suppose you are West and hear the following auction:

WEST (YOU)	NORTH	EAST (PARTNER)	SOUTH
	1♠	Pass	3♣
Pass	3♠	Pass	4 NT
Pass	5♥	Pass	6 NT
Pass	Pass	Pass	

You find yourself on lead with the following hand:

♠ Q 4
♥ J 10 9 8
♦ A 7 2
♣ 8 6 5 3

The ♥J, top of a sequence, looks like a nice safe lead but is it? The opponents have bid quite strongly to their slam contract and it is likely that they have about 33 HCPs between them, meaning that you probably have the only high cards for your side. With North bidding spades twice, it is unlikely that you are going to get a trick with your ♠Q. In fact, the only trick you are likely to get is the ♦A. Playing matchpoint duplicate, you should lead the ♦A to make sure that you get it. The complete hand might look something like this:

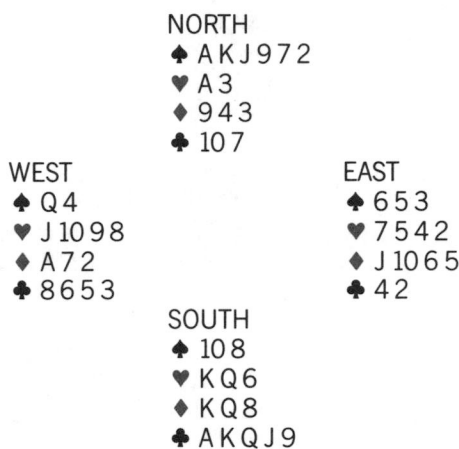

NORTH
♠ A K J 9 7 2
♥ A 3
♦ 9 4 3
♣ 10 7

WEST
♠ Q 4
♥ J 10 9 8
♦ A 7 2
♣ 8 6 5 3

EAST
♠ 6 5 3
♥ 7 5 4 2
♦ J 10 6 5
♣ 4 2

SOUTH
♠ 10 8
♥ K Q 6
♦ K Q 8
♣ A K Q J 9

If you lead anything but the ♦A, declarer can take all 13 tricks, making an overtrick. Leading an ace against a small slam is often a good idea. It may give you a chance to win the first two tricks if partner happens to hold the king in the same suit, or you may still have a trick in another suit. When playing matchpoint duplicate, taking your ace may give you a good result even when declarer takes the rest of the tricks.

Taking a Chance

It is not always good enough to merely take your tricks. Sometimes, you have to go all out to try to defeat the contract, even when it risks letting declarer make an overtrick. A typical situation is when you have doubled the opponents' contract. You are unlikely to get many matchpoints if they make the contract so you must try to find a way to defeat it. For example, suppose you are West and have the following hand:

♠ K J 3
♥ A Q 8 2
♦ A K 7 5 3
♣ 9

The auction proceeds:

WEST	NORTH (PARTNER)	EAST	SOUTH (**YOU**)
1 ♦	Pass	1 ♥	1 ♠
4 ♥	4 ♠	Pass	Pass
Double	Pass	Pass	Pass

With part of your strength being in the opponents' suit, you elect to double their 4♠ bid rather than bid on to 5♥. You lead the ♦A and see the following cards:

NORTH (DUMMY)
♠ Q 8 6 2
♥ 9 4 3
♦ J
♣ K 10 8 4 2

WEST (**YOU**)
♠ K J 3
♥ A Q 8 2
♦ A K 7 5 3
♣ 9

Dummy does not have much, but the singleton diamond means that you may have some difficulty defeating the contract. You have a sure trump trick and a likely heart trick but still need one more trick. There are a couple of possibilities. If partner has the ♥K and only a four-card heart suit, you will be able to take two heart tricks since declarer will have two heart losers. Alternatively, partner might have a club trick. If partner has the ♣A, you will be able to get a ruff as well and defeat the contract at least two tricks.

Suppose you decide to lead your singleton club at trick two, hoping partner has the ♣A and can give you a ruff. Unfortunately, declarer wins the trick with the ♣Q and plays the ♠A and a low spade toward dummy's ♠Q. You win this trick with the ♠K and have to decide what to do. It is now apparent that your partner does not have any club tricks and, if declarer has a singleton heart, you may not defeat the contract. Should you take your ♥A before declarer has a chance to discard any heart losers on dummy's long club suit? That would prevent any overtricks but you are going to get a very poor result if the opponents make their 4♠ doubled contract. Your only hope is that partner has the ♥K, quite likely since he has not shown up with any points so far. In case declarer has a singleton heart, you must lead a **low** heart to partner's king so that he can win the trick and lead back a club for you to ruff with your last trump, defeating the contract. You are hoping the complete hand looks something like this:

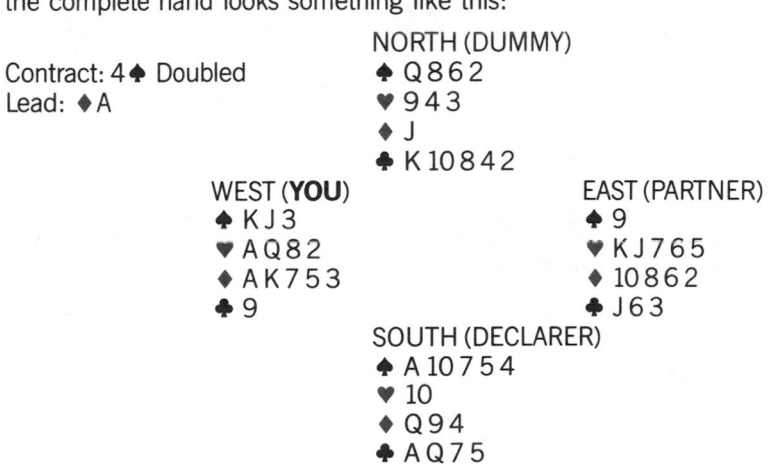

Contract: 4♠ Doubled
Lead: ♦A

NORTH (DUMMY)
♠ Q 8 6 2
♥ 9 4 3
♦ J
♣ K 10 8 4 2

WEST (**YOU**)
♠ K J 3
♥ A Q 8 2
♦ A K 7 5 3
♣ 9

EAST (PARTNER)
♠ 9
♥ K J 7 6 5
♦ 10 8 6 2
♣ J 6 3

SOUTH (DECLARER)
♠ A 10 7 5 4
♥ 10
♦ Q 9 4
♣ A Q 7 5

Of course, after winning a trick with the ♥K, partner will have to be alert enough to realize why you did not play your ♥A and lead back a club, rather than play another heart. What if declarer, rather than partner, held the ♥K? He would end up making an overtrick in his doubled contract. That, however, would not make much difference since you were probably going to get a very bad result anyway if the opponents made their contract.

♠ SUMMARY ♠

Duplicate bridge in North America is organized by the American Contract Bridge League, or ACBL. If you regularly play duplicate bridge, you will want to become a member of ACBL and benefit from its many programs. ACBL can also help you find a local game at your level when you are starting out. Once you have started, you will never turn back.

When you are defending in a matchpoint duplicate game, it is important to try to take all the tricks to which you are entitled, even if you cannot defeat the contract. Preventing declarer from making overtricks will increase the number of matchpoints you get for the result. On the other hand, if you can see that declarer will get an excellent result if you do not take enough tricks, it is worthwhile taking a chance, even if it risks letting declarer make an extra trick.

♠ GROUP ACTIVITIES ♠

Exercise One — Pre-duplicated Boards

Before the game begins, the director places two or more pre-printed hand records on each table. He asks the players to "pre-duplicate" the boards on their table by making up the hands to match those on the hand records. Why might this be necessary?

Exercise Two — Defensive Tactics

You (West) are defending 4♠ and lead the ♥A. What do you do next when dummy comes down and you see the following layout?

```
                    NORTH (DUMMY)
                    ♠ K Q 7 3
                    ♥ 7
                    ♦ A K Q 10 5
                    ♣ K Q 6

          WEST (YOU)
          ♠ 9 4
          ♥ A K 8 3 2
          ♦ J 6 2
          ♣ A 9 3
```

♠ *SAMPLE BOARDS* ♠

In this lesson, the sample boards are a collection of boards taken from the 1988 Epson Pairs game. In this event, the boards were randomly dealt before the event and records were then made so that the same boards could be played in countries all around the world. Before the event, the boards were analyzed by Omar Sharif and his comments were written up in a special booklet for distribution to the participants after the game was over.

In this type of event, the different possible results, and their expected frequency of occurrence, are determined before the game. "Matchpoints" from 0–100 are assigned to each result and pre-printed on the scoreslips. In this manner, pairs can see immediately after they have played the board how well they have done. Here is a sample of the results appearing on a scoreslip:

Score N-S	E-W	Points N-S	E-W	Score N-S	E-W	Points N-S	E-W	Score N-S	E-W	Points N-S	E-W
	...	100	0	630	...	81	19		...	34	66
800	...	99	1	**620**	...	**75**	**25**	150	...	32	68
	...	99	1	600	...	65	35		...	32	68
690	...	98	2		...	48	52		**100** ...	**30**	**70**
	...	**91**	**9**	200	...	40	60		...	10	90
660	...	89	11		...	38	62		**200** ...	**5**	**95**
650	...	85	15	180	...	36	64		...	0	100
	...	83	17	170	...	35	65				

If North-South end up in a vulnerable contract of 4♠ and make it, scoring 620 points, this translates into 75 matchpoints. If they are defeated one trick, losing 100 points, they would get 30 matchpoints. If they were doubled and defeated one trick, losing 200 points, they would get only 5 matchpoints. If North-South end up with a result that is not shown on the scoreslip, they get the number of matchpoints awarded in the space between the next higher and next lower results shown on the scoreslip. For example, if North-South made a contract of 2♠ doubled for a score of 670, they would get 91 matchpoints — the award for scores between 660 and 690. A score higher than 800 points would get North-South all 100 matchpoints.

The East-West result is the complement of the North-South result. For example, if North-South get 75 points out of 100, the East-West pair gets 25 (100 – 75 = 25).

♠ *SAMPLE BOARDS* ♠

BOARD #1

Dealer: North
Vulnerable: None

NORTH
♠ A Q J 7 4
♥ A 6 3 2
♦ Q 10
♣ 7 5

WEST
♠ 8 2
♥ J 10
♦ 6 5 2
♣ K 8 6 4 3 2

EAST
♠ K 5
♥ 9 7 5 4
♦ A K 8 4
♣ J 10 9

SOUTH
♠ 10 9 6 3
♥ K Q 8
♦ J 9 7 3
♣ A Q

Score		Points		Score		Points		Score	Points
N-S	E-W	N-S	E-W	N-S	E-W	N-S	E-W	N-S E-W	N-S E-W
	. . .	100	0	50	. . .	36	64		
450	. . .	99	1		. . .	3	97		
	. . .	99	1	150	. . .	2	98		
430	. . .	97	3		. . .	1	99		
420	. . .	84	16	300	. . .	1	99		
	. . .	73	27		. . .	0	100		
140	. . .	71	29						
	. . .	69	31						

Suggested Bidding

WEST	NORTH	EAST	SOUTH
	1♠	Pass	2♦
Pass	2♥	Pass	4♠
Pass	Pass	Pass	

After North opens the bidding 1♠, South can value his hand in support for spades. With 12 HCPs plus 1 point for the doubleton club, South has enough to want to make sure the partnership gets to game. Players who use limit raises of major suits are too strong to jump to 3♠, since that is only invitational. Instead, they can start by bidding a new suit and then jump to game over partner's rebid. Players using forcing raises can respond 3♠ and North, with a minimum opening bid can simply bid 4♠. In his analysis, Omar Sharif adds that South could simply jump directly to 4♠ if the partnership has no other way to show enough strength to raise to game. Omar sums up his analysis with: "Despite the many thousands of tables in play, this contract (4♠) will surely be almost universal."

Suggested Play

This hand presents the defenders with a good opportunity to combine their efforts to defeat the contract. East should lead the ♦A. Having no interest in the diamond suit, West should make a discouraging signal by playing the ♦2, his lowest diamond. The spotlight now turns to East. Looking at his partner's discouraging signal, he should stop to consider how the defense is going to defeat the contract.

East can see he is going to get a trick with the ♠K as well as two diamond tricks. The defenders might be able to defeat the contract if West has either the ♥A or the ♣K. If West has the ♥A, the defenders will probably get another chance to take it but, if West has the ♣K, East should lead a club right away. Since West has the ♣K on the actual hand, declarer cannot make the contract if East leads the ♣J at trick two. The defenders get a spade trick, two diamond tricks and a club trick.

What if East ignores his partner's discouraging signal and takes the ♦K at trick two? This gives North an opportunity to make the contract. When East belatedly switches to a club, declarer can win the trick with the ♣A, refusing the finesse, and use dummy's established ♦J to discard his club loser before taking the trump finesse.

Notes

As reflected on the scoreslip, the result on this hand is largely in the hands of the defense. If East-West defeat the contract they earn 64 matchpoints, a better than average score, while North-South collect 36. On the other hand, if declarer is allowed to make 4♠, East-West get 16 matchpoints and North-South 84 matchpoints.

BOARD #2

Dealer: East
Vulnerable: North-South

NORTH
♠ 10 2
♥ A 6 5
♦ A Q J 8
♣ 10 8 5 3

WEST
♠ 7 4 3
♥ 10 9 4 3
♦ 6 2
♣ A K 7 2

EAST
♠ K J 9
♥ J 8
♦ 10 7 5 4
♣ Q 9 6 4

SOUTH
♠ A Q 8 6 5
♥ K Q 7 2
♦ K 9 3
♣ J

Score		Points		Score		Points		Score		Points	
N-S	E-W	N-S	E-W	N-S	E-W	N-S	E-W	N-S	E-W	N-S	E-W
	...	100	0	630	...	81	19		...	24	76
1440	...	99	1	620	...	74	26	150	...	24	76
	...	99	1	600	...	51	49		...	23	77
690	...	98	2		...	30	70	100	...	13	87
	...	97	3	200	...	29	71		...	4	96
660	...	97	3		...	28	72	200	...	2	98
650	...	91	9	180	...	28	72		...	0	100
	...	86	14	170	...	26	74				

Suggested Bidding

WEST	NORTH	EAST	SOUTH
		Pass	1♠
Pass	2♣	Pass	2♥
Pass	2NT	Pass	3NT
Pass	Pass	Pass	

With 11 HCPs, North has enough to bid one of his suits at the two level in response to South's 1♠ opening bid. With a choice of four-card suits, North would normally bid the lower-ranking, bidding his suits "up the line." By responding 2♣, North gives the partnership the opportunity to find a fit in either clubs or diamonds. If South has support for clubs, he can raise. If South has a four-card or longer diamond suit, he can rebid 2♦ and North can raise. On the actual hand, South rebids 2♥, showing his second suit, and North can finish describing his hand by making an invitational rebid of 2NT, showing 11–12 points. With 15 HCPs and a five-card suit, South has enough to accept the invitation. Having found no major suit fit, South raises to 3NT.

Suggested Play

If North bid 2♣, East is likely to prefer a diamond lead to a club lead since he wants to avoid helping declarer by leading his suit when he has a suitable alternative. After a diamond lead, North can count eight sure tricks — one spade, three hearts, and four diamonds. There are two chances for a ninth trick. Declarer can try the spade finesse by leading a low spade toward dummy and finessing the ♠Q, hoping East has the ♠K. Alternatively, declarer can play the ♥A, ♥K and ♥Q, hoping the missing hearts are divided 3–3 and dummy's remaining heart will be a winner.

The best plan is to try the hearts first and, if they do not divide 3–3, try the spade finesse. The danger of trying the spade finesse first is that, if it loses, the defenders may be able to take enough club tricks to defeat the contract before declarer has a second chance to try the hearts.

Declarer has to be careful to keep an entry to his hand so that he can take the spade finesse after playing the hearts. On the actual hand, the hearts do not divide but the spade finesse works, so declarer should end up with nine tricks.

Notes

Bidding and making 3NT is the average result, giving North-South 51 matchpoints and East-West 49. North-South get a poor result if they do not bid game or if they do not make it. East-West get a poor result if they let North make an overtrick in the 3NT contract.

BOARD #3

Dealer: South
Vulnerable: East-West

NORTH
♠ 10 7 6 5 4
♥ A K 7 4
♦ A 9
♣ K 8

WEST
♠ 3
♥ Q 10 6 3 2
♦ J 10 8
♣ A J 9 6

EAST
♠ 9 2
♥ J 8
♦ K Q 6 5 4 2
♣ 10 7 2

SOUTH
♠ A K Q J 8
♥ 9 5
♦ 7 3
♣ Q 5 4 3

Score		Points		Score		Points		Score		Points	
N-S	E-W	N-S	E-W	N-S	E-W	N-S	E-W	N-S	E-W	N-S	E-W
		... 100	0			... 22	78				
980		... 91	9	50		... 12	88				
		... 82	18			... 1	99				
480		... 74	26	500		... 1	99				
		... 67	33			... 0	100				
450		... 45	55								
		... 24	76								
420		... 23	77								

Suggested Bidding

WEST	NORTH	EAST	SOUTH
			1♠
Pass	2♥	Pass	2♠
Pass	4♠	Pass	Pass
Pass	Pass		

Over South's 1♠ opening, West does not really have enough to compete and will likely pass. If North-South are playing limit raises, North can start by bidding a new suit since he is too strong to make a limit raise. South can rebid 2♠ to show a minimum opening bid and North can jump to game. If North-South are playing forcing raises, North could bid 3♠ directly and South would carry on to game. In either case, North-South should reach 4♠.

As pointed out by Omar Sharif, some North players might consider their hand too strong to stop in a game contract and might use the Blackwood 4NT convention to ask South how many aces he has. After South's 5♦ response, showing one ace, North might bid 6♠, hoping that the only loser will be the missing ace. Omar comments: "A purist might object, with justice, that North has bid this slam all by himself."

Suggested Play

In a spade contract, South has to lose a club trick but can trump his remaining club losers with dummy's trumps. His other potential loser is in the diamond suit. If the defenders are careful, South has no way to get rid of the diamond loser, but West may give declarer a chance. A lot depends on the opening lead. If West leads the ♦J, top of a sequence, South has no chance. If, instead, West leads the ♣A before leading a diamond, declarer can get rid of his diamond loser. He can win the ♦A and, after drawing trumps, take dummy's ♣K and come back to his hand to lead the ♣Q and discard dummy's low diamond. He can then trump his diamond loser in dummy, making 12 tricks.

Notes

The normal result of making 4♠ with an overtrick is slightly below average for North-South, worth 45 matchpoints. As noted above, some defenders may let declarer take 12 tricks. This will be very unfortunate if North-South are in 6♠, where it is very tempting for West to lead the ♣A, hoping the defenders have two quick tricks or that the lead will prevent South from making an overtrick.

BOARD #4

Dealer: West
Vulnerable: Both

NORTH
♠ 1062
♥ 985
♦ 9763
♣ K65

WEST
♠ AJ74
♥ A76
♦ K1042
♣ A9

EAST
♠ KQ85
♥ Q4
♦ AQ5
♣ QJ74

SOUTH
♠ 93
♥ KJ1032
♦ J8
♣ 10832

Score		Points		Score		Points		Score		Points	
N-S	E-W	N-S	E-W	N-S	E-W	N-S	E-W	N-S	E-W	N-S	E-W
	...	100	0		...	68	32	1440	...	6	94
300		... 97	3	650	...	65	35	1460	...	1	99
	...	95	5	660	...	61	39		...	0	100
200		... 90	10		...	60	40				
	...	86	14	680	...	55	45				
100		... 79	21	690	...	47	53				
	...	71	29		...	45	55				
	630 ...	70	30	1430	...	28	72				

Suggested Bidding

WEST	NORTH	EAST	SOUTH
1 NT	Pass	2♣	Pass
2♠	Pass	6♠	Pass
Pass	Pass		

If East-West are using a range of 16–18 points for an opening notrump bid, West will start with 1 NT. With interest in finding a major suit fit, East can make use of the Stayman convention by responding 2♣ to ask West if he has a four-card major. When West shows the four-card spade suit by bidding 2♠, East knows there is an eight-card fit. In support of spades, East has 16 HCPs and one point for the doubleton heart. Since West has at least 16 points, the combined partnership strength should be at least 33 points, enough for a slam contract. Omar's comment on the direct jump to 6♠ over 2♠ is the following: "When the spade fit is uncovered, so eager is East that he bids slam without further ceremony, brushing aside the trifling matter of aces. Impulsive, yes — but the direct raise does cut out any possible misunderstanding. 4 NT in this sequence has been known to be passed, with disastrous results."

Suggested Play

If West is in 6♠, he has two potential heart losers and one club loser. Since one of the heart losers can be trumped in dummy, North must be careful not to make West's task too easy. If North leads a club, West will win the first trick with dummy's ♣J (or ♣Q) and will have only one heart trick to lose.

Against the slam contract, North should probably choose a safer lead, perhaps the "when in doubt" lead of a trump. If North does not lead a club, declarer should still make the contract. After drawing trumps, declarer can start by playing the diamond suit. When South's ♦J appears on the second round, West's remaining diamonds are sure tricks and he can discard dummy's small heart on his last diamond. Now, declarer can play the ♣A and a club toward dummy. The only trick the defenders get is North's ♣K.

Notes

If East-West do not bid the slam, they get an approximately average result, 45 matchpoints, as long as they make 12 tricks. By bidding and making the slam, they get well above average, 72 matchpoints.

BOARD #5

Dealer: North
Vulnerable: North-South

NORTH
♠ 954
♥ J842
♦ A K3
♣ Q83

WEST
♠ 83
♥ A 1053
♦ 10642
♣ A72

EAST
♠ K Q J62
♥ 96
♦ J87
♣ K65

SOUTH
♠ A 107
♥ K Q7
♦ Q95
♣ J1094

Score N-S	E-W	Points N-S	E-W	Score N-S	E-W	Points N-S	E-W	Score N-S	E-W	Points N-S	E-W
		... 100	0	50		... 73	27			... 21	79
300		... 99	1	pass		... 63	37	180		... 21	79
		... 99	1			... 56	44			... 20	80
150		... 97	3	80		... 55	45	200		... 11	89
		... 95	5			... 55	45			... 3	97
120		... 93	7	100		... 41	59	300		... 2	98
110		... 89	11	110		... 25	75			... 1	99
100		... 85	15	120		... 23	77	500		... 1	99
90		... 80	20			... 23	77			... 0	100
		... 77	23	160		... 22	78				

Suggested Bidding

WEST	NORTH	EAST	SOUTH
	Pass	Pass	1♣
Pass	1♥	1♠	1NT
Pass	Pass	Pass	

This hand could well get passed out since no player has 13 or more points. However, South is likely to open light in third position with his 12 HCPs, hoping to get a small plus score. After North's 1♥ response, East will probably compete with an overcall of 1♠. With a very minimum hand, South could pass at this point but might rebid 1NT to describe his balanced hand. South might also consider raising to 2♥, even though he has only three-card support. Whatever call South makes, it is likely to end the auction since none of the other players has enough to bid further. In such a competitive auction, however, anything can happen. The partnerships are likely to end up in a number of different part-score contracts in the actual game.

Suggested Play

If South plays in 1NT, East's overcall of 1♠ should get West off to the best lead for the defense, the ♠8. Once declarer's ♠A is driven out, the defenders should end up with four spade tricks, a heart trick and two club tricks to defeat the contract by one trick.

If East is allowed to play in a spade contract, he has a spade loser, a heart loser, three diamond losers and a club loser. North-South will have to be careful, however, to get their club trick established before taking their three diamond tricks. Otherwise, East will be able to discard his club loser on dummy's remaining diamond winner after trumps are drawn.

Notes

The scoreslip reflects the fact that, although they have the balance of power on this hand, North-South are unlikely to be able to make a partscore, and it is more likely that East-West will end up with a plus score. North-South will get 80 matchpoints if they manage to make 1NT or 73 matchpoints if they can defeat any East-West contract by one trick. On the other hand, North-South still gets 41 matchpoints if they are defeated only one trick in any contract they reach.

BOARD #6

Dealer: East
Vulnerable: East-West

NORTH
♠ K Q 6 4
♥ 4
♦ K Q 7 5
♣ J 10 8 6

WEST
♠ A J
♥ A K Q 8
♦ 10 8 6 4 2
♣ A 4

EAST
♠ 9 5
♥ J 9 7 6 5
♦ A J
♣ K 9 7 5

SOUTH
♠ 10 8 7 3 2
♥ 10 3 2
♦ 9 3
♣ Q 3 2

Score N-S	E-W	Points N-S	E-W	Score N-S	E-W	Points N-S	E-W	Score N-S	E-W	Points N-S	E-W
		. . . 100	0	620 . . .	79	21		1430 . . .		2	98
100		. . . 98	2	630 . . .	77	23			. . .	0	100
		. . . 96	4		76	24					
50		. . . 95	5	650 . . .	62	38					
		. . . 95	5	660 . . .	47	53					
	300	. . . 93	7		47	53					
		. . . 91	9	680 . . .	27	73					
	500	. . . 86	14		8	92					
		. . . 81	19	710 . . .	6	94					
	600	. . . 81	19		4	96					

Suggested Bidding

WEST	NORTH	EAST	SOUTH
		Pass	Pass
1♦	Pass	1♥	Pass
4♥	Pass	Pass	Pass

When West opens in his long suit, North's hand is unsuited to making either an overcall or a takeout double. After East's 1♥ response, West can value his hand in support of hearts. With 18 HCPs plus 1 point for each of the doubletons, West has a maximum hand and can jump all the way to 4♥.

Suggested Play

East has a spade loser, a diamond loser and two club losers in his four heart contract. The club losers could be trumped in dummy or, perhaps, discarded on dummy's diamond suit if declarer can establish winners in that suit. South will probably choose between leading a spade and a club, since the opponents have bid both hearts and diamonds. If South leads a spade originally, the defenders can establish a spade winner to go along with the diamond trick they will get when declarer tries to establish the diamond suit.

If South's opening lead is a club, declarer has a chance to make two overtricks by establishing dummy's diamonds so that he can discard his spade loser as well as his other losers. Declarer can win the club with dummy's ♣A and lead a low diamond toward his hand. If North does not split his honors (play the ♦K or ♦Q), declarer can play the ♦J and win the trick, ending up with no diamond losers. If North plays a diamond honor, South can win the ♦A and lead the ♦J to drive out North's remaining diamond honor, establishing dummy's ♦10 as a trick. Now, it is too late for North to lead a spade. Declarer can win dummy's ♣A, draw trumps and discard his spade loser on dummy's ♦10. By this point, dummy's ♦8 and remaining low diamond will also be winners, since South's ♦9 had to be played on the second round of the suit. East can discard his remaining club losers and end up with 12 tricks for an excellent result.

Notes

The scoreslip reflects the importance of overtricks at duplicate bridge. For collecting 620 points for bidding and making exactly 4♥, East-West get only 21 matchpoints. In order to do well, declarer has to try to take all twelve tricks. For scoring 680, East-West get 73 matchpoints.

BOARD #7

Dealer: South
Vulnerable: Both

NORTH
♠ 10 5
♥ K 10 9 6
♦ A 8 4 3
♣ 10 6 5

WEST
♠ A K 7 4 3 2
♥ A J 7 2
♦ K 2
♣ 8

EAST
♠ Q 8
♥ Q 8 4 3
♦ J 9 7
♣ Q 9 7 3

SOUTH
♠ J 9 6
♥ 5
♦ Q 10 6 5
♣ A K J 4 2

Score N-S	Score E-W	Points N-S	Points E-W	Score N-S	Score E-W	Points N-S	Points E-W	Score N-S	Score E-W	Points N-S	Points E-W
		. . . 100	0			. . . 62	38			. . . 4	96
800		. . . 99	1	110		. . . 60	40	600		3	97
		. . . 99	1	100		. . . 47	53			. . . 3	97
500		. . . 96	4			. . . 37	63	620		2	98
		. . . 93	7		100	. . . 35	65			. . . 1	99
400		. . . 93	7		110	. . . 31	69	870		1	99
		. . . 92	8			. . . 28	72			. . . 0	100
300		. . . 84	16		140	. . . 18	82				
		. . . 76	24			. . . 9	91				
200		. . . 69	31		170	. . . 6	94				

Suggested Bidding

WEST	NORTH	EAST	SOUTH
			Pass
1♠	Pass	1 NT	Pass
2♥	Pass	Pass	Double
Pass	3♦	3♥	Pass
Pass	Pass		

The way the auction actually proceeds may differ considerably, depending on the action South takes at each opportunity. With only 11 HCPs and a five-card suit, most players will pass originally with the South hand, but some may open the bidding 1♣. Even if South passes originally, he may overcall 2♣ after the 1♠ opening bid and 1 NT response. The above auction shows another variation if South passes at both his first and second opportunities. When the opponents settle in a partscore, South might make a takeout double for the unbid suits. North will assume this is not a penalty double since South has passed twice and the opponents are only in partscore. Once North-South have found their diamond fit, East-West will probably bid on to 3♥, preferring to play the contract rather than defend 3♦.

Either side may bid higher, but they are likely to get doubled.

Suggested Play

If West ends up in 3♥, North will probably lead a low club. North will not want to lead a spade or a heart, since those are the opponents' suits. Against a suit contract, North should not lead a low diamond when he holds the ♦A and may not want to lead the ♦A in case it establishes the ♦K as a trick for the opponents.

After a club lead, West will have to be careful in order to make the contract. Since the missing spades are divided 3-2, West has no spade losers but, with North holding the ♥K and the missing hearts dividing 4–1, West will have to lose two heart tricks. There are also two potential diamond losers and a club loser. West's best chance is to hold his diamond losers to one trick. If he tries leading a diamond from dummy toward his ♦K, he will not be successful. However, North may lead the ♦A originally or, if South wins the first club trick and leads a diamond, West can play the ♦2 and North will have to play the ♦A to stop dummy from getting a trick with the ♦J.

Notes

East-West will get a very good result, 82 matchpoints, if they can make nine tricks in a heart or spade partscore. North-South must try to push them up to at least the three level, where they have a chance of defeating them and receiving a good result.

BOARD #8

Dealer: West
Vulnerable: None

NORTH
♠ 5
♥ K Q
♦ J 9 8 7 5
♣ A 6 5 4 2

WEST
♠ A J 3 2
♥ 1 0 8 7 4
♦ A 4
♣ 1 0 9 3

EAST
♠ Q 9 7 6 4
♥ A J 6 3 2
♦ K 3
♣ 7

SOUTH
♠ K 1 0 8
♥ 9 5
♦ Q 1 0 6 2
♣ K Q J 8

Score		Points		Score		Points		Score		Points	
N-S	E-W	N-S	E-W	N-S	E-W	N-S	E-W	N-S	E-W	N-S	E-W
	. . .	100	0	140	. . .	68	32		. . .	8	92
110	. . .	99	1	150	. . .	67	33	590	. . .	4	96
100	. . .	97	3		. . .	66	34		. . .	0	100
	. . .	96	4	170	. . .	55	45				
50	. . .	93	7		. . .	43	57				
	pass . . .	86	14	300	. . .	36	64				
	50 . . .	78	22		. . .	29	71				
	. . .	73	27	420	. . .	19	81				
	100 . . .	71	29		. . .	9	91				
	. . .	69	31	450	. . .	8	92				

Suggested Bidding

WEST	NORTH	EAST	SOUTH
Pass	Pass	1♠	Pass
2♠	3♦	Pass	Pass
3♠	Pass	Pass	Pass

This is another hand that might get passed out, since none of the players has a full opening bid. In a duplicate game, however, most East players, holding 10 HCPs and two five-card major suits, will open in third chair, hoping to get a plus score. After West's raise to 2♠, North has a problem. With two five-card minor suits, he would like to compete. He cannot make a takeout double, since he does not have support for hearts and neither of his suits is particularly attractive for an overcall at the three level. Some North players might risk an overcall of 3♦, hoping their partner will not get too excited since they passed originally. This will probably drive West on to 3♠. North-South must be careful not to compete too aggressively. If they bid on to 4♣, East-West may bid 4♠ and, on the lucky lie of the cards, will end up making it.

Suggested Play

Although East-West have only 19 HCPs between them, East should have no trouble taking 10 tricks in either spades or hearts. Although the spade finesse works, there is still one spade loser. If East leads the ♠Q, South should cover with the ♠K to eventually promote a spade winner for the defense. If South fails to cover the ♠Q, East would end up with no spade losers by repeating the finesse! East has to lose only one heart trick, since the missing hearts divide 2–2. There are no diamond losers and only one club loser.

Notes

East-West get only slightly below average, 45 matchpoints, for playing in partscore and making 10 tricks. Some East-West pairs may be pushed to the aggressive game contract and end up making it, collecting 81 matchpoints for scoring 420. If North-South are allowed to play a partscore in diamonds or clubs, they will get an excellent result, even if they do not make their contract.

BOARD #9

Dealer: North
Vulnerable: East-West

NORTH
♠ J 10 5 4
♥ 9
♦ A 10 9 7 4
♣ J 4 2

WEST
♠ A K Q
♥ A K 8
♦ J 6 5
♣ A Q 10 7

EAST
♠ 9 7 3 2
♥ Q 6 3
♦ Q 8
♣ 9 8 6 5

SOUTH
♠ 8 6
♥ J 10 7 5 4 2
♦ K 3 2
♣ K 3

Score N-S	E-W		Points N-S	E-W	Score N-S	E-W		Points N-S	E-W	Score N-S	E-W		Points N-S	E-W
		. . .	100	0	120	. . .		65	35			. . .	55	45
400		. . .	99	1	130	. . .		63	37	600	. . .		41	59
		. . .	99	1		. . .		63	37			. . .	27	73
300		. . .	97	3	150	. . .		61	39	620	. . .		26	74
		. . .	95	5		. . .		59	41	630	. . .		21	79
200		. . .	92	8	180	. . .		58	42			. . .	16	84
		. . .	89	11		. . .		57	43	660	. . .		9	91
100		. . .	79	21	300	. . .		57	43			. . .	3	97
		. . .	68	32		. . .		56	44	700	. . .		1	99
	110	. . .	67	33	500	. . .		55	45			. . .	0	100

Suggested Bidding

WEST	NORTH	EAST	SOUTH
	Pass	Pass	Pass
2NT	Pass	3♣	Pass
3♦	Pass	3NT	Pass
Pass	Pass		

West can open with 2 NT to show a balanced hand of 22–24 points. With 4 HCPs and a four-card spade suit, West can use the Stayman convention to find out if opener has a four-card spade suit. Opener's 3♦ response shows no four-card major and East can settle for 3NT. East's spades are so poor that Omar suggests that some East players will simply raise to 3NT, ignoring the possibility of playing in a spade fit.

Suggested Play

North should lead the ♦10, top of an interior sequence. Declarer has seven sure tricks: three spade tricks, three heart tricks and a club trick. Provided he plays a low diamond from dummy on the first trick, declarer will get a diamond trick. If South plays a low diamond, keeping dummy's ♦Q trapped, West will win a trick with the ♦J. If South wins the first trick with the ♦K and leads a diamond back, declarer will get a trick with either the ♦Q or ♦J. If South does play the ♦K on the first trick and leads one back, North should probably let declarer win the trick with dummy's ♦Q, keeping the ♦A as an entry to his winners in case South regains the lead. After winning a diamond trick, West needs one more trick. His best play is to start by taking the ♠A, ♠K and ♠Q, hoping the missing spades are divided 3–3, in which case dummy's ♠9 would become his ninth trick. When this does not work, West can fall back on his second chance of playing a low heart to dummy's ♥Q and leading a low club to his ♣Q, taking a finesse against South's ♣K. When this works, declarer has nine tricks.

Notes

Bidding and making 3NT is a little above average result for East-West. If declarer goes down in 3NT, East-West will end up with only 21 matchpoints, while North-South get 79.

BOARD #10

Dealer: East
Vulnerable: Both

NORTH
♠ 7 4 2
♥ J 6 3
♦ A K 3 2
♣ K 8 7

WEST
♠ J 8 6
♥ A K Q 9
♦ J
♣ Q 9 5 4 3

EAST
♠ A 10 5
♥ 10 8 2
♦ 7 6 4
♣ A J 10 2

SOUTH
♠ K Q 9 3
♥ 7 5 4
♦ Q 10 9 8 5
♣ 6

Score		Points		Score		Points		Score		Points	
N-S	E-W	N-S	E-W	N-S	E-W	N-S	E-W	N-S	E-W	N-S	E-W
	...	100	0	120	...	74	26		...	9	91
200		99	1	130	...	66	34	600	...	6	94
	...	99	1	140	...	62	38	620	...	3	97
110		97	3	150	...	42	58	630	...	1	99
100		93	7		...	23	77		...	0	100
90		90	10	170	...	19	81				
	...	89	11	180	...	14	86				
	90 ...	86	14		...	12	88				
	100 ...	81	19	200	...	11	89				
	...	78	22	210	...	10	90				

Suggested Bidding

WEST	NORTH	EAST	SOUTH
		Pass	Pass
1♣	Pass	1 NT	Pass
Pass	Pass		

In responding to partner's 1♣ opening, East will probably choose 1 NT rather than raise to 2♣. Playing five-card majors, West might have only a three-card club suit, and notrump contracts are usually worth more than contracts played in clubs, even if more tricks can be made playing with clubs as trumps. West will have a similar decision when the bidding comes back to him. Although he has an unbalanced hand, he knows there is no eight-card major suit fit since East would have bid 1♥, rather than 1 NT, if he held a four-card heart suit. West could rebid 2♣ — East must have support for clubs since he had no suit to bid at the one level — but will probably pass, being lured by the same consideration as East that a notrump contract is usually worth more than a minor suit contract.

Suggested Play

Against 1 NT, South should lead the ♦10, top of the interior sequence in his long suit. The defenders should have no trouble taking the first five diamond tricks but that should be all. East can take the remainder with the help of a successful finesse for the ♣K.

Notes

Making an overtrick in 1 NT turns out to be worth only 26 matchpoints for East-West. Some defenders will fail to get their five diamond tricks. If South does not lead a diamond, East will end up with 10 tricks: one spade trick, four heart tricks (when the suit divides 3–3) and five club tricks (after trapping North's ♣K). East-West might do better by playing in their club fit, since they will end up with at least 10 tricks, scoring 130 points, and may make 11 tricks, scoring 150 points. Playing in notrump rather than a minor suit does not always pay off!

BOARD #11

Dealer: South
Vulnerable: None

NORTH
♠ Q
♥ K 8 4
♦ Q 9 7 3 2
♣ A K 5 2

WEST
♠ J 7 6 3
♥ J 2
♦ J 6 5 4
♣ 8 4 3

EAST
♠ K 10 8 5 4
♥ A Q 6 3
♦ K 8
♣ Q J

SOUTH
♠ A 9 2
♥ 10 9 7 5
♦ A 10
♣ 10 9 7 6

Score N-S	E-W	Points N-S	E-W	Score N-S	E-W	Points N-S	E-W	Score N-S	E-W	Points N-S	E-W
	...	100	0	140		... 79	21		...	25	75
500	...	98	2	130		... 75	25	100	...	23	77
	...	96	4			... 73	27	110	...	16	84
340	...	95	5	110		... 66	34		...	10	90
	...	94	6	100		... 56	44	140	...	7	93
300	...	92	8	90		... 51	49	150	...	3	97
	...	91	9			... 51	49		...	1	99
200	...	90	10	50		... 43	57	300	...	1	99
	...	90	10		pass	... 35	65		...	0	100
150	...	84	16		50	... 30	70				

Suggested Bidding

WEST	NORTH	EAST	SOUTH
			Pass
Pass	1♦	1♠	1 NT
Pass	2♣	2♥	3 ♣
3♠	Pass	Pass	Pass

After East's 1♠ overcall, South does not have enough strength to bid a new suit at the two level and will have to settle for 1 NT. When the bidding gets back to North, he can show his second suit. With 15 HCPs, East will likely continue to compete by bidding his other suit. North-South will have to decide whether to defend or push on in their eight-card club fit. Likely, one of them will bid 3♣. If they do, West may come to life, even though he has only 3 HCPs. Having passed twice already, he may decide to show some support for partner by competing with 3♠. This will likely end the auction since none of the players has enough to bid more.

Suggested Play

If East ends up as declarer in a spade contract, he will likely have difficulty making it unless the defenders help him out. He initially starts with two losers each in spades, diamonds and clubs and three in hearts. The difficulty in getting rid of some of the losers is that there are no sure entries to the dummy so that he can lead toward his hand. If East could lead a low spade from dummy, planning to take a finesse, he would end up with only one spade loser once North's ♠Q appears. If he has to play spades starting from his hand, he will have to find the difficult play of leading the ♠K, driving out South's ♠A and catching North's singleton ♠Q at the same time. Now East can get to dummy with the ♠J and take the heart finesse. Once this succeeds, he can trump one of his heart losers in dummy. If East tries leading a diamond toward his ♦K, he will not be as lucky since South has the ♦A. Declarer will get a trick with the ♦K only if the defenders lead the suit first and he guesses right.

Notes

If East-West choose to defend 3♣, they will get only 34 matchpoints if North-South make the contract, scoring 110 points. East-West are probably better off to bid on, even if they go down a trick or two. Since they are not vulnerable, going down one trick will cost them only 50 points and they will end up with 57 matchpoints. Of course, North-South may not make their 3♣ contract.

BOARD #12

Dealer: West
Vulnerable: North-South

NORTH
♠ 3 2
♥ 10 8
♦ Q 10 9 8 5 3
♣ Q J 2

WEST
♠ K Q 9 8 6 4
♥ A K 7
♦ J
♣ 8 6 5

EAST
♠ A J 10 7
♥ 4 3
♦ A 7 4 2
♣ K 9 7

SOUTH
♠ 5
♥ Q J 9 6 5 2
♦ K 6
♣ A 10 4 3

Score		Points		Score		Points		Score		Points	
N-S	E-W	N-S	E-W	N-S	E-W	N-S	E-W	N-S	E-W	N-S	E-W
	. . .	100	0		. . .	4	96				
100	. . .	99	1	480	. . .	3	97				
	. . .	99	1		. . .	3	97				
50	. . .	97	3	800	. . .	1	99				
	. . .	96	4		. . .	0	100				
	200 . . .	95	5								
	. . .	95	5								
	420 . . .	65	35								
	. . .	36	64								
	450 . . .	20	80								

Suggested Bidding

WEST	NORTH	EAST	SOUTH
1♠	Pass	2♦	Pass
2♠	Pass	4♠	Pass
Pass	Pass		

With 12 HCPs and a doubleton heart, East is too strong to make a limit raise over partner's 1♠ opening. Instead, he starts with a new suit and raises to game over partner's minimum rebid. If East-West are playing forcing jump raises, East will jump to 3♠. West, with a minimum, will merely carry on to 4♠.

Suggested Play

After an auction such as the one above, North will probably choose the ♣Q as the opening lead, the top of his touching honors in an unbid suit. This will trap East's ♣K and the defenders will take the first three club tricks. Even if North does not lead a club initially, there is not much West can do to avoid losing three club tricks sooner or later. He can trump his heart loser in dummy so he should end up making exactly 10 tricks.

Notes

4♠ should be a fairly normal contract for East-West. However, if they get any higher, perhaps exploring the possibility of a slam, they will be defeated and get a poor result. North-South are vulnerable and, if they find their way into the auction, they cannot afford to get too high or they may get doubled and lose a large penalty if East-West defend carefully.

APPENDIX

Glossary of Terms

Answers to Exercises

The General Convention Card

Duplicate Scoring Summary

GLOSSARY OF TERMS

American Contract Bridge League (ACBL) — The organization which sanctions duplicate bridge games at all levels across North America.

ACBL *BULLETIN* — A monthly magazine containing articles on bridge, schedules of upcoming events, winners of tournaments, etc., which is published by ACBL for the benefit of its members.

ACBL Membership Number — The number assigned to each member of the ACBL, against which masterpoints are recorded.

ACBL Standard Yellow Card — A convention card designed to be used in events where players are all playing exactly the same conventions. The players must play the conventions marked on the card and are limited to playing only those conventions.

Advance Sacrifice — A sacrifice bid made before the opponents have had an opportunity to arrive at their optimum contract.

Alert — A warning by an opponent that the last call by his partner has been assigned some conventional message, rather than the natural or literal meaning one might expect.

Attitude Signal — A high card played to encourage partner to lead a suit, or a low card played to discourage partner from leading a suit.

Average — The median result on a board, worth exactly half the maximum matchpoints available on the board.

Average Minus — 40% of the maximum matchpoints available on a board. Sometimes awarded by the director to the offending pair for some infraction when a normal result cannot be obtained on a board.

Average Plus — 60% of the maximum matchpoints available on a board. Sometimes awarded by the director to the non-offending pair for some infraction when a normal result cannot be obtained on a board.

Bid Out Of Turn — A bid by a player when it is his partner's or an opponent's turn to bid.

Black Points — The masterpoint awards normally given out at club games for winning or placing in an event.

Blackwood Convention — An artificial bid of 4 NT used to ask partner for the number of aces he holds.

Board Number — The number on each duplicate board used to keep track of the hand played and the corresponding result.

Board-a-Match — A form of team game played in a similar fashion to a regular duplicate game.

Book — The first six tricks taken by declarer in a contract.

Bottom (On a Board) — A result on a board worse than those of all the other pairs sitting in the same direction.

Bridge Plus⁺ — A special form of duplicate game for beginning players and run by ACBL accredited teachers.

Bump — Temporary replacement of one pair by another during a duplicate movement. It is used to accommodate an extra pair in the game.

Bye-Stand — The location of a set of boards which is not in play during a particular round.

CDIN Director — A club director of Intermediates/Novices earns this title by taking a special course offered by ACBL at the NABCs.

Certified Director — A director who has passed the ACBL's written test covering the mechanics of the movements, scoring, and the Laws of the game.

Claim — A declaration by declarer or one of the defenders stating how many of the remaining tricks will be won by his side.

Class A Game — A duplicate game in which the allowable conventions are restricted to a few well known ones such as Stayman, Blackwood and Gerber.

Club Masterpoint Slip — A record of the masterpoints awarded in a club game. Slips are sent to ACBL to be registered against a player's ACBL membership number.

Committee — A panel of three or more of the players' peers convened at a duplicate game to rule on an infraction of the rules.

Constructive Auction — An auction in which all bids are designed to reach the best contract, rather than to interfere with the opponents' bidding.

Convention — A bid that conveys a meaning other than that which would literally be attributed to it.

Convention Card — A form used to describe a partnership's general style of bidding and defense and any artificial bids that are used.

Count Signal — A signal telling partner how many cards you have in a suit. A high card followed by a low card normally shows an even number and a low card followed by a high card normally shows an odd number.

Cuebid of the Opponents' Suit — A bid in a denomination already mentioned by an opponent, usually used to show strength rather than a desire to play in that suit.

Cut (the Cards) — Divide the deck into two parts and interchange the top and bottom sections, prior to dealing out the cards.

Dangerous Opponent — A defender is dangerous if he can lead a card that might set your contract.

Director — The person in charge of running the game.

District — One of the 25 geographical divisions of ACBL, responsible for running events within its boundaries and for electing a representative to ACBL Board of Directors.

Double Game Swing — In a team game, a game made in both directions on the same board.

Double Raise — A raise of partner's suit, skipping a level on the Bidding Scale. An immediate double raise is usually used to show the strength for a limit or forcing raise, depending on the partnership style.

Duck — To play a low card, surrendering a trick to the opponents when the trick could be won.

Duplicate Board — A container used to hold each player's cards for a hand, designed to keep the original deal intact and make it easy to pass it on to another table.

Duplicate (Bridge) — A form of bridge in which each deal is bid and played at one table and then the same deal is bid and played at a number of other tables.

Duplicate Bridge Club — One of the more than 4,000 clubs in North America which run bridge games sanctioned by the ACBL.

Entry Form — A form showing the starting table and direction to which a player, or partnership, is assigned.

Field — All the pairs sitting in one direction (*e.g.,* the North-South pairs).

Flat (Board) — A board on which the result is the same at every table.

Flighted Event — An event with different sections restricted to players within a specific range of number of masterpoints.

Follow Suit — Play a card of the same denomination as the one led.

Forcing (Bid) — A bid that requires partner to bid again.

Forcing Raise — A raise, usually a jump raise, which indicates that the partnership has enough combined strength for a game contract.

Fractional — .01 of a masterpoint.

Game Bonus — The score awarded for making a game contract: 300 points if the partnership is non-vulnerable; 500 points if it is vulnerable.

Gerber Convention — An artificial bid of 4♣ used to ask partner how many aces he holds. Usually used directly over opening notrump bids.

Gold Points — Special masterpoint awards, usually won at one of the three North American Bridge Championships (NABCs) held each year and at Regional tournaments.

Grand Slam Bonus — The bonus awarded for bidding and making a seven-level contract (7♣, 7♦, 7♥, 7♠ or 7 NT): 1000 points if not vulnerable; 1500 points if vulnerable.

Guide Card — A card which indicates the table number and the direction of each of the players for every round of play.

Hand Record — A diagram of all four hands used before a game when pre-duplicating boards, or a sheet of all boards in play used after the game so the players can review the deals.

Hold Up (Play) — Declining to win a trick which could be won.

Home Table — In a team game, the table to which the North-South team members are assigned.

Honor (Card) — One of the top five cards in a suit. (A, K, Q, J, 10.)

Howell Movement — A duplicate game in which the pairs change direction from time to time, playing in both the North-South and East-West directions.

International Match Points (IMPs) — A scaling of the results on a board, usually used in team events.

Individual Movement — A duplicate game in which each player plays with a different partner every round.

Insufficient Bid — A bid which is lower than or equal to the preceding bid on the Bidding Scale.

Invitational (Bid) — A bid that invites partner to bid again.

Jump Raise — A raise of partner's suit, skipping a level on the Bidding Scale. An immediate jump raise to the three level is usually used to show the strength for a limit or forcing raise, depending on the partnership style.

Kibitz — Watch other people play the game.

Kibitzer — A spectator.

Knockout Team — A team event in which a team is eliminated as soon as it loses a match.

Landy Convention — A bid of 2♣ over an opponent's 1 NT opening bid to ask partner to bid a major suit.

Life Master — A player who has won over 300 masterpoints in club and tournament play in addition to fulfilling other prescribed conditions.

Limit Raise — A raise which skips one level of bidding and is invitational only.

Make (a Board) — Shuffle and deal out the cards and place them in a duplicate board prior to or at the start of the game.

Masterpoints — Awards given to players who win or place in ACBL sanctioned events. A member's masterpoints are recorded by ACBL.

Matchpoint — Players get a matchpoint for each pair sitting in their direction which has a worse result on the board and half a matchpoint for each pair they tie. Their overall result is the sum of the matchpoints received on each of the boards they played.

Mitchell Movement — A duplicate game in which the North-South pairs remain stationary at their starting tables throughout the game and the East-West pairs move from table to table.

NABC — North American Bridge Championships (see National Tournament).

National Tournament — An out-of-date term once used to describe one of the three major tournaments run each year by ACBL, at which the North American Championship events are held. These tournaments are now called the NABCs (North American Bridge Championships).

Negative Response — A conventional response used to indicate a very weak hand (*e.g.,* a response of 2 NT to a strong two-bid).

Negative Scoring — A quick form of matchpointing in which each East-West pairs is given the same matchpoints as the North-South pair against which it played the board. The East-West pairs now want the lowest overall total of matchpoints, rather than the highest.

Non-forcing Stayman — The normal form of the Stayman convention in which the 2♣ response does not force the partnership to the game level and could be the start of only an invitational sequence.

Not vulnerable — In rubber bridge, a side which has not yet won a game. In duplicate bridge, the vulnerability is assigned on each board. The bonuses and penalties for a non-vulnerable side are less than those for a vulnerable side.

Novice Game — A club or tournament game restricted to players with less than a set number of masterpoints, usually 5 or 20.

Open Game — A club or tournament game with no limitation on the number of master-points held by the participants.

Overtrick — A trick taken by declarer in excess of those required to fulfill the contract.

Pair Number — The number assigned to each pair in a duplicate game. It determines their starting position and is used to record their results.

Pairs (Game) — A duplicate game in which a partnership plays together throughout, with their results being compared to those of the other players sitting in the same direction.

Partscore Bonus — The bonus awarded for making a partscore contract: 50 points.

Passed Out — A deal on which none of the players opens the bidding. The hand is not reshuffled and re-dealt but scored up with a result of 0 points for both sides.

Penalty Card — A card prematurely exposed by a defender. It must be left face up on the table until it can be legally played or picked up.

Penalty Double — A double of an opponent's contract, with the intention of defeating the contract. It increases the size of the penalty if the contract is defeated or the score if the contract is fulfilled.

Pick-up Slip — A piece of paper on which results are entered and which is taken away to be recorded on the recap sheet at the end of the round, rather than at the end of the game.

Playing Matchpoints — Playing in a duplicate event in which the overall result is determined by matchpointing the boards.

Pre-duplicated Hand — A deal prepared from hand records before the game starts.

Preemptive (Bid) — A bid made to interfere with the opponents' auction, usually done with a long suit and a weak hand.

Qualified Director — A director with some experience running the various duplicate movements, enough to keep the game moving smoothly. The title is earned by passing ACBL's Qualified Director exam.

Recap (Recapitulation) Sheet — The sheet on which each pair's results on every board are entered and the overall scores are totalled.

Red Points — Special masterpoints, usually won at regional or North American tournaments.

Redouble — A bid made after the opponents have doubled. Originally used to increase the scoring value of overtricks or undertricks. In modern bidding methods it can be used for other purposes.

Regional Tournament — A large tournament, held annually in a major metropolitan center.

Relay — Share the same set of boards between two tables.

Revoke — Fail to follow suit when one could have.

Round — A set of boards played against the same opponents.

Round-robin Teams — A team event in which each team plays a match against every other team in the same group.

Rubber Bridge — The type of bridge commonly played in the home, where each deal is dealt at the table and played only once.

Sacrifice — A bid made without the intention of fulfilling the contract but of preventing the opponents from playing and making their contract. The assumption is that you will lose fewer points by going down in your bid than the opponents would have received for making their contract.

Safety Play — A play that guarantees making the contract, even if it gives up the chance of making overtricks.

Scoreslip — The piece of paper on which the results of a board are entered after the board has been played. This paper is called a "traveling score" and remains with the duplicate board until the game is over.

Section — A group of tables which constitutes a self-contained unit for playing a duplicate game. When there are multiple sections, each section is identified by a different letter or number.

Sectional Tournaments — A small tournament, held mainly for the benefit of players from local clubs.

Set (of Boards) — The boards a pair plays against the same opponents during a round.

Silver Points — Special masterpoints, usually won at sectional tournaments.

Sit-out — A round during the game when a pair has no opponents to play against. This occurs when there is an odd number of pairs in the game.

Skip (a Table) — A point in an even-tabled Mitchell movement when the East-West pairs move two tables higher at the end of a round, rather than one.

Skip Bid — A bid which skips over one or more levels on the Bidding Scale.

Skip Bid Warning — A warning to the opponents that you are about to make a bid which skips one or more levels on the Bidding Scale.

Small Slam Bonus — The bonus awarded for bidding and making a contract at the six level (6♣, 6♦, 6♥, 6♠ or 6 NT): 500 points if not vulnerable; 750 points if vulnerable.

Stayman (Convention) — An artificial response of 2♣ to an opening bid of 1 NT (or 3♣ in response to a 2 NT opening), asking opener to bid a four-card major suit if he has one and otherwise to bid 2♦.

Student Game — A special game for graduates from bridge classes. (See Bridge Plus⁺.)

Strong Two-Bid — An opening suit bid at the two level, showing a hand too strong to open the bidding at the one level, usually a hand worth about 22 or more points.

Suit Preference (Signal) — The conventional choice of a card by a defender to indicate a desire to have his partner lead one suit rather than another, when his partner has a choice of two suits.

Swiss Teams — A team game format in which each team plays several matches, meeting opponents in each round with a similar record of wins and losses.

Table Number — The number assigned to each table in a duplicate game, usually found on the guide card.

Takeout Double — A double of an opponent's bid which asks partner to bid a suit not yet bid by the opponents.

Team Game — A format in which two partnerships form a team-of-four and play a match consisting of a pre-arranged number of boards against another team.

Top (On a Board) — A result on a board better than that of all the other pairs sitting in the same direction.

Total Point Scoring — A team game in which the overall result is determined by adding up each side's plus scores. Whichever team scores the most points is the winner.

Traveling Scoreslip (Traveler) — The scoreslip which travels around with a board and on which the results for the board are recorded each time it is played.

Unauthorized Information — Information given through a means other than the actual bids made or cards played.

Unblock (a Suit) — Play the high card(s) from the shorter holding in a suit first so that the remaining cards from the longer side opposite can be played later.

Undertricks — The number of tricks by which a contract is defeated.

Unit — A bridge organizational group within ACBL consisting of volunteers from the local area who have been elected by the membership and are responsible for the promotion and advancement of bridge in the local community.

Unit Education Liaison — The Unit officer working with the ACBL Education Department.

Victory Points — A scaling of the IMP results from a match, used in some team events.

Vulnerable — In rubber bridge, a side which has won a game. In duplicate bridge, the vulnerability is assigned on each hand. The bonuses and penalties for a vulnerable side are larger than those for a non-vulnerable side.

Weak Two-Bid — A conventional opening bid in a suit at the two level which is similar to a preemptive opening bid at the three level.

ANSWERS TO EXERCISES

Lesson One: Getting Started

Exercise One

1) The table number is found on the guide card.
2) The direction is found on the guide card.
3) North will (usually) be in the same position at each table.
4) The section identifier is found on the guide card.

Exercise Two

1) The board number is found on the duplicate board.
2) North on the board should match North on the guide card.
3) The player marked as DEALER bids first.
4) VUL (or a red pocket) is marked on the board in front of the vulnerable pair(s).

Exercise Four

Contract	Vulner-ability	Result	Trick Score	Game/Partscore Bonus	Over-tricks	Penalty Score	Slam Bonus	Total Score
2♥	Not vul	8 tricks	60	50	–	–	–	110
3NT	Not vul	11 tricks	100	300	60	–	–	460
6♣	Not vul	12 tricks	120	300	–	–	500	920
4♥	Not vul	9 tricks	–	–	–	50 (–)	–	50 (–)
1NT	Vul	8 tricks	40	50	30	–	–	120
4♠	Vul	10 tricks	120	500	–	–	–	620
3♦	Vul	7 tricks	–	–	–	200 (–)	–	200 (–)

Exercise Five

Contract	Vulnerability	Result	Total Score
4♥ Doubled	Not vul	10 tricks	590
7♠	Not vul	13 tricks	1510
2♠ Doubled	Not vul	9 tricks	570
5♦ Redoubled	Vul	10 tricks	400 (−)
1 NT	Vul	11 tricks	210

Exercise Six

ACBL SHORT TRAVELING SCORE
(Mitchell or Howell)

Board No. 8

N-S Pair No.	Contract	By	Made	Down	SCORE N-S	SCORE E-W	N-S Match-points	E-W Pair No.	E-W Match-points
1	4 H	N	4		420			6	
2	2 H	N	4		170			8	
3	3 S X	E		2	300			2	
4	4 H	N	5		450			4	
5	4 H	N		1		50		7	
6	3NT	S		2		100		1	
7	3 C	N	4		130			3	
8	3NT	S		1		50		5	

Exercise Seven

ACBL SHORT TRAVELING SCORE (Mitchell or Howell)									

Board No. **8**

N-S Pair No.	Contract	By	M a d e	D o w n	SCORE N-S	SCORE E-W	N-S Match-points	E-W Pair No.	E-W Match-points
1	4 H	N	4		420			6	
2	2 H	N	4		170		4	8	
3	3SX	E		2	300			2	
4	4H	N	5		450		7	4	0
5	4H	N		1		50	1–	7	
6	3NT	S		2		100	0	1	7
7	3C	N	4		130			3	
8	3NT	S		1		50	1–	5	

1) 4; Seven; 7   2) 6; 0
3) 4   4) 1½
5) 1; 7; The North-South pair get a bottom, 0.
6) 4; The North-South pair get a top, 7

Lesson Two: The Convention Card

Exercise One, Two and Three

There is an example of a completed card in the text.

Lesson Three: The Mitchell Movement

Exercise One

1) Table #6.   2) Table #4.   3) North.
4) Pair #6 E-W   5) Table #1.

Exercise Two

1) Putting out the guide cards; selling the entry forms; arranging partnerships; getting the players seated, ready to start; determining the format of the game; putting the starting boards on the table.
2) Calling the rounds; giving rulings; helping determine the score.
3) Determining the matchpoints on each board; determining the overall winner.

Exercise Three

1) Call the director.
2) Explain the options available to your opponent.
3) Make a face-down opening lead.

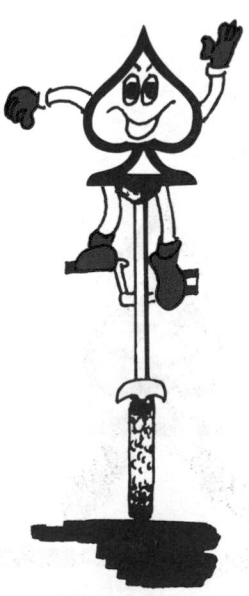

Lesson Four: Winning the Game

Exercise One

1) Third	2) Pair #2 N-S	3) 20
4) Above average.	5) 3	6) Worse
7) Better		

Exercise Two

1) 18	2) 82	3) Second
4) Nine	5) Three	

Exercise Three

- Talking during the bidding or play.
- Bidding with undue emphasis or with gestures.
- Hesitating unduly during the bidding or play.
- Smiling or frowning when partner makes a call or plays a card.
- Asking questions when it is not your turn to call or play a card.
- When dummy, looking at other players' hands during the play.
- Consistently taking too much time during the bidding or play.

Exercise Four

1) I am about to make a skip bid. Please wait. 3♣.
2) The opponent cannot pass quickly to show a weak hand.

Lesson Five: The Howell Movement

Exercise One

1) Table #2 N-S.
2) Pairs in a Howell Movement play in both directions.
3) In a Howell Movement, each pair is assigned a unique number not directly related to their starting table.
4) Boards 13, 14 and 15.
5) North. North always keeps score.

Exercise Two

1) The first hand the kibitzer was looking at does not have enough strength to take part in the auction.
2) That is not the play the kibitzer would have made.
3) The result of the hand is a foregone conclusion, no matter what declarer or the defenders do.

Exercise Three

Look at the opponents convention card to see the description of the 2♣ bid, ask opener's partner for an explanation, or bid or pass without asking for any further information.

Lesson Six: The Team Game

Exercise One

1) East-West.
2) Exchange them for the boards at your teammates' table.
3) Back to your teammates' table (your home table).
4) Yes, so that you can compare results with your teammates to determine which team won the match.

Exercise Two

Table #1 (N-S)				Table #2 (E-W)				Net Score	IMPs
Board	Contract	Result	Score	Board	Contract	Result	Score		
1	3NT N	3	+400	1	3NT N	3	–400	0	0
2	2♦ E	3	–140	2	4♠ E	–2	–100	–240	–6
3	4♥ S	4	+420	3	3NT N	3	–400	+20	+1
4	5♣ X W	–1	+200	4	3NT E	3	+600	+800	+13
									+8

Exercise Three

1) Three
2) Two spade losers, one heart loser and one club loser.
3) Discard them on dummy's extra diamond winners.
4) By taking a winning heart finesse.
5) Discard it on one of the extra diamond winners in the dummy.
6) Drawing trumps.
7) Yes, the opponents might be able to ruff one of your diamond winners if the finesse loses.
8) By playing the ♥A and then the ♥Q, drawing trumps as quickly as possible, even if it means giving up a trick to the ♥K. The danger in taking a heart finesse is that it might lose and the opponents might be able to ruff a diamond to defeat the contract.
9) Take the heart finesse. The small risk of a diamond ruff is more than compensated for by the chance for overtricks if the finesse is successful.

Lesson Seven: The Individual

Exercise One

1) Player A, sitting North   2) Player B, sitting West.
3) Player C, now sitting West   4) North

Exercise Two

1) Do you use the Stayman convention?
2) Do you play limit or forcing jump raises?

Exercise Three

1) The opponents will bid to a game — or even a slam — in hearts or clubs.
2) Eight or nine: seven spades and one or two diamond tricks.
3) One or two: a spade and/or a diamond.
4) Bid 4♠ to make it difficult for the opponents to bid their best contract.

Lesson Eight: Putting It Together

Exercise One

* The same deals can be played in more than one section.
* The same deals can be played at a number of different locations.
* Hand records can be distributed to the participants after the game.
* Printed analyses of the deals can be prepared beforehand and passed out after the game.

Exercise Two

Take the ♣A. Otherwise, you may not get any more tricks.

THE GENERAL CONVENTION CARD

A. THE GENERAL CONVENTION CARD

All conventions marked in red and all non-standard partnership agreements must be alerted.

SPECIAL DOUBLES (Describe)
Negative _____
_____
Responsive _____
Other _____
_____

DIRECT NT OVERCALLS
1NT _____ to _____ HCP
Jump to 2NT: ____ to ____ HCP
Unusual for Minors ☐
2 Lower Unbid ☐
Other _____

Names _____
General Approach _____ Pair # _____
Strong Forcing Opening: 2♣ ☐ 2 bids ☐ 1♣ ☐ Other_____

NOTRUMP OPENING BIDS
1NT _____ to _____   2NT _____ to _____ HCP
1NT _____ to _____   3NT _____ to _____ HCP
2♣ Forc.☐ Non-Forc.☐ Stayman   Solid Suit ☐: _____
2◊ Forc.☐ Non-Forc.☐ Stayman   _____
Transfers: Jacoby☐ Texas☐ Other☐ _____
1NT - 3♣/3◊   Is Invitational ☐   Preemptive ☐   Forcing ☐
Other _____

SIMPLE OVERCALL
____ to ____ HCP (occ. light ☐)
Responses: New Suit Forcing ☐
Cuebid Is: One-Round Force ☐
Game Force ☐ Limit Raise ☐
Other _____

Vs. Wk.☐ Strong☐ NT Opening
	Direct ☐		Balance ☐	
2♣ shows	♣	◊	♡	♠
2◊ shows	♣	◊	♡	♠
2♡ shows	♣	◊	♡	♠
2♠ shows	♣	◊	♡	♠

Other _____

JUMP OVERCALL
Strong ☐ Interm ☐ Preempt ☐
Special Responses _____
_____

OVER OPP'S TAKEOUT DOUBLE
New Suit Force 1-level ☐ 2-level ☐
Jp. Shift Force☐ Good☐ Weak☐
Redouble Implies No Fit ☐
Other _____

MAJOR OPENINGS
1♡-1♠ Opening on 4 Cards

	Often	Seldom	Never
1st-2nd	☐	☐	☐
3rd-4th	☐	☐	☐

MINOR OPENINGS
Length Promised

	4+	3+	Shorter
1♣	☐	☐	☐
1◊	☐	☐	☐

OPENING PREEMPTS
Sound Light Solid Minor
3-bids ☐ ☐ ☐
Other _____

Vs. Opening Preempts Dbl. Is
	Takeout	Opt.	Penalty
Wk. 2's	☐	☐	☐
3 Bids	☐	☐	☐
Conv. takeout	_____		

RESPONSES
Double Raise Forcing ☐ Limit ☐
Preemptive ☐ Limit in Comp. ☐
Conv. Raise: 2NT ☐ 3NT ☐
Swiss ☐ Splinter ☐
Conv. Responses: 1NT Forcing ☐
Drury ☐ Single Raise Constr. ☐
Other _____

RESPONSES
Double Raise
Forcing ☐ Limit ☐ Preempt☐
Single Raise Forcing ☐
1NT/1♣ _____ to _____ HCP
1◊ Resp. Conv. _____
Other _____

PSYCHICS
Never   Rare   Occ.   Frequent
☐   ☐   ☐   ☐
Describe: _____
_____

DIRECT CUEBID
Strong Takeout: Minor ☐ Major ☐
Natural: ♠ ☐ ◊ ☐ Artif. Bids ☐
Two Suits ☐ _____

2♣   WK ☐ ☐ ____ to ____HCP. Describe _____
   INT ☐ ☐ Conv. Resp. & Rebids _____
   STR ☐ ☐ _____ 2◊ Neg. ☐ 2 NT Neg. ☐

2◊   WK ☐ ☐ ____ to ____HCP. Describe _____
   INT ☐ ☐ Conv. Resp. & Rebids _____
   STR ☐ ☐ _____ 2 NT Force ☐ 2 NT·Neg. ☐

SLAM CONVENTIONS
Gerber ☐ _____ 4NT Var. ☐ _____
Interference over 4♣ or 4NT ☐ [*Describe*] _____

2♡   WK ☐ ☐ ____ to ____HCP. Describe _____
   INT ☐ ☐ Conv. Resp. & Rebids _____
   STR ☐ ☐ _____ 2 NT Force ☐ 2 NT Neg. ☐

2♠   WK ☐ ☐ ____ to ____HCP. Describe _____
   INT ☐ ☐ Conv. Resp. & Rebids _____
   STR ☐ ☐ _____ 2 NT Force ☐ 2 NT Neg. ☐

DEFENSIVE CARD PLAY
Opening lead vs. SUITS: 3rd best ☐ 4th best ☐ 5th best ☐ Other ☐
Mark card led: x x x   A K x   K Q x   Q J x   J 10 x   10 9 x
K J 10 x   K 10 9 x   Q 10 9 x   x x x x x
Opening lead vs. NT: 3rd best ☐ 4th best ☐ Other ☐

(Red Dot)
Mark card led: x x x   A K J x   A Q J x   A J 10 9
A 10 9 8   K Q J x   K Q 10 9   K J 10 9   K 10 9 8
Q J 10 x   Q 10 9 8   J 10 9 x   10 9 8 x   x x x x x

OTHER CONVENTIONAL CALLS
_____
_____
_____
_____

Special Carding _____ Frequent Count Signals ☐ _____

If in doubt as to the meaning of a conventional call — ASK AT YOUR TURN!

Bid	Made	Not Vulnerable			Vulnerable		
		Undbl	Dbl	Rdbl	Undbl	Dbl	Rdbl
5♡ – 5♠	5	450	650	1000	650	850	1200
	6	480	750	1200	680	1050	1600
	7	510	850	1400	710	1250	2000
5 NT	5	460	670	1040	660	870	1240
	6	490	770	1240	690	1070	1640
	7	520	870	1440	720	1270	2040
6♣ – 6♢	6	920	1090	1380	1370	1540	1830
	7	940	1190	1580	1390	1740	2230
6♡ – 6♠	6	980	1210	1620	1430	1660	2070
	7	1010	1310	1820	1460	1860	2470
6 NT	6	990	1230	1660	1440	1680	2110
	7	1020	1330	1860	1470	1880	2510
7♣ – 7♢	7	1440	1630	1960	2140	2330	2660
7♡ – 7♠	7	1510	1770	2240	2210	2470	2940
7 NT	7	1520	1790	2280	2220	2490	2980

DEFEATED CONTRACTS

Down	Not Vulnerable			Vulnerable		
	Undbl	Dbl	Rdbl	Undbl	Dbl	Rdbl
1	50	100	200	100	200	400
2	100	300	600	200	500	1000
3	150	500	1000	300	800	1600
4	200	800	1600	400	1100	2200
5	250	1100	2200	500	1400	2800
6	300	1400	2800	600	1700	3400
7	350	1700	3400	700	2000	4000
8	400	2000	4000	800	2300	4600
9	450	2300	4600	900	2600	5200
10	500	2600	5200	1000	2900	5800
11	550	2900	5800	1100	3200	6400
12	600	3200	6400	1200	3500	7000
13	650	3500	7000	1300	3800	7600

S21—Rev. 3/87

ACBL DUPLICATE INSTANT SCORER

Arranged by

American Contract Bridge League
P.O. Box 161192
Memphis, Tennessee 38186
901–332–5586

For additional copy, send
Self-addressed stamped envelope.

LEGEND
Dbl = Doubled
Undbl = Not Doubled
Rdbl = Redoubled

304

Scoring Summary

Bid	Made	Not Vulnerable Undbl	Dbl	Rdbl	Vulnerable Undbl	Dbl	Rdbl
1♣ - 1◇	1	70	140	230	70	140	230
	2	90	240	430	90	340	630
	3	110	340	630	110	540	1030
	4	130	440	830	130	740	1430
	5	150	540	1030	150	940	1830
	6	170	640	1230	170	1140	2230
	7	190	740	1430	190	1340	2630
1♡ - 1♠	1	80	160	520	80	160	720
	2	110	260	720	110	360	1120
	3	140	360	920	140	560	1520
	4	170	460	1120	170	760	1920
	5	200	560	1320	200	960	2320
	6	230	660	1520	230	1160	2720
	7	260	760	1720	260	1360	3120
1 NT	1	90	180	560	90	180	760
	2	120	280	760	120	380	1160
	3	150	380	960	150	580	1560
	4	180	480	1160	180	780	1960
	5	210	580	1360	210	980	2360
	6	240	680	1560	240	1180	2760
	7	270	780	1760	270	1380	3160
2♣ - 2◇	2	90	180	560	90	180	760
	3	110	280	760	110	380	1160
	4	130	380	960	130	580	1560
	5	150	480	1160	150	780	1960
	6	170	580	1360	170	980	2360
	7	190	680	1560	190	1180	2760
2♡ - 2♠	2	110	470	640	110	670	840
	3	140	570	840	140	870	1240
	4	170	670	1040	170	1070	1640
	5	200	770	1240	200	1270	2040
	6	230	870	1440	230	1470	2440
	7	260	970	1640	260	1670	2840

Bid	Made	Not Vulnerable Undbl	Dbl	Rdbl	Vulnerable Undbl	Dbl	Rdbl
2 NT	2	120	490	680	120	690	880
	3	150	590	880	150	890	1280
	4	180	690	1080	180	1090	1680
	5	210	790	1280	210	1290	2080
	6	240	890	1480	240	1490	2480
	7	270	990	1680	270	1690	2880
3♣ - 3◇	3	110	470	640	110	670	840
	4	130	570	840	130	870	1240
	5	150	670	1040	150	1070	1640
	6	170	770	1240	170	1270	2040
	7	190	870	1440	190	1470	2440
3♡ - 3♠	3	140	530	760	140	730	960
	4	170	630	960	170	930	1360
	5	200	730	1160	200	1130	1760
	6	230	830	1360	230	1330	2160
	7	260	930	1560	260	1530	2560
3 NT	3	400	550	800	600	750	1000
	4	430	650	1000	630	950	1400
	5	460	750	1200	660	1150	1800
	6	490	850	1400	690	1350	2200
	7	520	950	1600	720	1550	2600
4♣ - 4◇	4	130	510	720	130	710	920
	5	150	610	920	150	910	1320
	6	170	710	1120	170	1110	1720
	7	190	810	1320	190	1310	2120
4♡ - 4♠	4	420	590	880	620	790	1080
	5	450	690	1080	650	990	1480
	6	480	790	1280	680	1190	1880
	7	510	890	1480	710	1390	2280
4 NT	4	430	610	920	630	810	1120
	5	460	710	1120	660	1010	1520
	6	490	810	1320	690	1210	1920
	7	520	910	1520	720	1410	2320
5♣ - 5◇	5	400	550	800	600	750	1000
	6	420	650	1000	620	950	1400
	7	440	750	1200	640	1150	1800

Dickinson Public Library
Dickinson, North Dakota

Presented by

Southwest Duplicate

Bridge Club